CISCO ROUTERS FOR THE DESPERATE, 2ND EDITION

"For me, reading this book was like having one of the guys in my company who lives and breathes Cisco sitting down with me for a day and explaining everything I need to know to handle problems or issues likely to come my way."
—IT WORLD

"This really ought to be the book inside every Cisco Router box for the very slim chance things go goofy and help is needed 'right now.'"
—MACCOMPANION

PGP & GPG

"Excellent tutorial, quick read, and enough humor to make it enjoyable."
—INFOWORLD

"An excellent book that shows the end-user in an easy to read and often entertaining style just about everything they need to know to effectively and properly use PGP and OpenPGP."
—SLASHDOT

"The world's first user-friendly book on email privacy. Unless you're a cryptographer, or never use email, you should read this book."
—LEN SASSAMAN, CODECON FOUNDER

NETWORK FLOW ANALYSIS

by Michael W. Lucas

no starch
press

San Francisco

NETWORK FLOW ANALYSIS. Copyright © 2010 by Michael W. Lucas.

14 13 12 11 10   1 2 3 4 5 6 7 8 9

ISBN-10: 1-59327-203-0
ISBN-13: 978-1-59327-203-6

Publisher: William Pollock
Production Editor: Ansel Staton
Cover and Interior Design: Octopod Studios
Developmental Editor: William Pollock
Technical Reviewer: Richard Bejtlich
Copyeditor: Kim Wimpsett
Compositors: Riley Hoffman and Ansel Staton
Proofreader: Linda Seifert
Indexer: Nancy Guenther

For information on book distributors or translations, please contact No Starch Press, Inc. directly:

No Starch Press, Inc.
38 Ringold Street, San Francisco, CA 94103
phone: 415.863.9900; fax: 415.863.9950; info@nostarch.com; www.nostarch.com

Library of Congress Cataloging-in-Publication Data

Lucas, Michael, 1967-
 Network flow analysis / by Michael W. Lucas.
      p. cm.
 Includes index.
 ISBN-13: 978-1-59327-203-6
 ISBN-10: 1-59327-203-0
1. Network analysis (Planning)--Data processing. I. Title. T57.85.L83 2010
 658.4'032--dc22
                                      2010015790

For Liz

BRIEF CONTENTS

CONTENTS IN DETAIL

6
PERL, FLOWSCAN, AND CFLOW.PM 117

7
FLOWVIEWER 139

ACKNOWLEDGMENTS

Thanks to all the folks who have attended my network flow analysis tutorial over the years, and whose questions, comments, and ideas motivated this book. Now that the book is out, I'll have to find something else to teach. And a special thanks to Mike O'Connor, who helped with the manuscript when he really should have been doing other things.

INTRODUCTION

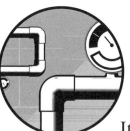

Network administrators of all backgrounds share one underlying, overwhelming desire. It doesn't matter if you manage a network with 400 separate manufacturing plants connected by a global MPLS mesh or if you're responsible for three computers and an elderly printer. Network administrators all share an abiding and passionate desire for just one thing: We want our users to shut up.

Blaming the network is easy. The network touches everything. Businesses assume that the network will work perfectly and make decisions accordingly. A user can't open that 900MB Excel spreadsheet on the file server on another continent from his 20th-century PC? Network problem. A website in Farawayistan is slow? Network problem. A user can't get a faster response over a 33.6Kbps modem? Network problem. In general, users don't care about trivialities such as the cost of bandwidth, the physical layout of transcontinental fiber, or the speed of light. They want the network to work the way they think it should.

This problem is exacerbated by the network's invisibility. Routers and switches are black boxes. You feed cables to the network, and it gives connectivity back. Traditionally, servers have much better activity logging and reporting than network devices. Sysadmins can write scripts to announce when a server process fails and try to remedy the situation, but very few network administrators have equipment that can monitor or repair itself. The usage information stored on a network device shows only the last few minutes at best. When a user reports an application failure, many systems administrators check their logs and report, "I have no problems. It must be the network." More sophisticated network administrators have traffic measurement tools such as MRTG, CiscoWorks, or OpenView, but these don't prove a network has no problems. They merely show whether the network has or lacks the particular set of problems that the software can report. The lack of media errors on a switch's uplink port says nothing about TCP/IP errors or firewall issues. With such minimal logging, blaming the network becomes very easy and hard to disprove.

In addition, modern-day network administrators typically have no formal certification or training process. The days of needing a computer science degree to manage a network are long gone. What network administration certifications exist are frequently for systems administration. An "operating system vendor–certified" network administrator is actually certified in the services that the operating system offers to the network, not the network itself. When you study for a Microsoft DHCP Server certification, for example, you learn some things about networking but a whole lot more about that particular DHCP implementation. Network service management is a useful skill, mind you, but it's not the same as managing the lowest level of the network. Network administrators learn the hard way—and it's a very hard way indeed.

This is a shame, because network administrators can claim a powerful role in any organization. The network administrator can help resolve almost every technical issue. The network administrator can make himself an invaluable, indispensable, and irreplaceable component of the organization. A network administrator who masters the tools, understands the protocols, and restrains his natural contempt for the lesser minds surrounding him will not be fired until the company dissolves around him.

Some network administrators understand this and are always ready to help. If a user or sysadmin reports an issue, this network admin is always ready to leap in with a packet analyzer or firewall log and offer insights. This is great customer service, *if* the user can replicate the problem at the time the network administrator is watching. Replicating problems consumes endless time and makes everyone involved testy.

What if you had a tool that could tell you specifically what happened on the network yesterday or last week or last year? Imagine being able to precisely identify the network impact of server and hardware changes. Suppose you could tell systems administrators exactly what bogus traffic their new server transmitted? Just for a moment, dream about being able to categorically and without risk of repudiation state, "That problem was not the network." Then think about doing all that by taking advantage of your existing equipment.

Network flow analysis lets you do exactly that. Perhaps you won't completely silence your users—nothing short of divine intervention can manage that. But you can identify problems on your network before they happen. You can answer questions authoritatively, definitively, and decisively. People will no longer automatically blame the network. Your work will become less stressful because you will no longer *think* you know what happened. You'll *know*.

This book will take network administrators through building a flow-based network management system out of any free Unix-like operating system, freely available software, and existing network hardware.

Network Administration and Network Management

What's the difference between a network administrator and a network manager?

Network administration involves configuring hardware, phoning tech support, and running cables. *Network management* involves making decisions about the network. Network managers usually start off as network administrators and may still perform network administration duties, but their technical knowledge guides managerial decisions.

Although changing your job title requires intervention from management, any network administrator can transform into a network manager by doing the work required. You're in charge of your equipment, and you can probably scrounge up access to some computing resources somewhere. The most difficult investment will be your time. Once you start providing fact-based answers and diagnoses, however, people will notice the change. Over time, company management will start involving you in decisions about the network or even seek your advice about business processes built on top of the network, making you the de facto network manager no matter what your business card says.

Network Management Tools

These are some pretty heady claims for a network management system, especially if you are familiar with existing network management tools. Many people are justifiably proud of their extensive network management systems. Let's take a look at some of the popular free network management tools and see how they fit together and how flow analysis can improve on them.

MRTG, Cricket, and Cacti

MRTG, Cricket, and Cacti use SNMP to generate graphs of network traffic across device interfaces and store the results in a fixed-size database. Knowing how much traffic crosses your network at any time is an absolute necessity, and I make heavy use of such tools myself. The fixed-size databases mean that you don't need to worry about database administration; they're easy to set up, and they quickly produce useful information.

Knowing that your circuits are full explains why connectivity is slow, but the obvious next question is "full of what?" MRTG-style tools cannot answer that question. Flows can. Also, these tools normally use five-minute averages of traffic. They obscure brief spikes and valleys. Finally, these tools compress historical data into long-term averages. If you want to know the details of traffic six months ago, you must either extensively reconfigure these tools or use another tool.

RTG

Like the previous tools, RTG uses SNMP to measure network traffic crossing device interfaces and graphs the data. Unlike MRTG and its descendants, RTG measures much briefer intervals of traffic and stores each individual result in a database. It provides much more detailed visibility into traffic congestion. If you want to see how traffic has varied on a network interface throughout a single minute, RTG is your friend. You can also perform detailed comparisons with historical data.

The presence of a database means that you must either know something about databases or have an infinite amount of disk space. Also, RTG can't show you the contents of the traffic, only how much there was. It resolves one problem with MRTG-style tools but not the others.

Nagios and Big Brother

If you step away from measuring the quantity of traffic, you also need to check the health of your network gear. Free software such as Nagios and Big Brother is very useful in this regard; you can get an alarm when a switch's redundant power supply fails, when a port starts spewing CRC errors, or when a switch reboots itself. You must have this information to maintain a reliable network.

Knowing that your hardware is operating correctly is vital, but the fact that a switch is operating correctly doesn't mean that the traffic passing through it isn't having trouble. A functional switch or router will transmit undesirable traffic just as reliably as desirable traffic.

CiscoWorks, OpenView, and More

Then you have the commercial network management suites. Most of these products are either tool kits with pretty frontends or limited to simple networks. These tools are seductive. They look like anyone can use them. But these tools often want to control your entire computing infrastructure, from router to desktop, and attempts to deploy them in production usually fail.

What most people don't realize is that by the time you've set up these software suites to work the way you need, you've done just as much work as you would through building your own flow analysis system. You have had the satisfaction of giving some other company money that rightfully belongs in your pocket, however. (It's the boss's money, you say? Get a price quote for the commercial stuff. During your performance review, tell your manager that you got the same results without spending that cash and you'd like a slice of it. It's more likely to work than asking for a raise after spending that money.)

Enough Griping: What's the Solution?

Resolved: Network administration sucks. The tools are all inadequate, expensive, or both. How do you escape this pit? *You record the traffic that passes across your network.*

Yes, this is a tall order. Fortunately, you don't have to record the entire contents of every network transaction. For a moment, think about the duties of a network administrator. Part of your responsibilities include providing network services, such as DNS and DHCP. You probably have to feed your proxy server every few days and dust the script kiddies out of the intrusion detection system each Monday morning. But set aside the services that run on the network for a moment, and consider the base network.

The network exists to carry traffic from one host to another. That's it. The network administrator makes that happen.

Perhaps you're the only IT person at your company, and you are also responsible for everything else. Most of the time, however, network administrators work on a team with system administrators, a database administrator or two, a help desk, and other IT professionals. In this case, the network administrator's responsibility is to deliver packets in a timely manner. Successful delivery of those packets completes your responsibilities.

Being able to prove that packets arrived at their destination and were accepted will completely change your relationship with your co-workers. All of a sudden, you have *proof*. The network is no longer something that indiscriminately accepts the blame whenever something goes askew. Some of the errors will be your responsibility, of course. But many won't, and there's nothing like the glorious feeling of conclusively demonstrating for the very first time that not only is a problem not yours, but you can rigorously demonstrate where the problem lies. (The trick here lies in not alienating those same co-workers with said proof, but I'll talk about that later.)

You don't need a complete record of the contents of traffic to demonstrate your point. All you need is proof that successful network-level communication occurred between hosts. If a user cannot display a page on your internal web server, for example, you don't need a full record of the contents of the network connections between the user's desktop and the server. You only need a record that a network conversation occurred between the client and the server, that the network carried data between the two, and that the conversation concluded normally and without error at the network level. You don't need to record every individual image or chunk of text in that conversation. That's not the network administrator's responsibility. Proving that the network carried web traffic between the client and the server demonstrates that the network functioned correctly. Mind you, as the network administrator, you're still on the hook for helping solve the problem; it's just that nobody will be blaming you as you work.

Flow-Tools and Its Prerequisites

Flow-tools is the standard freely available flow management and analysis tool kit. Although you can find many other tools for flow management, flow-tools has been around for the longest time and is the most widely deployed free toolkit. Many people have written flow analysis interfaces based on flow-tools, and I'll cover several of them in this book.

Flow-tools is written for Unix-like systems such as Linux, OpenSolaris, various BSDs, commercial options such as AIX, and many others. My reference platform is FreeBSD, but everything in this book also works on Linux. You might have difficulties using more challenging or unique platforms. This book provides examples of the commands for the flow management tools, but you must know how to invoke superuser privilege, navigate the file system, and so on.

Much of this software uses Perl. You don't need to write your own Perl, but you'll need to edit Perl scripts to set variables such as your company name and your IP addresses. Some flow software includes specific Perl hooks, and I'll cover them for Perl aficionados.

If you want to perform ad hoc reporting of flow data with flow-tools, you'll want a plotting program. I discuss gnuplot. You'll be most comfortable using gnuplot if you have an X server installed on your desktop, but that's not mandatory.

In addition, to use flow-tools, you must understand Unix epoch time. Epoch time is the number of seconds since 00:00:00 on January 1, 1970, in the UTC time zone. Any number of websites offer epoch-to-date converters. You can convert epoch seconds to a date on the command line with the date command, but the syntax varies among Unix-like operating systems.

Speaking of time, having good time on your network will enhance your network management capabilities. Therefore, I recommend installing and using Network Time Protocol. Use authoritative time sources for your network. If the timestamps in your server logs match the timestamps in your network traffic records, your analysis will be much easier.

Flows can include Border Gateway Protocol (BGP) information. I discuss how to manage flow BGP data, but those explanations assume basic BGP knowledge. If you don't use BGP, your flow data will not contain any BGP data. You can safely skip discussions of BGP-based flow data.

Finally, you must understand networking. If you don't have a strong grip on networking fundamentals now, however, you'll have one by the time you finish your flow management implementation.

Flows and This Book

Before you can manage your network with flow information, you must understand how flows work, where the data comes from, how it is gathered and processed, and the strengths and limitations of flow-based management. Chapter 1 introduces flows.

Many routers and switches can perform *flow export*, where the hardware tracks flow data and transmits it to a management system. If your hardware cannot export flows, you can perform flow export in software. Chapter 2 discusses flow export and how to configure it in both hardware and software, as well as how to collect those flow records from many different network devices using the industry-standard flow-tools software package.

Chapter 3 teaches you how to view the flow records you've gathered. Flow records contain vast amounts of information, and choosing the proper viewing format will help you get the insight you need.

Flow records include all the traffic that passes over your network, but you'll often be interested only in very specific information, such as the traffic over a particular circuit or to a certain host. Chapter 4 demonstrates filtering flows to display only interesting data.

At times you'll be interested in reporting on the aggregated flow data rather than individual flows. What hosts sent the most traffic? What are the most popular UDP ports on your network? Which hosts connect to the most other hosts? Flow-tools supports a wide variety of reports, which I'll cover in Chapter 5.

Another common requirement is for simple visualization of network traffic; in other words, presenting the flow records in graphical format. Chapter 6 covers FlowScan, web-based software that offers traffic graphs to your users. It also covers the `Cflow.pm` Perl module used to write FlowScan so you can write your own flow analysis software if you're so inclined.

Although FlowScan works well for users, network administrators need something more powerful. Chapter 7 covers FlowViewer, another web-based tool that lets you deeply dissect your traffic.

Web-based software can handle many network visualization tasks, but automating visuals and graphing ad hoc data aren't among them. At times, you'll need to prepare graphs that show today's traffic compared to last week's or last year's. In Chapter 8, you'll use `gnuplot` to create graphs of truly arbitrary flow data.

Finally, Chapter 9 discusses some flow collection edge cases and talks about how you can use flow records to proactively improve your network.

Before doing all the advanced stuff, however, let's take a deep, hard look at flows in Chapter 1.

1

FLOW FUNDAMENTALS

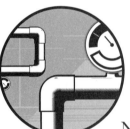 I'll assume at this point that you're sold on the idea that flows can solve your problems. Now, let's get specific about what flows are, what they're good for, and how you can implement and analyze them. This chapter focuses on the flows commonly found on TCP/IP networks, specifically, TCP, UDP, and ICMP flows.

This chapter assumes you have a basic understanding of TCP/IP and tries to drag you into a deeper understanding of it. If you find yourself growing confused, I suggest you consult an introductory book such as Charles M. Kozierok's *The TCP/IP Guide* (No Starch Press, 2005). I also encourage you to spend quality time with a packet sniffer watching TCP/IP transactions in the real world because there's no better way to learn network protocols than observing them carrying out real work.

What Is a Flow?

Strictly speaking, a *flow* is a series of packets that share the same source and destination IP addresses, source and destination ports, and IP protocol. This is also called a *five-tuple IP flow*. The word *flow* is also sometimes used to mean an aggregate of individual flows. A *flow record* is a summary of information about a flow, recording which hosts communicated with which other hosts, when this communication occurred, how the traffic was transmitted, and other basic information about the network conversation. A flow analysis system collects flow information and gives you a system to search, filter, and print flow information. Flow records summarize every connection on your network.

Do you want to know what kind of traffic is filling your Internet T1, what a client PC is doing, or what kind of errors are reaching a server? Check the flow records. Want to know what happened on the network yesterday between 3 AM and 3:05 AM, when the file server mysteriously crashed and rebooted? Check yesterday's flow records.

The good news is that most network hardware can report traffic as flows. Having that hardware send flow information to a recording host imposes only a small overhead; you don't need to install anything.

Because flow records do not include the data exchanged by a network connection, flow records are small. For example, as I write this, my data center has a DS3, several T1s, a gigabit Ethernet backbone, and assorted smaller subnets and DMZs. Still, three complete years of flow records use less than 100GB of disk space. Granted, that's not trivial, but it's a small amount of disk space by modern standards and far less than that required to capture the complete contents of every exchange.

Even with gigabytes of data, flow records do not allow unlimited troubleshooting. Anyone who has ever used a packet sniffer to watch a telnet or unencrypted web session understands that everything that traverses the network can be captured, analyzed, and reconstructed. A snooper can see exactly which websites a user visits, what files the user downloads, what the user transmits back to the site, and any usernames and passwords used in the exchange. Flow records do not contain this data; they simply tell the network administrator that a client visited a website running at a particular IP address, how many connections the user made to that site, how much data was exchanged, but not the contents of those exchanges.

Recording only flow information rather than complete packets might sound limited, but the NSA performs similar analysis on phone records to catch criminals and terrorists. Similarly, the wireless wiretapping at AT&T was discovered through netflow analysis. Knowing who talked to whom, when they talked, and how much each party said is terribly valuable.

Flow System Architecture

A typical flow-based management system has three components: a sensor (or sensors), a collector, and a reporting system. Components can be combined as well, as you'll learn in Chapter 2.

A *sensor*, also known as a *probe*, is a device that listens to the network and captures traffic data. The sensor may be a switch, router, or firewall with integrated flow export capability, or it might be a piece of software listening to an Ethernet tap or a switch port in monitor mode. The sensor tracks network connections, and after it believes a connection has finished or the connection reaches a timeout, it transmits the data.

The *collector* is software that receives sensor records and writes them to disk. The collector is an absolutely critical piece of your flow-based management infrastructure. Unfortunately, there's no universally accepted on-disk format for storing flow records. This complicates analysis and restricts the reporting tools you can use, but you'll learn how to work around that in this book.

Finally, the *reporting system* reads the collector files and produces human-friendly reports. The reporting system must understand the file format used by the collector.

You can find many different implementations of each component of a flow-based management system. Each hardware vendor's higher-end equipment has a flow sensor, and many people have written or implemented flow sensors for their preferred operating system. Several different collectors have come into prominence and faded, such as cflowd, and many people who wanted to demonstrate their mastery of the latest cool scripting language have written reporting systems to meet their particular needs.

A newcomer might look at the vast array of options and decide that flow management is too complicated to even begin to attempt. What's worse, much of this software is obsolete, but Internet mailing list archives from, say, 1998 strongly recommend it. The neophyte can spend hours tracking down software only to discover that it can no longer be built with a modern compiler. Additionally, many possible combinations are subtly incompatible.

This situation is beyond frustrating, and it makes many people abandon investigations into flow-based network management after only a couple hours.

This book presents a single set of software components that work together. The components either are still actively developed or have a widespread user base. The core platform is the flow-tools tool kit (*http://code.google.com/p/flow-tools/*). Flow-tools has been the standard freely available flow collector and reporting software for many years now and is compatible with all common sensors. Additionally, many reporting tools leverage flow-tools' data format when correctly configured. You'll learn how to make flow-tools integrate with some other popular tools in this book.

The History of Network Flow

High-speed router and switch hardware directs traffic without going to the operating system, in other words, without making each forwarding decision in software. Decisions on packet routing are made at the lowest level possible, generally within the hardware itself. Circa 1996, Cisco invented a method by which routing decisions were guided by flows. Subsequently, the value of flow information was realized, and it was made accessible to network administrators as a feature called NetFlow.

NetFlow Versions

NetFlow has undergone several revisions through its history.

NetFlow Version 1

NetFlow version 1 was the earliest Cisco release. Other vendors reverse-engineered the NetFlow reporting protocol and released their own NetFlow-compatible reporting systems. A few vendors still support NetFlow version 1, and if this is all you have, it will still solve many problems for you. It contains only the minimal flow information.

NetFlow Version 5

The oldest widely deployed flow record format is NetFlow version 5. Many vendors, such as Juniper and Nokia, implemented this protocol.

NetFlow version 5 includes seven key values: source IP address, destination IP address, source port (TCP and UDP protocols only), destination port, IP protocol, the interface the flow arrived on the system on, and the IP type of service. It also includes information about BGP, the exporter IP address, and a few other traffic characteristics. Although flow records have become more detailed over the years, NetFlow version 5 suffices for most environments.

NetFlow Version 7

NetFlow version 7 is supported only by high-end Cisco Catalyst switches. Its flow record format includes switching and routing information not available in version 5, such as the IP address of the next hop address for the flow. If you have hardware that supports NetFlow version 7, this book will show you how to take advantage of it.

NetFlow Version 8

NetFlow version 8 is a cluster of similar formats that aggregate information. If you have many high-bandwidth connections and you must minimize the amount of resources you spend collecting and analyzing flow records, NetFlow version 8 might be useful. Cisco is the only vendor that supports it, however, and it's used only rarely. Given our ever-increasing computing power and disk capacity, however, NetFlow version 8 is usually not compelling.

NetFlow Version 9

NetFlow version 9 is Cisco's final version. It is template-based and extensible, meaning that third-party vendors can add arbitrary information into a NetFlow record. Version 9 is also the first version to support IP version 6 (IPv6). NetFlow version 9 is deployed in only a few commercial products.

NetFlow Competition

As Cisco deployed more and more NetFlow versions, other networking companies saw the benefit of exporting and reporting on flow data. For example, Cisco developed NetFlow based on the needs of its own customers, which were not necessarily the needs of the global networking community. Other vendors implemented similar flow-based reporting based on the needs of their customers. As a result, NetFlow competitors appeared, the best known of which is sFlow. Some equipment from vendors such as 3Com, HP, Extreme, and Juniper support sFlow.

NOTE   *sFlow is specifically not NetFlow because Cisco owns that word. People began to refer to* flow export *instead of* NetFlow *about the same time that sFlow was released.*

As the number of competitors grew, the networking community saw the advantages of a common standards-defined flow export protocol. Current efforts focus on this standards-based approach.

The Latest Standards

In the early 2000s, the Internet Engineering Task Force created a working group to define flow formats and prevent further flow format fragmentation. The working group chose to use NetFlow version 9 as the base protocol, with minor changes to make it friendlier. Cisco is still involved but now as a member rather than the sole controlling interest.

The latest version of the network flow standard is called IP Flow Information eXport (IPFIX). Although many hardware vendors are implementing IPFIX support as well as support for older versions, the format is rarely deployed. IPFIX is much more complicated than earlier flow versions and uses more system resources. The differences between earlier NetFlow versions are evolutionary, but NetFlow version 9 and IPFIX represent dramatic breaks from earlier versions. People are also investigating using IPFIX to manage non-network data, such as security events.

The solutions you'll explore in this book address NetFlow versions 1 through 7. Versions 8 and 9 are rarely needed, and although IPv6 requires NetFlow version 9 or newer, most of the world is not interested in IPv6 and will remain disinterested until IP version 4 address space shortages become intolerable. Once IPv6 is no longer optional, I expect vendors to jump directly to IPFIX. When IPFIX becomes more widespread, I have no doubt that the user community will add IPFIX support to the tools covered in this book.

NETFLOW VS. FLOW EXPORT

Sometimes in this book I use the word *NetFlow*; other times I use *flow management* or *flow export*. The difference between them is that Cisco owns the word NetFlow, while other vendors support a NetFlow-compatible flow export technology. You might be using NetFlow, or you might be using a NetFlow-compatible flow export system, depending on your equipment. The difference is only semantic, but whenever possible, I avoid annoying any multinational firm that could crush me like a bug.

Flows in the Real World

"A *flow* is a series of packets that all share the same source and destination IP addresses, source and destination ports, and IP protocol." What the heck does that mean, really? Let's pull this description apart and see what it really means in a few places in the real world. I'll start with the simplest network traffic, a ping request and response, and then proceed to more complicated examples of DNS and HTTP requests.

ICMP Flows

Although ICMP is most commonly associated with ping requests, it also carries the most basic instructions for Internet routing and management. Certain individual flows, such as ICMP redirects, can carry useful information, but to keep things simple, I'll cover the common ping.

ICMP has no TCP-style flags and does not have ports like TCP and UDP do. Instead, ICMP packets are assigned an *ICMP type* and an optional *ICMP code*. The ICMP type identifies the general purpose of the packet. Ping requests and response messages have their own ICMP types, and an ICMP type might have associated ICMP codes that offer more detail. (You'll learn more about ICMP types and codes in Chapter 3.)

To ping a server, the client creates an ICMP packet with a source address of the client and a destination address of the server. The client sets the ICMP type to 8, or echo-request, and sends the packet onto the network. This ping packet is the entirety of the first flow.

In response, the server creates an ICMP packet with the server's source address, the client's destination address, and an ICMP type of 0, or echo-response. This is the complete second flow.

That said, if your client sends multiple ping requests, the flow system assigns subsequent pings to the same flow. A Windows system, for example, normally sends five ping requests and expects five ping replies. Your flow system records a single flow containing five requests and a separate flow containing five responses.

A flow sensor has no way of knowing when ICMP flows are complete, because the traffic contains no internal markers that say "No further packets will arrive." The sensor holds ICMP flows in memory until a timeout expires, at which point the sensor marks the flows as complete and transmits them to the collector.

UDP Flows

Now consider a basic DNS request to see how UDP flows function. UDP sessions are slightly more complex than ICMP flows: Although UDP doesn't use types and codes like ICMP and doesn't have flags like TCP, UDP uses TCP-style port numbers. Also, UDP has no built-in concept of a session or transaction, which is why people describe it as *connectionless*. UDP does carry useful application-level data, however, and most UDP traffic is part of some sort of session or transaction. The most common UDP flows on the average network are DNS requests. A DNS request is among the simplest possible network requests and produces the shortest flows you'll see. Other UDP network protocols, such as bootp, generate many more packets per flow, but to understand flows, you'll look at the humble DNS request here.

A client connecting to a DNS server creates a UDP packet with a source IP of the client and a destination IP of the server. As with TCP, the UDP request originates from an unused port on the client side and uses the standard DNS port 53 as its destination. A simple DNS query, such as a request for the address of *www.nostarch.com*, fits entirely within one packet. This single packet is the start of the third sample flow.

The fourth flow begins when a server responds by creating a UDP packet with a source IP of the server and a destination IP of the client. Similarly, the source and destination ports are reversed from the packet sent by the client. A DNS response containing the information for a typical site also fits entirely within one packet.

These flows are now complete, and no more traffic will be passed as part of them. You can see these flows in Figure 1-1.

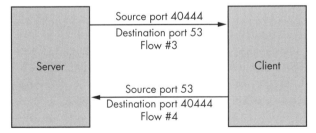

Figure 1-1: UDP network transaction with flow memberships

Because UDP is connectionless, the network traffic contains no markers to tell an observer that a particular conversation is complete. The packets have no TCP-esque FIN flag that announces "I'm done, so hang up now," so a flow sensor has no way to know that the flows are complete. The sensor holds those flows in memory until a timeout expires, at which point the sensor marks the flows as complete and transmits them to the collector.

TCP Flows

The most complicated network flows that I'll cover are TCP flows, such as those used by web servers and browsers. The TCP protocol includes ports such as those used by UDP but also includes internal flags that indicate the state of the connection. TCP tells the client and the server whether a connection is being requested, ongoing, or being torn down. For example, now that you have an IP address for *www.nostarch.com*, let's look at a web client requesting a single, static, simple web object from that site.[1]

The fifth flow begins when a client connecting to a web server sends a single packet to the server with a source IP of the client and a destination IP of the server. The client allocates an unused port on the local system for exclusive use by this connection, which is the packet's *source port*. Web servers typically run on port 80, so this is the packet's destination port. On the first packet in the connection, the client sets the synchronization (SYN) request flag (this initial packet is usually referred to as a *SYN request*). The client is contacting the server, saying "Hey, can I talk to you?"

When the server receives a SYN request on port 80 and decides to accept the connection, it prepares a *response packet*. This response packet has a source address of the server and a destination address of the client. The source port is 80, the port requested by the client; the destination port is the earlier packet's source port.

The sixth flow is the packet sent as a response to a SYN packet, so the server sets the acknowledgment (ACK) flag. Because the server hasn't sent any packets in this TCP/IP conversation before, it also sets the SYN flag to request synchronization (commonly called the *SYN-ACK packet*).

A second flow in one network transaction? Yep. Remember, a single flow shares the same source and destination IP addresses, among other things. You have one flow with a source address of the client and a second with the source address of the server. The source port of one flow matches the destination port of the other flow, permitting you to match the two together, but these are two separate flows. Flows let you determine how much traffic goes in each direction in any given transaction.

When the client receives the server's response, it matches the incoming packet with the connection it's trying to establish with that server. The client responds with a packet to the server from the assigned local port. The connection is now synchronized: Both the client and the server know the IP addresses involved in the connection and the port numbers on each side

---

1. Of course, the No Starch Press website is fully dynamic, interactive, and individually generated for each viewer by a sophisticated self-modifying artificial intelligence, and it doesn't have any simple "individual objects." You should check it out. Buy something while you're there.

(as well as sequence numbers and other assorted characteristics that uniquely identify this connection). Because this packet is part of an existing connection, the SYN flag is not required. The client must acknowledge the SYN request the server included in its last packet, however, so this next packet includes the ACK flag.

This packet from client to server might be the third in the transaction, but it's the second sent by the client to the server. It shares the source and destination IP addresses and port numbers of the first packet in the transaction, both of which are using the same IP protocol (TCP). This third packet is the second packet in the first flow. (Figure 1-2 illustrates this three-way handshake, noting the flows to which each packet is assigned.)

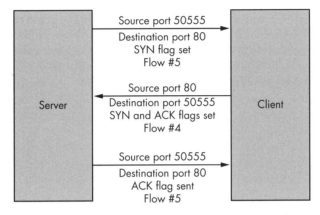

Figure 1-2: TCP three-way handshake with flow memberships

Now that a connection exists, the client may transmit actual data, such as an HTTP GET request. The GET request is part of the first flow, from client to server. The server's response, including any HTML, images, or error codes, becomes part of the second flow, from server to client. Packets now stream back and forth, including ACKs as required to acknowledge receipt of earlier packets.

At the end of the transaction, one side or the other sends a packet with the "finish" (FIN) flag set. This packet is called a *FIN request*, and it marks the end of the TCP/IP session. The other system sends an ACK and then a FIN of its own. The client sends an ACK to the final FIN, closing the connection. The flow sensor sees the FINs and ACKs, terminates both flows, and immediately transmits the TCP flow records to the collector.

Other Protocols

Flow management systems can track protocols other than ICMP, UDP, and TCP, but these three protocols comprise the overwhelming majority of network traffic. Your flow system will record traffic for protocols such as the AH and ESP protocols used for IPSec VPNs, but flows do not record the internal characteristics of this traffic.

For these less common protocols, a flow system records the protocol, time, number of packets, and other vital flow information.

Flow Export and Timeouts

Most medium to high-end routers and switches store flow data, but they don't necessarily provide a way for a human being to look at the flow data locally. Instead, to analyze flow records, you must first *export* the flow records from the hardware to a computer. Flow sensors export their records when the corresponding network activity is complete or when a timeout expires.

The exported record is not necessarily a complete TCP/IP session, however. For example, downloading an ISO image from an Internet site can take a very long time, and that session will probably be represented in several consecutive flow records.

Why break long-running sessions into multiple records? Suppose your router exported flow records only when each TCP/IP session finished. Now assume that one of your users started a large download likely to saturate your Internet connection for several hours. As the network administrator, you'll quickly get a call complaining that the Internet is really, really slow. To solve this problem, you'll want to identify what's happened on your network over the past few minutes, not just once the big download is complete. By breaking up the records of long-running connections into discrete flow records every few minutes, the router lets you view the data in close to real time. You can look at the flow records while this big download is still going on and identify the issue before it lasts all day. You can either shut down the offending user or, if the user is an executive or on the IT team, inform the caller the Internet will be slow for a while because of solar radiation interference and that they just have to wait.

Network hardware creates flow records based on a configured *timeout*, or the maximum amount of time the device can track an individual flow. When a particular connection lasts as long as the timeout, the device exports a flow record and creates a new record. For example, if your router had a one-minute flow timeout, it would export a record of the big download every minute. Although this record would not include the complete TCP session, you could look at your flow records and say, "During this minute, the biggest bandwidth user was this particular workstation downloading from this particular website." You have time to intervene if necessary.

Timeouts also help manage flow records for UDP, ICMP, and other non-TCP flows. The network device would create a flow record for each of these transactions. When the timeout expires, the device exports the flow record. Although a network device can't tell exactly when a UDP flow is finished, the timeout guarantees that the record of that is eventually exported.

You can change the timeout to fit your needs. I'll discuss the reasons for doing so later in this book, but you should know that changing the timeout impacts system resources. Increasing the timeout increases the memory and CPU the device needs for flow tracking.

Packet-Sampled Flows

Flow export first appeared on routers with very limited hardware resources. On many of these devices, as interface bandwidths increased, tracking every packet required more horsepower than the router or tap could supply. Instead, the hardware *sampled* packets to create flow data, recording and exporting only a specified fraction of the traffic passing through the device. This flow data was necessarily incomplete.

Today, most hardware can track most or all flows going through a machine in most small and medium-sized environments.[2] Once you start to get into 10 gigabit networks, sampling 1 in 100 or 1 in 1,000 packets is the norm. As hardware capacity increases, we'll sample more fully, but bandwidth will increase similarly. Once terabit Ethernet becomes commonplace, I expect we'll have the capacity to perform flow capture on 10 gigabit Ethernet, if we'd even want that much data!

Should you sample your network flows or record all of them? If at all possible, you should record all traffic that passes through your network. You should sample only if your hardware cannot support complete flow tracking. Sampling some data is better than not having any data, but recording as much detail as possible is far more useful for troubleshooting.

You should now have a good idea of how a flow system works, how its components fit together, and how to assemble a flow analysis system. Let's start with your flow-tools collector and your first sensor.

---

2. I had a conversation with one of the senior techs at the Internet Software Consortium (ISC) about its flow export system. The ISC samples from its multiple gigabit Internet uplinks. If you, like ISC, have an amount of bandwidth that can be described only as "You have *got* to be (bleep)ing kidding," you'll probably need to sample as well.

2

COLLECTORS AND SENSORS

The collector and sensors are the irreplaceable components of any flow system. Why? You can analyze data in innumerable ways, but before you do, you must gather and store the data, and you do that with sensors and the collector.

Because these pieces of your flow system are so critical, you'll begin your implementation with the collector and proceed to the first sensor.

Collector Considerations

The *collector* is the host that receives records from network equipment and is where you'll perform most of your work. You must practice good systems administration on your collector, but you have a lot of flexibility on your hardware, operating system, and software.

Operating System

The collector runs on a Unix-like operating system. Almost any modern Unix-like operating system will suffice. I recommend a BSD operating system. (If you've never worked with BSD, permit me to suggest you buy one of my BSD books, such as *Absolute FreeBSD* or *Absolute OpenBSD*.)

That said, Linux, OpenSolaris, or any standard 32-bit or 64-bit Unix-like system with a recent GCC compiler and libraries will work just fine. The more unusual your operating system, however, the more trouble you will have with your collector and reporting system. Some commercial Unix-like operating systems are noted for behavior that technically complies with the standards but differs from every other Unix-like operating system in bizarre or down-right unspeakable ways.[1] Pick something known for playing well with others.

Whichever system you choose, it must be secure. Every active Unix-like operating system has a current security and hardening guide. Get it. Read it. Use it. Your collector should provide no other services except for those related to flow management. This will let you harden the system much more than a multipurpose machine permits.

System Resources

Flow collection uses very few system resources other than disk space. (I've run flow collectors on Pentium Pro servers.)

The amount of disk space needed depends on the type of traffic on your network and how long you want to retain your records. In my environment, a data flow averaging 5Mbps uses about 2GB of disk a month. Today, disk capacity expands faster than network utilization. I've found that it's possible to retain all data for the indefinite future if you keep buying larger disks.

Additional memory and CPU resources will accelerate flow reporting. When provisioning a machine for flow collection, I suggest using a slower but larger hard drive (like one of the "green" drives) and adding memory. The slower hard drive will save you money and power, and additional memory will improve the system's buffer cache and let you analyze data more quickly.

Get at least 4GB or more of RAM for your collector. Any modern Unix-like OS caches recently accessed disk files in RAM. Large amounts of memory will accelerate running multiple reports on the same data more than anything else.

Sensor Considerations

The sensor is the device or program that captures flow data from your network and forwards it to the collector. Flow sensors are perhaps the most difficult portion of a flow-based management system to implement, especially on a geographically large network. You don't want to drive across the continent just to install a flow sensor!

---

1. I would name names, but IBM has better lawyers than I do.

The good news is, you don't need to worry about making those road trips. In fact, you probably already have flow sensors installed that you just haven't configured yet. Do you have Internet border routers? Have them act as sensors. Got a high-end Cisco switch? Great, use that.

If you don't have hardware that can do the job, you can implement a flow sensor in software.

Location

If you have even a medium-sized network, you'll quickly realize that you need to be selective about your sensor locations. Perhaps you have a couple dozen small switches and a hefty central core switch at your headquarters, half a dozen DMZs, an Internet border, and several remote facilities connected via VPN or MPLS. You could conceivably have sensors at each of these locations. Which are worth the effort?

Internet Border

Start with your Internet border. Almost all modern commercial-grade routers can export flow records. Analyzing those flows will tell you how you're using your Internet access. Knowing how much of your traffic is web surfing versus how much of your traffic is accessing your VPN will immediately help you make better decisions.

Ethernet Core

Look at your network's Ethernet core next. The internal LAN will have much more traffic than the wide-area Internet connection. Analyzing flow data from your internal network will quickly expose problems, misconfigurations, and performance issues. Your network architecture dictates sensor placement.

If you have a single large core switch, such as a Cisco 4000 or 7000, the switch itself can probably export flow information.

If you have multiple switches in your Ethernet core, you might think you need flow export on every one of them, but that's overly ambitious. You do not need a complete record of every last packet that passes through every switch on your office network.

When considering where to capture data, think about how traffic flows from device to device, and configure flow export only from central "choke" points. For example, my main data center has a configuration common in large enterprises: a large Cisco switch at its core and client switches in wiring closets on each floor. Every closet switch and every server is attached directly to the core switch. Any traffic that leaves a local switch must pass through the core switch.

I collect flow data only from the central switch. This means that I'm blind to any traffic that remains entirely on a closet switch, but I capture all client broadcast traffic and anything that goes to servers or leaves the network. Even if a client uses a printer attached to the local switch, the print job traverses the print server attached to the core switch. One single flow export point offers adequate visibility into the entire network.

If your Ethernet core is only one or two small switches and none of the switches can export flow information, you can still implement flow-based network management if one of the switches has a "sniffer" or "monitor" port. One of the switches is effectively the network core. If you haven't designated a particular switch as the core, use the switch that serves the highest number of servers. Attach a software flow sensor to the monitor port (see "Configuring Software Flow Sensors" on page 32).

From Remote Facilities

Apply similar reasoning to remote facilities. Each remote facility has at least one router connecting it to the global network. It might be connected to an MPLS cloud or the Internet, but it's still your link into the outside world. Capture flows from that device.

If a remote facility has a export-capable core switch, use it as well. If the site reports many problems and the central switch cannot export flows, consider implementing a software sensor or upgrading the core switch.

Have remote sites export their flows to your central collector. Maintaining multiple collectors increases your workload with very little gain.

From Private Network Segments/DMZs

Tracking flows from your core network, and your Internet border provides insight into your entire network, including servers on isolated or private network segments such as DMZs. You can see the traffic DMZ servers exchange with your core network and the Internet. What you cannot see is the traffic among DMZ servers.

If you have only one or two servers on a DMZ, you probably don't need flow export on that network segment. If you have several servers, you'll want flow export. You don't need to decide right away, however. Fine-tune your flow management installation on your core and border networks, and then implement flow export on your DMZs.

Implementing the Collector

Enough theory, enough planning. Let's install something!

An Internet search reveals any number of freely available flow collectors. The big three are cflowd, flowd, and flow-tools. Cflowd is obsolete, is unsupported, and doesn't compile on 64-bit systems. I have high hopes for flowd, but it's a comparatively new tool and doesn't yet have broad support among users or third-party software. That leaves us with flow-tools, the most commonly used flow management tool kit.

Flow-tools is older but has a very broad user community. The original author (Mark Fullmer) released version 0.68 in 2005 and went on to other projects. Any unmaintained software slowly becomes obsolete, but a group of users assumed responsibility for flow-tools in 2007. These users collect improvements and bug fixes, and they release updated versions as needed. Although you'll still find occasional bugs, as with any software, flow-tools has a broad base of users.

NOTE *Do not use version 0.68 of flow-tools. It has many small problems and does not function correctly on 64-bit systems. (It seems to work on 64-bit systems, but actually corrupts data, which is even worse than completely failing to work!) Take the time to install the newer version, 0.68.5 as of this writing.*

Installing Flow-tools

You can install flow-tools from an operating system package or from source. Before installing it, visit the flow-tools website at *http://code.google.com/p/flow-tools/* to download the most recent version.

Installing from Packages

Most Unix-like operating systems offer prepackaged versions of freely available software. If you can use precompiled, prepackaged software, do so.

However, many operating systems include only flow-tools version 0.68 rather than the newer version with its the bug fixes. Some operating systems, such as FreeBSD, include the newer software as a package called *flow-tools-ng*.

Fine details in the flow-tools package names are important. For example, flow-tools was recently at version 0.68.4. A search for a CentOS flow-tools RPM revealed version 0.68-4, which is actually revision 4 of flow-tools package 0.68. At first glance, this might look like the correct package, but it's not.

By the time this book reaches print, ideally major OS vendors will provide an updated package. If not, you get to install from source.

Installing from Source

To install the latest version of flow-tools from source, download the source code from *http://code.google.com/p/flow-tools/*, and extract it. You'll need GNU make and GCC, as well as the libraries and header files for your operating system.

```
# tar -xf flow-tools-0.68.4.tar.bz2
```

Now go into the *flow-tools* directory, and read the *INSTALL* file for the current compiling instructions. The process probably includes the steps configure, make, and make install.

Before installing, run **./configure --help** to list the build and installation options. The option I find most useful when installing is prefix, which allows you to specify where you want the software installed.

Most Unix-like operating systems install prepackaged software in */usr/local/bin*, */usr/local/sbin*, and so on. When you build a package such as flow-tools from source, however, your installation is not tightly integrated with the system's package management system. I suggest installing it in a location not used by the rest of the system because you don't want an operating system update to overwrite part of flow-tools or, worse, revert it to the obsolete version shipped with your OS! (Don't forget to update your PATH and MANPATH environment variables to include your new directories.)

In the following example, you'll install flow-tools under */usr/local/flow*. I'll use this directory for the examples throughout this book.

```
# ./configure --prefix=/usr/local/flow
# make
# make install
```

If your system is missing any prerequisites, the installation process will produce an error after the first command. After a successful install, you will find commands under */usr/local/flow/bin*, manual pages under */usr/local/flow/share/man*, and so on.

DON'T CLEAN UP

Do not run make clean after building flow-tools from source. I find that I occasionally need to return to the source code for troubleshooting.

Running flow-capture

The flow-capture program listens on a specified UDP port for incoming flow exports. It then captures the data and writes flow records to disk. flow-capture must know where to write the files, how often to start a new file, who to accept flow information from, and so on. The flow-capture manual page offers many options, but the following example suffices for many situations:

```
# flow-capture -p /var/run/flow-capture.pid -n 287 -w /var/db/flows -S 5 192.0.2.1/192.0.2.10/5678
```

The -p argument tells flow-capture where to store its process ID (PID) file. The location */var/run/flow-capture.pid* is a common default for most Unix-like operating systems.

The -n option tells flow-capture how many times it should rotate its log files in a 24-hour period. 287 tells flow-capture to create a new log file every five minutes. (The astute among you will notice that a day contains 288 five-minute periods. Flow-capture creates one file and then rotates to a new one 287 times in a day, for a total of 288 log files per day.) Many of the add-on reporting programs you'll use expect log files in five-minute increments.

Tell flow-capture where to write its files with -w. The directory */var/db/flows* is a common choice, though some prefer */var/log/flows*. Either way, each collector needs its own directory, so you might want to use something like */var/db/flows/internet* or */var/log/internet_flows*.

The -S 5 option tells flow-capture to log messages to syslog, telling how many flows it has processed, how many packets it has received, and how many flows it believes it has dropped. The argument (5) is the number of minutes between log messages.

flow-capture uses the syslog facility LOCAL6. (Check a syslog tutorial to learn how to manage syslog messages.) You cannot change this facility without delving deep into the flow-capture source code.

The last command line argument (192.0.2.10/192.0.2.1/5678) specifies flow-capture's network configuration. The first address is the IP address on the local machine that flow-capture listens to. As you can see in the listing above, our sample collector runs on the IP address 192.0.2.10. If you put a 0 in this space, the collector will accept traffic on all IP addresses on the machine. Even if your collector has only one IP address, I recommend explicitly assigning that address to your collector. You might add more IP addresses to your collector at a later date, and you probably don't want flow-capture attaching to those addresses as well.

The second IP, 192.0.2.1, is the address of the sensor that is permitted to send data to this collector. If you were to put 0 here (or eliminate it) instead of an IP address , flow-capture would accept flow data from any address. Doing so increases the risk that an intruder will send bogus data to your collector but also permits you to accept flows from multiple sources simultaneously. (Almost all Unix-like operating systems have packet filter functions that would let you protect this port from all but sensors you specify, however.)

Finally, 5678 is the UDP port flow-capture listens to. Because no authority has formally assigned a UDP port for Cisco NetFlow, you should use any high-numbered port not reserved by any other service. Port 6434 is assigned to sFlow, and ports 4739–4740 have been assigned to IPFIX, so you might want to use one of those ports. Also, many Cisco NetFlow products use port 2055, which was assigned to Cisco for a product never publicly released.

Try to start flow-capture on your system with options appropriate for your system. Confirm that it continues to run for a few minutes. This validates that you haven't made any fundamental mistakes in building or installing the software and that your command line is basically correct.

Starting flow-capture at Boot

Your operating system must start flow-capture at boot time, just as it does any other critical service. The process for doing so varies widely with operating systems. If you installed flow-tools from a package provided by your operating system vendor, it almost certainly includes a startup script. For example, the Red Hat Linux RPM installs a startup script in */etc/init.d.* The FreeBSD package includes a startup script configured in */etc/rc.local.* You'll need to tell the script where to store the captured flow files, how often to rotate them, and what hosts to accept flow data from—in fact, all of the things you set in the flow-capture command in the previous section.

If the package for your chosen operating system doesn't include a startup script, add your flow-capture command into the computer's startup system appropriately. Check your operating system documentation. Sometimes this is as simple as copying the command into /etc/rc.local. flow-capture should start only after the network and local storage are started.

Reboot your system to verify that flow-capture starts on boot.

How Many Collectors?

Now that you have one instance of `flow-capture` running, it's time to decide how to handle incoming data. You can choose to have all your sensors feed data to a single collector or have each sensor feed data to its own collector instance.

Having all sensors feed records to one collector is simple. Configure one and only one collector, and do not restrict the addresses that can send to it. Configure all your sensors to use that single collector. The collector will intermingle all the flow records from all sensors into one common log file. But how do you tell whether flows are from one part of the network or another? You can differentiate flows by the sensor IP address, but this adds steps to the analysis.

In the absence of compelling reasons otherwise, I recommend running a separate collector for each flow sensor to help you keep your data separate. All the `flow-capture` instances can run on the same server and use the same IP address, and you can assign each `flow-capture` process its own UDP port and data directory so that you can analyze traffic from each network segment separately. Combining separated data is much easier than separating combined data.

Collector Log Files

Your collector won't record anything until a sensor starts sending data. Once data reaches the collector, however, the collector creates a log file of the following format:

tmp-v05.2009-11-15.134501-0500

The leading *tmp* in this filename indicates that this is a temporary file. `flow-capture` is still writing to this file. The year, month, and day on which the flow file was created comes next, followed by the timestamp in 24-hour format. The time given is the time the flow file was created, not the time the log file was completed and closed off. This example flow file was created on November 15, 2009 (*2009-11-15*), at 13:45:01 or 1:45:01 PM (*134501*). The last number (*-0500*) is the time zone offset from UTC. My collector is running in Eastern standard time, negative five hours east of UTC. If your collector is in a time zone west of UTC, the time zone offset will have a + in front of it. If you have multiple collectors in multiple time zones, I recommend having them all use the same time zone, such as UTC.

When it's time to create a new file, `flow-capture` renames the current temporary file to begin with *ft-* and creates a new temporary file. The name otherwise remains the same, allowing you to easily identify and sort flow files by creation time.

Collector Troubleshooting

If you configure a sensor to send data to your collector but flow-capture isn't generating any log files within a few minutes, start troubleshooting. Either the sensor is not transmitting data, flow-capture is not writing the data to disk, or a firewall between the sensor and collector is blocking that port.

To begin troubleshooting, first verify that sensor data is reaching your collector with tcpdump in order to separate network problems from local software problems.

```
# tcpdump -p -n -i em0 udp and port 5678
```

The -p tells tcpdump to *not* put the interface into promiscuous mode. This means that the system will only sniff traffic that reaches the local interface. (A proper switch configuration should prevent promiscuous-mode sniffing, but using -p means that the machine won't even try.) The -i argument gives the name of the interface that you want to listen to, em0 in this case, which happens to be a network card on my system. (Most Linux distributions have a primary network interface of eth0.) Finally, specify the port your collector runs on, 5678 in this case.

This command should print information about every packet arriving at your collector host on the specified port. If you don't see any data reaching the collector host, check your sensor configuration and the configuration of any firewalls between the sensor and collector, and then use your packet sniffer progressively closer to the sensor until you find where the data stops. If you reach your sensor and find that it's not putting any flow exports on the wire, your sensor configuration is suspect. If necessary, contact your vendor for assistance.

If the system is receiving flow data but flow-capture is not writing any log files, check your flow-capture configuration to be sure that you specified the proper UDP port and directory. Verify that the user running flow-capture can write files to that directory. Also check the system logs, such as */var/log/ messages*, for error messages. (Remember, flow-capture uses LOCAL6. Be certain to configure syslog to log LOCAL6 messages to a file.)

Configuring Hardware Flow Sensors

Configuring hardware flow sensors is your simplest and best option in most cases. Many network hardware manufacturers, such as Cisco, include flow export in their products. Cisco routers have supported NetFlow since the 1990s. Some larger Cisco switches also support NetFlow, but for best results you must configure switches differently than routers. Juniper routers also support flow export, so I'll cover configuring them. A number of smaller router vendors also support flow export, but you'll need to check your vendor's documentation for configuration instructions.

The book's examples will assume that the flow collector is running on the host 10.10.10.10 on UDP port 5678. Replace these with appropriate values for your environment.

Cisco Routers

Configure NetFlow on a Cisco router interface by interface. You probably need NetFlow only on your upstream interface(s), not on the local Ethernet interface. (If you have a complex Ethernet infrastructure, such as an HSRP or VRRP cluster, you might want to monitor flows on the Ethernet interfaces as well.) In the following example, you activate NetFlow on the interface Serial0/0:

```
Router# conf t
Router(config)# int s0/0
Router(config-if)# ip route-cache flow
Router(config-if)# exit
```

Repeat this configuration on all upstream router interfaces, and then tell the router where to send flow data.

```
Router(config)# ip flow-export version 5
Router(config)# ip flow-export destination 10.10.10.10 5678
```

Now save your work. You should find that data goes to your collector almost immediately.

To see the flow information tracked on your router, use the IOS command `show ip cache flow`.

Some Cisco models use a slightly different syntax. If you have trouble, search Cisco's website or the Internet for suggestions.

Cisco Switches

NetFlow on Cisco switches is a comparatively recent development and is limited to higher-end models. As a rule, only modular switches such as the 4000, 6000, and their descendants support NetFlow export. Many switches also require an add-on NetFlow card that you might or might not have. Stackable switches do not, nor do smaller stand-alone managed switches. Enable or disable NetFlow for the switch as a whole, not on a per-interface basis.

NetFlow support varies widely by model and the IOS version installed. I'm providing a sample configuration here, but do not blindly install it on your switch! Cisco switches can perform many tasks in many different ways, and what works in my environment might not work in yours.

Before configuring NetFlow on your router, ask Cisco how to capture all flow data from your model of switch in your environment. Your configuration will probably look similar to the following sample.

NOTE   *If you decide that you want to just try this and see what happens, back up your config-uration first and try it while you have no users on the network.*

```
Switch# conf t
Switch(config)# ip route-cache flow
Switch(config)# ip flow ingress
Switch(config)# ip flow ingress layer2-switched
Switch(config)# ip flow-export version 7
Switch(config)# ip flow-export destination 10.10.10.10 5678
```

The second line's configuration statement (ip route-cache flow) tells the switch to activate flows, and the next one (ip flow ingress) tells the switch to track flows based on the route they take to enter the switch.

By default these routing-capable switches export information only about flows that they route, not switched Ethernet traffic. However, because you want to capture flow information about the local Ethernet traffic as well, you tell the switch to capture the layer 2 flows as well with **ip flow ingress layer2-switched**.

Cisco switches speak NetFlow version 7, so you might as well use it. Turn it on with **ip flow-export version 7**. Finally, you tell the switch where to send the flow data, to 10.10.10.10, port 5678.

Once you've completed your configuration, save your work. Data should arrive at your collector almost immediately. As with a Cisco router, use the command **show ip cache flow** to see current flow statistics.

Juniper Routers

Juniper configurations are much longer than Cisco configurations, but the configuration isn't that difficult. Start by telling the Juniper how to sample flow traffic and where you want the flows sent.

```
    forwarding-options {
      sampling {
        input {
          family inet {
❶         rate 1;
          run-length 9;
        }
      }
      output {
❷       cflowd 10.10.10.10 {
❸       port 5678
❹       source-address 172.16.16.16;
        version 5;
        no-local-dump;
        }
      }
    }
  }
```

Despite all the parentheses, this configuration isn't that hard to understand. You begin at ❶ by defining how heavily you want to sample flows. In this example, I've set the sampling rate to 1. This Juniper samples 1 flow out of every 1, or all, flows. If you were to set the sampling rate to 100, the Juniper would sample 1 out of every 100 packets. This example betrays my personal bias; I record all traffic, if possible. If complete traffic recording overloads your router, increase the sampling level until the hardware can support it. Those of you with 10GB networks almost certainly must sample! The only way to determine the lowest sustainable sampling rate on your network is through experimentation. Sampling too aggressively overloads the router and causes packet loss.

As you might remember, cflowd is an obsolete flow collector. Juniper hardware uses that name to specify where the router will send flows. At ❷ you tell the Juniper where to find your flow collector, the UDP port (❸) the collector runs on, and what address on the router (❹) to send packets from.

Now enable sampling on the interface(s) you want to capture flow data from.

```
...
  family inet {
    sampling {
      input;
      output;
    }
...
```

This configuration sends the incoming and outgoing traffic on this interface to the flow export (or sampling) engine.

Configuring Software Flow Sensors

Suppose you need flow export on a network but don't have any switches that support flow export. Never fear, you can implement a flow sensor in software instead of buying new hardware.

Using software instead of hardware for flow sensing has limitations. For one, software needs to run on a server, so it adds another device to your network. Also, you can only capture data from a managed Ethernet switch. The software might not capture all the traffic, and it might not tell you when it misses something. And flow sensor software is yet another thing that the network administrator must configure, patch, and maintain. Don't you have enough to do already? Still, for a small network, software is the only realistic choice.

Setting Up Sensor Server Hardware

Flow sensor software requires very few system resources. You can easily use a desktop that your management took out of production because it ran so slowly that the receptionist couldn't use it anymore. I've run effective flow sensors on tiny computers such as the Soekris (*http://www.soekris.com/*). Even a modest machine with a 266MHz CPU and 128MB of RAM was mostly idle while capturing traffic off a low-traffic LAN.

Whatever hardware you choose, your flow sensor machine needs at least two network interfaces. One interface must be capable of handling many packets per second. If you're recycling a discarded desktop machine with a network card embedded on the motherboard, assume that the built-in network card is not of sufficient quality. Very few desktop motherboard vendors use high-end network chipsets, preferring to use inexpensive chipsets that are just barely adequate for most users. If you're not sure what network card to buy, Intel's cards usually suffice for a flow sensor. The embedded network cards on server-grade systems are usually adequate; they're not great, but they're adequate.

Finally, if you recycle an old machine for flow sensor hardware, get a new hard drive. Flow sensors use very little hard drive space, but the hard drive is the system component most likely to fail with age. You don't want to install your flow sensor just to see your work evaporate in a few weeks because the hard drive shattered! (Senior systems administrators might consider building a flow sensor bootable CD out of a tool kit such as FreeSBIE so that you can mass-produce easily replaceable sensors.)

Finally, I recommend using the same operating system on both your flow sensor server and your collector. This is certainly not a requirement, but running multiple operating systems in production just because you can is a symptom of having too much time on your hands.

Network Setup

Using a software flow sensor requires that you have a switch capable of *port mirroring* or *port monitoring*. This is often called a *sniffer port*. The switch copies all traffic crossing the switch to the monitor interface. You might verify this with a packet sniffer before proceeding.

To configure a monitor port on a Cisco system, define the interfaces you want to monitor and the interface to which you want to direct traffic. In the following example, a Cisco switch is copying all traffic from VLAN 1 into interface Gi0/4. (Many switch vendors also offer web-based configuration tools.)

```
router# conf t
❶ router(config)# monitor session 1 source vlan 1
❷ router(config)# monitor session 1 destination interface Gi0/4
```

You start at ❶ by defining a monitor session and telling the switch which VLAN or ports to monitor. Then at ❷ you tell the switch where to replicate the monitored traffic. This small switch will now copy all traffic crossing the main VLAN to the monitor port.

A switch that can export flows should be large enough to allow you to connect all of your primary servers to it so that all critical traffic crosses that big switch and your flow exports capture pretty much everything vital. If you use a few smaller switches instead of one big one, ensure that the monitor port captures traffic from all critical servers.

Remember, any traffic that remains on a closet switch will not be captured. You could deploy a flow sensor on every switch, but that quickly becomes cumbersome.

Sensor Server Setup

A switch will not accept regular traffic on a monitor port, so the sensor machine cannot use the monitor port for its network traffic. (Go ahead, try it.) Sniffer ports are only for watching the network, not participating in the network. Your sensor box needs a second network card for regular network activity.

On Linux and BSD systems, you must activate the sniffer interface before it can sense traffic. It's also wise to disable ARP on the interface (with the up and -arp commands) so that your sniffer interface doesn't even try to participate in the network. Here, you start the interface em0 and disable ARP on it:

```
# ifconfig em0 up -arp
```

Substitute your sniffer interface for em0, and then use tcpdump to verify that you're seeing network traffic on your sniffer interface.

```
# tcpdump -n -i em0
```

You should see traffic records streaming across the screen. Press CTRL-C to stop the output.

Running the Sensor on the Collector

If your collector runs on higher-end hardware and you don't need many sensors, you might consider running the sensor on the collector machine. Add another network interface to the machine, have the sensor run on that interface, then configure the sensor to transmit to a UDP port on the localhost IP (127.0.0.1), and have the collector accept connections only from 127.0.0.1.

This machine becomes doubly security sensitive, however. Not only does the collector have a historical record of traffic through your network, but it can view all current network activity. Secure this machine!

The Sensor: softflowd

Again, an Internet search will reveal many different software flow sensors, but I recommend softflowd, from *http://www.mindrot.org/softflowd.html*. Go there to identify the current version; if you can find a current package for your operating system, use it. If you cannot find a package, download the source code, and install the program by hand.

Check the softflowd README file for instructions on how to build. Much like flow-tools, softflowd has a configure script. I prefer to install my add-on software in a different directory than the main system so I can easily keep it separate. Here I install softflowd under */usr/local/softflowd*:

```
# configure --prefix=/usr/local/softflowd
# gmake
# gmake install
```

This installs two programs (softflowd and softflowctl), a man page for each program, and a README file.

Running softflowd

To run softflowd, you must know the interface softflowd will listen to, the collector's hostname or IP address, and the port the collector is running on. Here, I'm having softflowd listen to the port em0 and transmit data to 10.10.10.10 on port 5678:

```
# softflowd -i em0 -t maxlife=300 -n 10.10.10.10:5678
```

The -t maxlife=300 in the middle of the command sets the flow timeout to 300 seconds, or five minutes.

softflowd is more flexible than a hardware flow sensor, which means you have more opportunities to misconfigure it. The manual page has a complete list of ways you can adjust softflowd's performance, but most of them are not useful in most environments. The one option that might be helpful, though, is the ability to change the upper limit on the number of flows soft-flowd will track at any one time.

By default softflowd tracks up to 8,192 flows at once, using about 800KB of memory. That's an awful lot of simultaneous connections, but if you're monitoring a high-bandwidth link, you might need to raise it. (The next section shows how to see how many flows softflowd is actually tracking at any given time.) Use the -m flag to specify the upper limit on the number of tracked flows.

```
# softflowd -i em0 -t 5m -m 16384 -n 10.10.10.10:5678
```

This example tracks twice the normal number of flows.

Watching softflowd

The softflowctl program allows the network administrator to manage a running softflowd process. You can use it to start and stop collecting flows, view currently tracked flows, and flush all flows being tracked to the collector. The softflowctl manual page gives instructions for all of softflowctl's features, but I'll cover only the functions used in normal circumstances.

The easy `softflowctl` commands are shutdown and exit. To tell `softflowd` to export all the flows it's currently tracking to the collector and shut itself down, use the `shutdown` command. This is the recommended way to terminate `softflowd`.

```
# softflowctl shutdown
```

If you want `softflowd` to shut itself off without sending any additional flows to the collector, use the `exit` command. You will lose any data `softflowd` has gathered but not exported.

```
# softflowctl exit
```

The more interesting features of `softflowctl` include the ability to view currently tracked flows and the ability to view the `softflowd`'s internal statistics on tracked flows.

Viewing Tracked Flows

If you want to see the flows that `softflowd` is currently tracking, use `softflowctl`'s `dump-flows` command. Each line is a single flow. If you see flows, `softflowd` is working.

```
# softflowctl dump-flows
softflowd[61946]: Dumping flow data:
ACTIVE seq:84 [❶192.0.2.253]:❷4234 <> [❸239.255.255.250]:❹1900 proto:❺17
octets>:314 packets>:1 octets<:0 packets<:0 start:2011-12-07T15:03:18.541
finish:2011-12-07T15:03:18.541 tcp>:00 tcp<:00 flowlabel>:00000000
flowlabel<:00000000
EXPIRY EVENT for flow 84 now
...
```

This flow involves a host with an IP of 192.0.2.253 (❶) and port 4234 (❷), and the other end of the connection is the host 239.255.255.250 (❸) on port 1900 (❹). This flow uses protocol 17 (❺), or UDP. Although you can see timing information as well, you'll have other ways to view this data more conveniently.

Viewing Flow Statistics

`softflowd` starts tracking flows immediately upon starting. You can use `softflowctl` to query `softflowd` about the characteristics of the flows it is currently tracking with the statistics command, as shown here:

```
# softflowctl statistics
```

I'll break up the lengthy output from this command into a few sections to make it easier to understand.

```
❶ softflowd[61946]: Accumulated statistics:
❷ Number of active flows: 16
❸ Packets processed: 11898
❹ Fragments: 0
❺ Ignored packets: 46 (46 non-IP, 0 too short)
❻ Flows expired: 759 (0 forced)
❼ Flows exported: 784 in 67 packets (0 failures)
❽ Packets received by libpcap: 12156
❾ Packets dropped by libpcap: 0
❿ Packets dropped by interface: 0
```

The first line at ❶ includes one interesting number: the process ID of the softflowd process you're querying. If you're running multiple instances of softflowd on one machine, this will help you verify that you're querying the correct one.

The number of active flows at ❷ tells you how many flows softflowd thinks are ongoing. This is not the same as the number of active connections on your network at the moment. Remember, a sensor tracks a flow unless either it has reason to think that the flow has ended or the timeout expires. A flow from a DNS or UDP NFS request remains in softflowd's list of tracked flows until the timeout expires, which may be long after the corresponding network activity has ceased.

The number of packets processed (❸) should always increase, and the number of fragments (❹) probably will increase but less quickly.

The number of packets dropped (❺) is much more interesting. Every network tends to have "odd stuff" fluttering across it now and then. Flow management only handles TCP/IP and its related protocols, including IPv6, SCTP, and other advanced protocols. When softflowd encounters packets that are not part of TCP/IP, such as DECNet, it counts them but doesn't otherwise process them. Dropped packets might come from bad hardware, badly scrambled TCP/IP stacks, unusual network protocols, or any other weird error. You might try netstat -s to get an idea about which part of your system is dropping packets, and why. softflowd also drops packets that are too short to contain actual data.

You can see at ❻ that the number of flows softflowd has expired, as well as at ❼ how many it has exported to the collector. These numbers do not necessarily equal each other, because the former is a softflowd internal statistic. The number of flows exported should match the number received on the collector, however. If you see that softflowd has forced some flows to expire, use -m to increase the number of flows softflowd may track.

Libpcap is the packet-capture software softflowd uses. At ❽, the number of packets libpcap receives should be roughly comparable to the number of packets softflowd has processed. At ❾, the number of packets dropped by libpcap should be very low for proper data capture. If this number is increasing, investigate. Your operating system or your hardware might not be adequate to the load being placed on it.

It's also possible that your network card might not be up to the task of capturing all the data from your network. Finally, at ❿, the packets dropped by interface counter should be zero, or at least very low.

The output continues with information about the expired flows.

Expired flow statistics:	minimum	average	maximum
Flow bytes:	❶ 221	❹ 263570	7564472
Flow packets:	❷ 1	345	9446
Duration:	❸ 0.00s	❺ 22.73s	307.47s

The smallest flow (❶) had 221 bytes. The smallest number of packets in a flow (❷) was 1. The briefest flow (❸) lasted less than one one-hundredth of a second.

You can make some guesses based on this data. For example, it's likely but not certain that the 221-byte flow was in a single packet, and it probably was the briefest as well. You might have many flows containing a small number of bytes in a single packet, though, and it's possible that the 221-byte flow was broken into multiple small packets. To reach any conclusions about particular flows, you must perform more detailed analysis. Treat the maximum values similarly; the flow with the greatest number of bytes was not necessarily the flow with the greatest number of packets.

The average flow (❹) was 263,570 bytes, or roughly 257KB, and lasted about 22 seconds (❺). Again, you cannot assume that the average-sized flows are the same as the flows with the average number of packets or the flows of average duration.

The statistics end with a count of the reasons why softflowd expired and exported each flow and a per-protocol statistics list.

```
Expired flow reasons:
            tcp =       10   tcp.rst =   ❶ 1   tcp.fin =   ❷ 1
            udp =      126      icmp =   ❸ 0   general =     0
  ❹   maxlife =        5
  ❺   over 2Gb =       0
  ❻   maxflows =       0
  ❼   flushed =        0

Per-protocol statistics:        Octets    Packets   Avg Life   Max Life
               tcp (6):       32994923      36899    195.36s    330.44s
              udp (17):          46014        135      0.00s      0.03s
```

TCP and UDP have their own entries, including the specific reasons why flows were expired. For example, as shown at ❶, TCP flows can be expired by a TCP RST indicating that a port is closed or by the TCP FIN (❷) that marks the end of a normal session. Similarly, a UDP request to a closed port can generate an ICMP response, as shown at ❸, or it might just time out.

softflowctl also displays the number of flows expired because the timeout elapsed (❹) and the number expired because they exceeded the maximum size of a single flow (❺).

The softflowd program tracks a maximum number of flows simultaneously. If softflowd detects more flows than it can track, it expires older idle flows until it has sufficient capacity to track active flows. If the maxflows number (❼) begins climbing, increase the number of flows softflowd can track at any time.

Finally, the flushed entry (❽) shows how many flows were expired when the administrator ran softflowctl expire-all.

The statistics section ends with per-protocol flow information.

Now that you've gathered some data, you'll learn how to look at it in Chapter 3.

3

VIEWING FLOWS

You have sensors transmitting data, and your collector is writing that data to disk. Now what? Flow-tools provides several programs for viewing flow data, generating statistical analysis, and generating reports. You'll start by displaying the data in the flow files.

Using flow-print

Flow files contain tightly packed binary data, and viewing a flow file with cat or more will scramble your terminal. To view flow data, you should use flow-print.

Each flow file contains header information that identifies the host that exported the data, the capture time, and so on. When you need to view multiple flow files, you should strip out these headers before feeding the data to flow-print so that they don't interfere with your viewing of the actual flow data. That's where flow-cat comes in. You'll use flow-cat to concatenate multiple flow files and present clean data to flow-print. Although using flow-cat is optional, I recommend that you always use it with `flow-print` unless you are specifically examining header data.

To examine a flow file, use `flow-cat` to feed the data to `flow-print`, and then pipe the result to a pager so that you can view all of the results, as shown in Listing 3-1.

```
# flow-cat ft-v05.2009-12-01.171500-0500 | flow-print | less
srcIP           dstIP           prot  srcPort  dstPort  octets    packets
36.85.32.9      158.43.192.1    17    2325     53       59        1
158.43.192.1    36.85.32.9      17    53       2325     134       1
36.85.32.37     83.243.35.204   6     25       4115     1035      14
83.243.35.204   36.85.32.37     6     4115     25       1527      12
...
```

Listing 3-1: Sample flow-print output

Each line in Listing 3-1 represents one flow. The first column, `srcIP`, shows the source IP address of the flow, and the second (`dstIP`) shows the destination address.

The `prot` column displays the protocol number for this flow. Protocol 17 is UDP, and protocol 6 is TCP. (Table 3-1 on page 44 describes the protocols most commonly seen on a network, and you'll find a mostly complete list of these protocols numbers in the */etc/protocols* file on your collector server.)

The `srcPort` column shows the source port of a TCP or UDP flow, and `dstPort` shows the destination port. Finally, the `octets` column shows the number of bytes in the flow, and `packets` shows the number of packets in the flow.

The first flow in Listing 3-1 comes from the address 36.85.32.9. This is an address on my network that's going to the IP 158.43.192.1. Off the top of my head, I haven't the foggiest idea what this address is or why I'm communicating with it, but I do know that protocol 17 is UDP, the source port is 2325, and the destination port is 53. Port 53 is the UDP port reserved for DNS transactions, so I know that this flow represents a DNS query, and I also know from the octets column that 59 bytes were sent in one packet.

Now look at the second flow in Listing 3-1. Notice that the source and destination IP addresses are reversed from our first flow: The remote end sent data from port 53 to port 2325 on my end, which is the reverse of the first flow. The response, 134 bytes in one packet, is almost certainly a DNS response to the query sent in the first flow, but I'd need to view the timing information to be absolutely certain.

The third flow in Listing 3-1 originates from a different IP on my network and is going to a different remote IP than either of the IPs in the first two flows. This flow represents a TCP/IP transaction that is separate and different from the first two flows. This transaction runs over protocol 6 (or TCP) and has a source port of 25 and a destination port of 4115. That's odd. TCP port 25 is used for SMTP, or email. You would expect an email connection to be *to* port 25, not *from* port 25. Why would a network transaction have a *source* port of 25? Remember, every network transaction includes two flows: one from the client to the server and another from the server to the client. This "source port 25" flow is the server's communication to the client.

Now look at the fourth and final flow. This flow is the reverse of the third flow and represents the other half of that SMTP transaction. The source port is 4115, and the destination is 25, which makes sense if someone is trying to send mail to the email server.

As these last two lines demonstrate, `flow-print` does not necessarily print flows in the order in which the traffic occurred. For example, if two hosts have very fast connectivity to each other, the flow record might show both the flow that initiates a connection and the flow that is the response to that connection request as starting simultaneously. In that case, `flow-print` displays the flows in the order in which they are recorded in the flow file. (We'll extract actual timing data from flow files later.)

BITS, BYTES, AND OCTETS

Most network management systems offer information about traffic in some multiple of bits—kilobits, megabits, and so on, all in base 10. However, some flow analysis systems, such as flow-tools, offer traffic information in *octets*, rather than bits or even bytes, because the byte is not always 8 bits.

Most computing professionals know a byte as 8 bits. But *very* strictly speaking, most computer professionals are wrong. A byte is the smallest unit of memory addressing on a particular hardware platform. The Intel 8086 CPU and its descendants, today's most common machines, have an 8-bit byte, which many other platforms adopted as a convenient standard. Commercially available hardware exists with bytes anywhere from 5 to 12 bits, and experimental hardware can have bytes of just about any size.

An octet is always eight bits, the same size as the normal byte. If you have systems where a byte is not 8 bits, the word *byte* is ambiguous. Some software, such as flow-tools, explicitly uses octets for disambiguation because almost all network administrators only have hardware with 8-bit bytes. (Most of us don't have odd hardware.) You just need to recognize octets when you see them and be grateful that some network administrators suffer from annoyances you'll never need to cope with.

Printing Protocol and Port Names

You probably remember that port 53 is for the Domain Name System, and port 25 is for email's SMTP protocol, but most of us haven't memorized the purpose of every port number. Similarly, you might remember that protocol 6 is TCP and 17 is UDP, but you can't bother memorizing all the other protocol numbers. The files */etc/protocols* and */etc/services* list port numbers and their associated names. Use the -n flag to have `flow-print` display ports and protocols using these names, as shown here:

```
# flow-cat ft-v05.2011-12-01.171500-0500 | flow-print -n | less
srcIP            dstIP            prot  srcPort   dstPort  octets    packets
36.85.32.9       158.43.192.1     udp   2325      domain   59        1
158.43.192.1     36.85.32.9       udp   domain    2325     134       1
36.85.32.37      83.243.35.204    tcp   smtp      4115     1035      14
83.243.35.204    36.85.32.37      tcp   4115      smtp     1527      12
...
```

These are the same results as in Listing 3-1, except that in the prot column tcp replaces 6 and udp replaces 17. Similarly, the numbers in the srcPort and dstPort columns have been replaced with service names such as domain and smtp. While using names for port numbers is reasonable, using hostnames instead of IP addresses introduces a dependency on the network. Also, getting hostnames for hundreds or thousands of IP addresses can take a very long time.

Not all flow-print formats support output with names, however. In those output formats, flow-print ignores the -n flag.

Common Protocol and Port Number Assignments

Once you've worked with flow information for a while, you'll begin to recognize port and protocol numbers automatically. Table 3-1 lists some protocols you'll commonly see on the Internet.

Table 3-1: Common Protocol Numbers

Number	Protocol
1	Internet Control Message Protocol (ICMP)
6	Transmission Control Protocol (TCP)
17	User Datagram Protocol (UDP)
47	Generic Routing Encapsulation (GRE)
50	Encapsulating Security Payload (ESP)
51	Authentication Header (AH)

Similarly, Table 3-2 lists a few of the commonly used TCP and UDP port assignments on internal and public networks. (For a more complete list, see */etc/services* on your collector host.)

Table 3-2: Common TCP and UDP Port Assignments

Number	Service
20	File Transfer Protocol (FTP) data channel
21	File Transfer Protocol (FTP) control channel
22	Secure Shell (SSH)
23	Telnet
25	Email (SMTP)
53	Domain Name Service (DNS)
80	Hypertext Transfer Protocol (HTTP, Web)
137	NetBIOS Naming Service (Windows file sharing)
138	NetBIOS Datagram Service (Windows file sharing)
139	NetBIOS Session Service (Windows file sharing)
161	Simple Network Management Protocol (SNMP)
389	Lightweight Directory Access Protocol (LDAP)
443	Secure HTTP (HTTPS)
445	SMB over TCP (Windows file sharing)

You'll find many more ports than this in use, of course, and if you find that a port isn't in this list or in */etc/services*, an Internet search should identify it. Some ports will stubbornly resist identification from the network, though: Some program on the host is using that port, and you'll need to use that host's native tools to identify that program.

PORTS VS. SERVICES

Always remember that a port assignment is not conclusive proof that a particular protocol is running over that port. A systems administrator can run any program on any port. For example, you can run a web server on port 25 (email) or an FTP server on port 443 (HTTPS). One of my servers runs SSH on ports 23, 25, 53, 80, 443, and more, which lets me evade most simple packet-filtering firewalls. If you discover suspicious traffic, such as very long TCP-based DNS requests, remember that users are tricky little buggers and will try just about anything to evade your access controls.

Viewing Flow Record Header Information with -p

Each flow file includes header data that records the collector hostname, timing and compression information, and other capture data. The -p flag prints the header information from a flow file before any of the flows to make it easier for you to identify the sensor host, start and stop time of a flow, how long a flow ran, how many flows flow-capture believes were lost in transit, and so on. This flow data is not frequently useful, but you can see it if you think it might help.

Remember, flow-cat specifically strips out this header data to avoid confusing other flow tools, which means that you can only effectively examine the headers of one flow file at a time, and you cannot use flow-cat.

```
# flow-print -p < ft-v05.2011-12-01.171500-0500 | less
```

Printing to a Wide Terminal

Many flow-print reports contain a lot of information and as such don't have very much whitespace between columns. The -w flag tells flow-print that you have a wide terminal, so it can add extra space between the columns to make the output easier to read. If you have a very wide terminal, however, I suggest you look at format 5 instead.

FLAGS AND CONTROL BITS

The TCP protocol includes *flags*, also known as *control bits*. flow-print provides the flags field for TCP flows, but this field is meaningless for other protocols. I'll call TCP flags by the name *control bits* to be consistent.

Setting flow-print Formats with -f

Because the default `flow-print` output might not include all the information you're interested in (and it certainly doesn't include all the information included within a flow file), `flow-print` supports a wide variety of output formats. You set the `flow-print` format with the `-f` flag.

Each format has a number. For example, format 3 is the default format most commonly used by `flow-print`. (If you are using NetFlow version 8, `flow-print` might choose a different default.) You can use these format options to present flow data in the manner that best suits you, as demonstrated in the following examples. I'll cover only the most useful ones, but you can learn about the other formats in the `flow-print` man page.

Showing Interfaces and Ports in Hex with Format -f 0

If you want to view the router interfaces the flows passed through, use format 0, as shown here:

```
# flow-cat ft-v05.2011-12-01.171500-0500 | flow-print -f 0 | less
Sif  SrcIPaddress     Dif DstIPaddress      Pr SrcP DstP Pkts     Octets
0000 36.85.32.9       0000 158.43.192.1     11 915  35   1        59
0000 158.43.192.1     0000 36.85.32.9       11 35   915  1        134
0000 36.85.32.37      0000 83.243.35.204    06 19   1013 14       1035
0000 83.243.35.204    0000 36.85.32.37      06 1013 19   12       1527
...
```

Much of this output looks the same as the default output, but notice the addition of the `Sif` and `Dif` columns. These represent the source (`Sif`) and destination (`Dif`) interfaces. Flow records include information on which interface a packet entered on and which interface the flow departed on. You can match these to router interfaces, as you'll see in Chapter 4 ("Identifying Interface Numbers Using SNMP" on page 68).

However, software flow sensors do *not* record interface information because they cannot access it. Software-based sensors listen to a monitor port on a switch, but they can't see interface information. The interface number is always 0 as far as they're concerned.

Format 0 adds interface numbers to the flow output by compressing some of the other columns. The protocol column is now `Pr`, for example. But take a look at the numbers. The first flow is protocol 11 (or Network Voice Protocol per */etc/protocols*), the source port is 915, and the destination port is 35. You're almost certainly not running NVP on your network! What's going on here?

What's happening is that this format creates space for interface numbers by printing port and protocol information in hexadecimal. For example, 11 is hex for 17, or UDP; 915 is hex for 2325; and 35 is hex for 53. As it turns out, all four of these flows are exactly the same flows shown in the earlier examples, just printed in hex and with the interface column added.

Printing the port numbers in hex is useful if you're looking at ICMP flows. If you're looking at TCP or UDP flows with ports and interfaces on something other than an old 80-column terminal, use the 132-column format instead.

Two Lines with Times, Flags, and Hex Ports Using -f 1

There is a better way to show all the information for a flow on a standard-width screen: Split each flow across two lines. Use format 1 to see interface information and times as well.

```
# flow-cat ft-v05.2011-12-01.171500-0500 | flow-print -n -f 1 | less
Sif  SrcIPaddress      DIf  DstIPaddress        Pr SrcP DstP  Pkts   Octets
    StartTime              EndTime             Active   B/Pk Ts Fl

0000 36.85.32.9        0000 158.43.192.1        11 915   35    1       59
❶  1201.17:09:46.750  1201.17:09:46.869         0.119 59  00 00

0000 158.43.192.1      0000 36.85.32.9          11 35    915   1      134
    1201.17:09:46.750  1201.17:09:46.869         0.119 134 00 00

0000 36.85.32.37       0000 83.243.35.204       06 19    1013  14    1035
    1201.17:09:46.912  1201.17:09:51.890         4.978 ❷73  00 1b

0000 83.243.35.204     0000 36.85.32.37         06 1013  19    12    1527
    1201.17:09:46.912  1201.17:09:51.890         4.978 ❸127 00 1b
...
```

These are the same flows that have appeared in all preceding examples, but they look very different. Each flow is shown on two lines, with a blank line separating individual flows. In addition, the entries on each line are slightly offset. This two-line format can be confusing at first glance, especially because it doesn't have actual columns: The header shows where information appears within each flow's two-line entry. The first line of each flow shows the source interface, source IP address, destination interface, destination IP address, protocol, source and destination ports, number of packets, and number of octets in the flow. (You've seen all of these before.) Take a moment to see how these appear in each of the four sample flows, and then you can look at the new items in the second line of each flow.

The StartTime and EndTime spaces give the time that a connection started and ended. Here, at ❶, 1201 represents the date, December 1. The next three values give the time in 24-hour-clock format: 17:09:46 is 5:09:46 PM. The last fraction is the millisecond the flow began, or .750 seconds. (If you need more precision than this, you're probably trying to solve the wrong problem.)

The Active column gives the number of seconds the flow was active, saving you the trouble of subtracting the StartTime from the EndTime (which would be easy with the first two flows but slightly more difficult as the flows grow longer).

The B/Pk space gives the average number of bytes per packet. The first flow had 59 bytes in 1 packet, so the math is pretty easy, but it's more difficult in larger flows. The third flow at ❷ averaged 73 bytes per packet, while the fourth at ❸ averaged 127 bytes per packet.

The Ts space gives the Type of Service (ToS), which is almost always 00 because most TCP/IP networks do not have to respect the ToS flag. Generally, a ToS in a packet indicates either that you're on an experimental network, that you're using complicated services such as VoIP or MPLS, or that someone is playing silly twits.[1]

The Fl space gives the flow's flags, the TCP control bits. Non-TCP flows, such as the first two, always show flags of zero. The third and fourth examples are TCP flows, and the flags are shown as 1b for both. See "TCP Control Bits and Flow Records" on page 50 to learn how to transform 1b into a meaningful value.

Printing BGP Information

Routers that speak Border Gateway Protocol (BGP) with multiple upstream ISPs transmit flow records that contain autonomous system numbers (ASNs). Format 4 prints this information instead of the port numbers. Otherwise, this format includes the usual source and destination addresses, protocol, octets, and packet information you've seen in other formats.

These are the same four flows used in Listing 3-1, displayed in format 4:

```
# flow-cat ft-v05.2011-12-01.171500-0500 | flow-print -n -f 4 | less
srcIP              dstIP              prot  srcAS  dstAS  octets      packets
36.85.32.9/0       158.43.192.1/0     udp   0      701    59          1
158.43.192.1/0     36.85.32.9/0       udp   701    0      134         1
36.85.32.37/0      83.243.35.204/0    tcp   0      4713   1035        14
83.243.35.204/0    36.85.32.37/0      tcp   4713   0      1527        12
...
```

Note in the previous listing that either the source (srcAS) or destination AS (dstAS) for each flow is 0. These flows are sourced locally. Flow sensors don't track your local AS.

If you're not using BGP, this format is irrelevant to you.

Wide-Screen Display

If you have a sufficiently wide monitor, working in 80 columns is an annoyance. Why not just have a single very wide format that can show the most useful stuff on a single line? While we're at it, let's get rid of that hexadecimal and print everything in decimal. That's what format 5 is for, the format I use most frequently when examining network problems.

---

1. Although Type of Service/Quality of Service are worthwhile topics and although flow-tools supports ToS/QoS, these topics are required by only a small fraction of networks. Including a proper discussion of them would make this book much longer. Once you understand how to search and report on flows based on ports and addresses, you won't have any trouble processing flows based on their ToS or QoS.

Like a summer special-effects blockbuster film, this format works nicely on a wide-screen monitor but less well on the printed page. But rather than provide an actual printed sample that would run across two facing pages of the book or have to be printed sideways, let's just walk through the fields this format shows.

```
# flow-cat ft-v05.2011-12-01.171500-0500 | flow-print -f 5 | less
```

Format 5 produces the columns Start, End, Sif, SrcIPaddress, SrcP, DstIPaddress, DstP, P, Fl, Pkts, and Octets.

Start and End give the times the flow begins and ends in millisecond resolution, just like format 1.

Then there's Sif (source interface), SrcIPaddress (source IP address), and SrcP (source port), followed by DIf (destination interface), DstIPAddress (destination IP address), and DstP (destination port). You should have no trouble reading these after understanding the earlier reports.

P is the protocol number.

Fl gives the TCP control bits printed in decimal.

At the end, Pkts gives you the number of packets in the flow, and Octets gives the bytes.

TIMES VS. TIMES

Flow record files are named after the time they were collected on the server. The times shown when printing flows are the time on the flow sensor. If your collector's clock and your sensor's clock don't match, the times shown in your flow records won't match the time the records were collected. Synchronize your clocks!

IP Accounting Format

Perhaps you have software that interprets Cisco IP accounting output or you've looked at the output for so long that you can process it without expending precious brainpower. Format 6, shown here, exists specifically to make you happy:

```
# flow-cat ft-v05.2011-12-01.171500-0500 | flow-print -f 6 | less
```

Source	Destination	Packets	Bytes
36.85.32.9	158.43.192.1	1	59
158.43.192.1	36.85.32.9	1	134
36.85.32.37	83.243.35.204	14	1035
83.243.35.204	36.85.32.37	12	1527
...			

For example, here are the four sample flows in Cisco format. If you sort this output by the number of bytes, you should be able to easily identify the hosts exchanging the most traffic.

```
# flow-cat ft-v05.2011-12-01.171500-0500  | flow-print -f 6 | sort -rnk 4 | less
  36.85.32.36      64.18.6.14             ❶ 12820      ❷ 19216320
  36.85.32.36      64.18.6.13               12820        19216320
  207.46.209.247   36.85.32.4               10977        16458558
  84.96.92.121     36.85.32.37               6904         9671951
...
```

By sorting the flows into order by the number of octets sent, you've ranked the flows from largest to smallest. What filled up your circuit? Here's the quick answer: The first line shows that the host 36.85.32.36 sent 64.18.6.14 (❶) 12,820 packets containing (❷) 19,216,320 bytes. The same host 36.85.32.36 sent 64.18.6.13 the same amount of traffic. Further filtering and reporting can identify the type of traffic between these busiest hosts, as you'll see in the next two chapters.

Now that you can view the traffic any way you want, let's take a closer look at some intricacies of TCP and ICMP connections.

> **WARNING: HEXADECIMAL MATH AHEAD!**
>
> The network is binary, and lots of it is in base 16. To understand TCP control bits and ICMP codes and types, you'll need to use basic hexadecimal math. Remember, a leading 0x indicates that a number is hexadecimal.

TCP Control Bits and Flow Records

Every TCP packet includes one or more control bits, which are on-off switches that tell the connection participants how to handle a particular packet. Flow records capture the control bits used by each TCP flow. These control bits are not terribly useful when a connection works correctly but are invaluable when identifying problems. If you're not familiar with TCP control bits, read a good TCP/IP primer such as Charles A. Kozierok's *The TCP/IP Guide* (No Starch Press, 2005).

Control bits are given this name because TCP has six bits set aside just for them. These bits are as follows:

- **The SYN (synchronize) bit** indicates a connection synchronization request. It permits the sender and receiver to synchronize TCP sequence numbers, allocate consistent ports on each end, and so on. This bit is always set on the first packet in a flow.

- **The ACK (acknowledge) bit** indicates that a packet contains acknowledgments of receiving specific earlier packets.

- **The PSH (push) bit** is set when the side transmitting data wants the client's network stack to immediately shove this data up the protocol stack. This bit requests that the client flush all hardware and kernel buffers and hand all data to the client.

- **The URG (urgent) bit** indicates that the URGENT pointer field contains data that needs to be interpreted. In everyday language, this means that this packet contains the glue that the receiver needs if it is to correctly process other packets in the flow.

- **RST (reset)** immediately terminates the connection.

- Finally, the **FIN (finish) bit** announces that this host will send no more data, but it will continue to listen for data from the other end. A FIN signals that it's time to tear down the connection.

Each control bit is expressed as a hexadecimal number, as shown in Table 3-3.

Table 3-3: TCP Control Bit Hexadecimal Values

Flag	Hexadecimal
FIN	0x01
SYN	0x02
RST	0x04
PSH	0x08
ACK	0x10
URG	0x20

Many people find this easier to understand as a diagram, such as Figure 3-1.

Field 0x20	Field 0x10	Field 0x08	Field 0x04	Field 0x02	Field 0x1
URG	ACK	PSH	RST	SYN	FIN

Figure 3-1: TCP control bits

Any combination of control bits in a packet can be represented as a unique number. If a control bit is set, add that flag's number to the packet's total control bit number. If you say that a packet's control bits are set to 18, that indicates a precise set of control bits. Only one possible combination of control bits adds up to 18. (Go ahead, try it. I'll wait.)

For example, Figure 3-2 shows how you would represent a typical SYN/ACK packet.

Field 0x20	Field 0x10	Field 0x08	Field 0x04	Field 0x02	Field 0x1
URG	ACK	PSH	RST	SYN	FIN
0	1	0	0	1	0

Figure 3-2: TCP control bits in a SYN/ACK packet

As you can see in Figure 3-2, this packet has the control bits SYN (0x2) and ACK (0x10) marked, and all other control bits are unmarked. Go ahead and add 0x2 and 0x10. Hexadecimal 10 plus hexadecimal 2 is hexadecimal 12; my calculator tells me that hexadecimal 12 is decimal 18.

The only way to get a packet with a control bits value of 18 is if SYN and ACK, and only these two control bits, are selected.

Flows don't track individual packets, so how can flow records sensibly track TCP control bits? The flow sensor tracks all control bits that appear in a single flow. For example, when a host that initiates a connection sends a SYN and an ACK during the connection, you'd reasonably expect to also see, say, a PSH and a FIN. When any of these flags appear in a flow, the flow sensor notes their appearance. Figure 3-3 shows how this would look in a bitmap.

Field 0x20	Field 0x10	Field 0x08	Field 0x04	Field 0x02	Field 0x1
URG	ACK	PSH	RST	SYN	FIN
0	1	1	0	1	1

Figure 3-3: TCP control bits in a flow with SYN, ACK, PSH, and FIN

So, we have 0x1 + 0x2 + 0x8 + 0x10 = 0x1b, or decimal 27.

Look back at the first view of TCP flags earlier this chapter (in "Two Lines with Times, Flags, and Hex Ports Using -f 1" on page 47). The Flags field of the third and fourth sample flows equals 1b, which tells you that this flow included all the TCP flags required for a normal connection (SYN, ACK, and FIN). It also tells you that this flow included a flag perfectly acceptable in a normal connection (PSH) and that it didn't include the flag that would indicate a problem (RST). This connection almost certainly worked. In Chapter 4 you'll search for flows that have combinations of control bits that indicate problems ("TCP Control Bit Primitives" on page 63).

CONVERTING HEX TO DECIMAL AND BINARY

The Calculator program in Windows can convert between the three bases. Open the Calculator, and select **View ▶ Scientific**. You'll see buttons for Hex(adecimal), Dec(imal), Oct(al), and Bin(ary). Select the base you want to convert from. Type in the number in that base. Select the base you want to convert to, and the Calculator will convert for you. You can also use the Calculator if you don't do hexadecimal math often enough to learn it. Most Unix-like desktop environments also include a hexadecimal/decimal calculator.

ICMP Types and Codes and Flow Records

Flow records also record ICMP types and codes, displaying them as destination port numbers. I'll review ICMP types and codes first and then discuss how flow records portray them.

Types and Codes in ICMP

Many people mentally pour the different ICMP requests into one large bucket and get by on generalizations such as "ICMP is ping." Although this might be fine for average users, you're not an average user, and you need a deeper understanding of ICMP to manage a network.

An ICMP *type* is a general class of ICMP request, such as ping requests and ping replies. Other ICMP types include messages such as "host unreachable," routing advertisements, traceroute requests, routing redirects, and so on. Some ICMP types prompt a response from the recipient, while others are received without comment.

Some ICMP types also include an ICMP *code* that allows an ICMP message to provide a more specific response. The meaning of each ICMP code varies with the message's ICMP type. For example, although ICMP types 3, 5, and 11 all offer an ICMP code of 1, that code has a completely different meaning with each type.

The Internet Assigned Numbers Authority (IANA) assigns ICMP types and codes and maintains a list of current assignments at *http://www.iana.org/ assignments/icmp-parameters/*. These assignments rarely change, so Table 3-4 offers the most commonly seen ICMP types and codes. Although an explanation of the meanings of different ICMP messages is best left for a book on TCP/IP (such as *The TCP/IP Guide*, mentioned earlier), this table provides an easy reference.

Table 3-4: Common ICMP Types and Associated Codes in Decimal and Hexadecimal

Type	Code	Decimal	Definition
0	0	0	Echo Reply
3			Destination Unreachable
	0	300	Network Unreachable
	1	301	Host Unreachable
	2	302	Protocol Unreachable
	3	303	Port Unreachable
	4	304	Fragmentation Needed, but Don't Fragment was Set
	6	306	Destination Network Unknown
	7	307	Destination Host Unknown
	9	309	Communication with Destination Network Administratively Prohibited
	10(a)	310	Communication with Destination Host Administratively Prohibited
	13(d)	313	Communication Administratively Prohibited

(continued)

Table 3-4: Common ICMP Types and Associated Codes in Decimal and Hexadecimal (continued)

Type	Code	Decimal	Definition
5			Redirect
	0	500	Redirect for Subnet
	1	501	Redirect for Host
8	0	800	Echo Request
11(b)			Time Exceeded
	0	2816	Time to Live exceeded in Transit
	1	2817	Fragment Reassembly Time Exceeded
12(c)		3072	Parameter Problem
13(d)		3328	Timestamp Request
14(e)		3584	Timestamp Reply

Flows and ICMP Details

Flow sensors encode the ICMP type and code in the flow's destination port. Destination (and source) ports are two bytes. The first byte of the port gives the type, and the second byte gives the code. Because ICMP has no concept of an originating port, the source port is always zero. In the following example, I've selected a few ICMP flows out of my test data.

This example uses a print format that displays destination ports in hexadecimal. You can use a format that displays ports in decimal, but you must convert the destination port from decimal to hex to interpret it.

```
# flow-cat ft* | flow-print -f 0 | less
Sif  SrcIPaddress     Dif  DstIPaddress      Pr SrcP DstP  Pkts      Octets
0000 80.95.220.173    0000 36.85.32.153      01 0   ❶800  2         122
0000 189.163.178.51   0000 36.85.32.130      01 0   ❷b00  1         56
0000 64.142.0.205     0000 36.85.32.5        01 0   ❸300  1         56
0000 201.144.13.170   0000 36.85.32.130      01 0   ❹303  1         144
0000 36.85.32.9       0000 194.125.246.213   01 0   ❺0    5         420
...
```

The first flow comes from the address 80.95.220.173 to 36.85.32.153 and has a destination port of hexadecimal 800 (❶). Although flow-print doesn't print leading zeros, you could think of this as 0800, just as you could think of port 25 as port 025. In this example, the ICMP type is 8, and the code is 00. ICMP type 8 has no associated codes, so flow-print gives the ICMP code as 00.

A look at Table 3-4 tells you that ICMP type 8 is an echo request, also known as a *ping attempt*. The host 80.95.220.173 is trying to ping 36.85.32.153.

The second ICMP flow has a destination port of b00 (❷), or an ICMP type of b and an ICMP code of 00. ICMP type b is "time exceeded." Unlike ICMP type 8, this ICMP type has codes with it. Code 0 means "time to live exceeded in transit." In this case, the IP 189.163.178.51 is informing the IP 36.85.32.130 that it's taking too long to reach a particular address, which usually means that a client has been disconnected.

The third flow, from 64.142.0.205 to 36.85.32.5, has a destination port of 300 (❸). ICMP type 3 messages indicate that a destination is unreachable. ICMP type 3's code 0 means "network unreachable." In this case, host 36.85.32.5 attempted to reach another host, and a router on the Internet is returning a message indicating that the target network is not reachable.

The fourth flow has a destination port of 303 (❹). ICMP type 3 indicates that a destination is unreachable, but code 03 means "port unreachable." When a client sends a UDP request to a server port that isn't open, the server returns this ICMP message. If you were to search these flow records, you would find a UDP request going in the other direction between these two hosts.

Our fifth flow has a destination port of 0 (❺). ICMP type 0 is an echo reply, or a response to a ping. If you search these flows, you'll find an echo request going in the other direction.

As you can see, ICMP messages are frequently responses to other types of network requests. They often show exactly what type of error occurred as a result of an attempted connection. Matching these messages to other flows frequently requires searching the flow records, which is best accomplished by filtering, as you'll see in Chapter 4.

4

FILTERING FLOWS

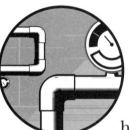

The good news is, you now have actual data about your network. The bad news is, you have far too much data about your network. An Internet T1 might generate millions of flow records in a single day, while a busy Ethernet core might generate billions or more. How can you possibly manage or evaluate that heap of data? You must filter your data to display only interesting flows. The `flow-nfilter` program lets you include or exclude flows as needed.

You can filter traffic in almost any way you can imagine. For example, if a particular server is behaving oddly, you can filter on its IP address. If you're interested in HTTP traffic, you can filter on TCP port 80. You can reduce your data to include only interesting traffic, which will help you evaluate and diagnose issues. For example, if you have a large internal corporate network, you might want to view only the traffic exchanged with a particular branch office, filtering on all of its network addresses.

In Chapter 3, you viewed flow information by running flow-cat and feeding the resulting data stream to flow-print. Filtering takes place between these two processes: flow-nfilter accepts the data stream from flow-cat and examines each flow. Flows that match the filter pass on to flow-print (or other flow-processing programs); flows that do not match the filter drop from the data stream.

Filter Fundamentals

In this chapter, you'll start by building a few simple filters. Once you understand the basics of filter construction, you'll examine the various filter types and functions in depth.

NOTE   *Define your filters in the file filter.cfg, which is probably in* /usr/local/flow-tools/etc/cfg/filter.cfg *or* /usr/local/etc/flow-tools/filter.cfg, *depending on your operating system and how you installed flow-tools.*

Common Primitives

You'll build your filters out of *primitives*. A primitive is a simple traffic characteristic, such as "port 80," "TCP," or "IP address 192.0.2.1." For example, those three primitives could be combined to create one filter that passes all TCP traffic to the host 192.0.2.1 on port 80.

flow-nfilter supports more than a dozen different primitives and can compare them with flows in more than two dozen different ways. A primitive looks much like this:

```
filter-primitive name
❶    type primitive-type
❷    permit value
```

The first line defines a filtering primitive and assigns the primitive a name.

The type at ❶ defines the characteristic you want to match on, such as an IP address, a port, or a time. (I'll cover the most commonly useful filter types.)

The permit statement at ❷ defines the values you're looking for. By default, a primitive denies everything, so you must explicitly state what your filter permits. Alternatively, you could use a deny statement to create a primitive that matches everything except what you're looking for and explicitly put a default permit statement at the end.

For example, a complete primitive that matches the IP address 192.168.1.1 looks like this:

```
filter-primitive ❶ 192.0.2.1
❷    type ip-address
❸    permit 192.0.2.1
```

At ❶ I've named my primitive after the address it matches. You can use any one-word name that makes sense to you, such as "mailserver" or "firewall," if you prefer. The ip-address primitive at ❷ matches network addresses. Finally, at ❸ this primitive matches any IP address equal to 192.0.2.1. If you include this primitive in a filter, it will pass traffic to or from this IP address only.

Similarly, the following primitive defines port 25:

```
filter-primitive ❶ port25
    type ❷ ip-port
    permit 25
```

Although I could have called this primitive 25, at ❶ I used the name port25 to make it absolutely clear that this primitive matches a port because the number 25 by itself could be a number of seconds, a count of octets or packets per second, an autonomous system, a floor number, and so on. (An IP address is unmistakable, so using the address as a name probably won't confuse you.)

The ip-port primitive at ❷ is another commonly used filter component. Including this primitive in a filter means that the filter will pass traffic only on port 25.

The default *filter.cfg* includes a primitive for TCP traffic, as shown here:

```
filter-primitive ❶ TCP
    type ❷ ip-protocol
    permit ❸ tcp
```

You're unlikely to mistake the name TCP at ❶ for anything other than the protocol, but the ip-protocol primitive at ❷ lets you create a primitive for any TCP/IP protocol. Of course, if you have obscure network protocols, you'll probably need to create additional protocol primitives, and your permit statements at ❸ can use either the protocol number or the protocol name from */etc/protocols*.

Each primitive can include only one type of match. For example, the following is invalid:

```
filter-primitive bogus-primitive
❶     type ip-port
      permit 25
❷     type ip-address
      permit 192.0.2.1
```

This primitive tries to match on both a port number (❶) and an IP address (❷). A primitive cannot do this. To filter out connections to the IP address 192.0.2.1 on port 25, you must assemble a filter from multiple primitives.

Now that you have a few primitives, you can create your first filter.

Creating a Simple Filter with Conditions and Primitives

Combine primitives into filters with the `filter-definition` keyword, like so:

```
❶ filter-definition name
❷     match condition primitive1
      match condition primitive1
      ...
```

Every filter begins with `filter-definition` (❶) and a name. Filters can share a name with a primitive but not with other filter definitions.

The filter contains a series of `match` keywords (❷), followed by conditions and primitives. The `match` keyword specifies the part of the flow this entry checks and the primitive to compare it to.

Conditions include things such as IP addresses, ports, protocols, types of service, and so on. All of the conditions listed must match for the filter to match a flow. For example, the following filter combines the `TCP` primitive and the `port25` primitive:

```
  filter-definition TCPport25
❶     match ip-protocol TCP
❷     match ip-source-port port25
```

This filter passes all flows coming from TCP port 25. Any flow that does not come from TCP port 25 will not pass through the filter.

Although primitives and conditions look similar, their names can differ. For example, both filter conditions and filter primitives use the `ip-protocol` keyword (❶). When matching ports, however, primitives use the `ip-port` keyword (❷), but filter definitions use the `ip-source-port` and `ip-destination-port` keywords instead.

NOTE   *The most common cause of filtering errors is using incorrect keywords. Use filter keywords only in filters, and use primitive keywords only in primitives.*

NAMING CONVENTIONS FOR FILTERS AND PRIMITIVES

Assign names to your filters and primitives carefully. If you initially choose ambiguous or confusing names, you'll trip over them when you have dozens or hundreds of filters! Make your names easy to recognize and unmistakable in purpose.

Primitives can share a name with a filter. For example, you can name a primitive TCP and a filter TCP, but you cannot name two primitives TCP or two filters UDP. Also, filter and primitive names are case insensitive. You cannot name one primitive tcp and another primitive TCP.

Using Your Filter

Use `flow-nfilter`'s `-F` option and the filter name to pass only the traffic that matches your filters. For example, here I'm printing only the flows that match the TCPport25 report:

```
# flow-cat * | flow-nfilter -F TCPport25 | flow-print | less
srcIP           dstIP           prot  srcPort  dstPort  octets     packets
192.0.2.37      216.82.253.163  6     25       62627    1294       12
192.0.2.36      81.30.219.92    6     25       63946    1064       15
203.16.60.9     192.0.2.36      6     25       1054     1628       31
...
```

In this example, you can see only the flows where the protocol is 6 (TCP) and the source port is 25. This filter would be useful if you were investigating mail issues, for example. The filter shows that the mail server sent traffic from port 25, and hence the network level of the mail system is functioning.

Useful Primitives

Now that you understand how primitives and filters work together, I'll discuss primitives in depth. `flow-nfilter` supports many different primitives, but I'll cover only the most commonly useful ones here. The `flow-nfilter` man page includes the complete primitive list, but this book contains every one that I have used during several years of flow analysis.

Protocol, Port, and Control Bit Primitives

Filtering on network protocol and port information is one of the most common ways to strip a list of flow records down to only interesting traffic.

IP Protocol Primitives

You saw a basic IP protocol primitive earlier, but you can check for protocols other than TCP. For example, if you use IPSec, OSPF, or other network protocols that run over IP but that are not over TCP or UDP, you'll eventually need to view them separately. Filtering by protocol is the only way to differentiate between network applications that share port numbers, such as syslog (UDP/514) and rsh (TCP/514).

When defining a protocol filter, you can use either the protocol number or name from */etc/protocols*. I prefer to use the number so that */etc/protocols* changes won't interfere with traffic analysis. For example, OSPF runs over protocol 89, so here's a filter to match it:

```
filter-primitive OSPF
    type ip-protocol
    permit 89
```

Similarly, IPSec uses two different protocols: ESP (protocol 50) and AH (protocol 51). The following primitive matches all IPSec traffic. (Separate multiple entries with commas.)

```
filter-primitive IPSec
    type ip-protocol
    permit 50,51
```

Although the IPSec protocols don't have port numbers, `flow-nfilter` can show you how much bandwidth an IPSec VPN between any two points uses and where your VPN clients connect from.

NOTE   *The default filter.cfg includes primitives for TCP, UDP, and ICMP.*

Port Number Primitives

Most network applications run on one or more ports. By filtering your output to include the port only for the network service you're interested in, you ease troubleshooting. To do so, use the `ip-port` primitive you saw earlier.

```
filter-primitive port80
    type ip-port
    permit 80
```

A single primitive can include multiple ports, separated with commas like so:

```
filter-primitive webPorts
    type ip-port
    permit 80,443
```

If you have a long list of ports, you can give each its own line and add comments. This example includes services that run over TCP (telnet and POP3) as well as UDP (SMB).

```
filter-primitive unwantedPorts
    type ip-port
    permit 23    #telnet
    permit 110   #unencrypted POP3
    permit 138   #Windows SMB
...
```

You can also create primitives for ranges of ports.

```
filter-primitive msSqlRpc
    type ip-port
    permit 1024-5000
```

IP port primitives can use names from */etc/services*, but I recommend using numbers to insulate you from changes or errors in that file. `flow-print` and `flow-report` can perform number-to-name translations if necessary.

TCP Control Bit Primitives

Filtering by TCP control bits identifies abnormal network flows. Use the `ip-tcp-flags` primitive to filter by control bits. (See "TCP Control Bits and Flow Records" on page 50.)

```
filter-primitive syn-only
    type ip-tcp-flags
    permit 0x2
```

This primitive matches flows with only a SYN control bit, also known as a *SYN-only flow*. Either the server never responded to the request, a firewall blocked the connection request, or no server exists at the destination address.

These flows are fairly common on the naked Internet, where viruses and automated port scanners constantly probe every Internet address, but they should be comparatively uncommon on your internal network. Numerous SYN-only flows on an internal network usually indicate misconfigured software, a virus infection, or actual intruder probes.

Similarly, you can filter on flows that contain only an RST. An RST-only flow indicates that a connection request was received and immediately rejected, generally because a host is requesting service on a TCP port that isn't open. For example, if you ask a host for a web page when that host doesn't run a web server, you'll probably get a TCP RST.

```
filter-primitive rst-only
    type ip-tcp-flags
    permit 0x4
```

Although a certain level of this activity is normal, identifying the peak senders of SYN-only and RST-only flows can narrow down performance problems and unnecessary network congestion.

To identify flows with multiple control bits set, add the control bits together. For example, flows that contain only the SYN and RST control bits indicate system problems. To identify these flows, write a filter that matches SYN+RST packets.

```
filter-primitive syn-rst
    type ip-tcp-flags
    permit 0x6  # 0x2 (SYN) plus 0x4 (RST)
```

Once you start examining TCP control bits on even a small network, you'll find all sorts of problems and quickly ruin your blissful ignorance.

ICMP Type and Code Primitives

Different ICMP type and code messages can illuminate network activity. Although you can filter flows based on ICMP type and code, it's not exactly easy to do so.

Flows encode the ICMP type and code as the destination port. A primitive that matches a particular type and code uses the ip-port primitive. ICMP type and code are usually expressed as hexadecimal, but ip-port takes decimal values. (Use Table 3-4 on page 53 to identify the appropriate decimal values.)

For example, suppose you're looking for hosts that send ICMP redirects. Redirects are ICMP type 5 and come in two codes, 0 (redirect subnet) and 1 (redirect host). In hexadecimal, these would be 500 and 501. Table 3-4 shows their decimal values as 1280 and 1281, so write a primitive like this:

```
filter-primitive redirects
    type ip-port
    permit 1280-1281
    default deny
```

Used in a filter by itself, this primitive would pass ICMP, TCP, and UDP flows. When you create the actual filter, use both this primitive and the ICMP primitive to see only ICMP redirects.

IP Address and Subnet Primitives

Filtering flows by addresses and subnets lets you narrow down data to hosts and networks of interest.

IP Addresses

Primitives for IP addresses use the ip-address type. It's reasonable to name primitives after the IP address they match, because IP addresses are difficult to confuse with other types of filter primitives.

```
filter-primitive 192.0.2.1
    type ip-address
    permit 192.0.2.1
```

One primitive can include any number of addresses.

```
filter-primitive MailServers
    type ip-address
    permit 192.0.2.10
    permit 192.0.2.11
```

A primitive such as this MailServers example lets you match multiple hosts that serve a particular function, such as "all web servers," "all file servers," and so on.

Subnet Primitives

Primitives can also match subnets using the ip-address-mask and ip-address-prefix primitives. Flow-tools provides two different formats for subnets, ip-address-mask and ip-address-prefix, to match the two common notations for expressing subnets.

The `ip-address-mask` primitive expects a full IP network address with the netmask in decimal form, as follows:

```
filter-primitive our-network
    type ip-address-mask
    permit 192.0.2.0 255.255.255.0
```

This primitive matches all hosts with an IP between 192.0.2.0 and 192.0.2.255.

The `ip-address-prefix` primitive uses prefix (slash) notation.

```
filter-primitive our-network
    type ip-address-prefix
    permit 192.168.0/24
    permit 192.168.1/24
```

You can include multiple subnets, each on its own line, in the subnet primitive, and the subnet masks or prefixes do not have to be equal in all the entries. For example, the following is a perfectly valid primitive:

```
filter-primitive mixed-netmasks
    type ip-address-prefix
    permit 192.168.0/23
    permit 192.168.2/24
```

This primitive matches any IP address between 192.168.0.0 and 192.168.2.255.

Time, Counter, and Double Primitives

You can filter flows by times during the day or by arbitrary counter values.

Comparison Operators in Primitives

Time and counter primitives use logical comparison operators, as shown in Table 4-1.

Table 4-1: Time and Counter Comparison Operators

Operator	Comparison	Time
gt	Greater than	Later than
ge	Greater than or equal to	This time or later
lt	Less than	Earlier than
le	Less than or equal to	Earlier than or equal to
eq	Equal	Exactly this time

Use these comparison operators *only* in time and counter primitives, not in filter definitions.

Time Primitives

To filter according to when flows began or stopped, use a `time` primitive. For example, here, you're looking for flows that stop or start some time during the minute of 8:03 AM.

```
filter-primitive 0803
    type time
    permit eq 08:03
```

NOTE   *Remember, flow records use a 24-hour clock, so 8:03 PM is filtered as 20:03.*

You can narrow down a time period even further. For example, if you know that the traffic you're interested in started and stopped during the second of 8:03:30 AM, you can write a primitive for that.

```
filter-primitive 0803
    type time
    permit eq 08:03:30
```

You cannot filter on millisecond time intervals. Sensors and collectors are rarely accurate to milliseconds, however.

To define a time interval, use other comparison operators. For example, suppose you know that something happened on your network between 7:58 AM and 8:03 AM. To filter traffic during this time period, define a time window from 7:58 to 8:03, inclusive, with the ge and lt operators, like so:

```
filter-primitive crashTime
    type time
    permit ge 07:58
    permit le 08:03
```

Although you can control the data you report on by selecting which flow files to analyze, using times helps narrow your searches even further. This is invaluable when examining large files, and it demonstrates the need for accurate time on your network.

NOTE   *flow-nfilter also supports the time-date primitive for a specific date and time, such as January 20, 2011, at 8:03 AM. If you're interested in a specific date, however, you're better off analyzing the flow files for that date. Flow files are named for the year, month, day, and time of their creation for a reason.*

Counter Primitives

The counter primitive lets you create filters like "more than 100 octets" or "between 500 and 700 packets." When creating filters of this sort, use one or more comparison operators with integers to define counters, as follows:

```
filter-primitive clipping
    type counter
    permit gt 10000
```

This particular filter would pass anything that has more than 10,000 of what you're trying to measure. As another example, suppose you want to look at flows that last only 1,000 milliseconds (1 second) or longer. Here's how you could do that:

```
filter-primitive 1second
    type counter
    permit ge 1000
```

Or, perhaps you want only flows of 1KB or larger.

```
filter-primitive 1kB
    type counter
    permit ge 1024
```

You can use multiple comparisons in a counter. For example, here, I'm permitting everything greater than 1,000 and less than 2,000:

```
filter-primitive average
    type counter
    permit gt 1000
    permit lt 2000
```

NOTE   *When using the counter primitive, keep in mind that counters work only when filtering based on octets, packets, and/or duration. Counters will not match TCP ports or IP addresses.*

Double Primitives

No, a double primitive isn't twice as primitive as the rest of flow-tools. A double primitive is a counter with a decimal point. It matches either packets per second or bits per second.

For example, suppose you want to ignore all connections that send 100 or more packets per second. You need a primitive to define the 100 part of that.

```
filter-primitive lessThan100
    type double
    permit lt 100.0
```

You'll see how to tie this to the number of packets per second in a filter definition, but this primitive defines the "less than 100" part of the filter.

Like the counter primitive, the double cannot match arbitrary data. It can match only octets, packets, and duration.

Interface and BGP Primitives

Flow records exported from a router include routing information, but most of this information is useful only if you're using dynamic routing such as Border Gateway Protocol (BGP). If you are not using BGP or other dynamic routing protocols, you can skip this section.

Identifying Interface Numbers Using SNMP

Most router configuration interfaces (such as Cisco's command line) give each router interface a human-friendly name such as FastEthernet0 or Serial1/0. Internally, the router knows each interface by a number. The router uses the interface number in flow records, rather than the human-friendly name.

The simplest way to get the list of interface names and their corresponding numbers is through Simple Network Management Protocol (SNMP). If you're using multiple Internet providers, you almost certainly have some sort of SNMP capability. Most Unix-like systems include the net-snmp software suite, so I'll use that as an example. Other SNMP browsers should present similar results.

Remember, SNMP presents information as a hierarchical tree. To get a list of network interfaces, check the RFC1213-MIB::ifDescr branch of the SNMP tree. To see interface names and numbers, use snmpwalk to query the router's RFC1213-MIB::ifDescr values. If your MIB browser doesn't support human-friendly names, RFC1213-MIB::ifDescr is equivalent to .1.3.6.1.2.1.2.2.1.2.

```
# snmpwalk -v ❶ 2 -c ❷ community ❸ router RFC1213-MIB::ifDescr
RFC1213-MIB::ifDescr.❹1 = STRING: ❺ "FastEthernet0/0"
RFC1213-MIB::ifDescr.2 = STRING: "FastEthernet0/1"
RFC1213-MIB::ifDescr.4 = STRING: "Null0"
RFC1213-MIB::ifDescr.5 = STRING: "T1 0/0/0"
RFC1213-MIB::ifDescr.6 = STRING: "T1 0/0/1"
RFC1213-MIB::ifDescr.7 = STRING: "Serial0/0/0:0"
RFC1213-MIB::ifDescr.8 = STRING: "Serial0/0/1:1"
RFC1213-MIB::ifDescr.9 = STRING: "Tunnel1"
```

In the previous example, at ❶ you query a router with SNMP version 2, using its community name (❷) and the router's hostname or IP address (❸). In response, you get a list of router interface names.

The SNMP index is the router's internal number for the interface. For example, at ❹ interface 1 is named *FastEthernet0/0* (❺). Interface 7 is named *Serial0/0/0:0*, and so on.

Network engineers should notice that of the eight interfaces listed, interface 4 (null0) is a logical interface and should never see any traffic. Similarly, interfaces 5 and 6 are not real interfaces; they are interface cards supporting interfaces 7 and 8. Only five of the eight interfaces should ever pass traffic.

By default, Cisco routers can change their interface numbering on a reboot, which prevents gaps in interface numbering when interfaces are added or removed. Interface numbers that change arbitrarily really confuse long-term reporting, however. I recommend making your router maintain consistent interface numbering across reboots. It's true that this leaves gaps in the interface list; note the absence of interface 3 on the example router. On the other hand, interface 7 is always Serial 0/0/0:0, even years later. Tell a Cisco device to leave interface numbering unchanged with the configuration option snmp-server ifindex persist.

Also, note that if you have multiple routers exporting data to a single collector, you must separate the data to get meaningful interface information. For example, interface 8 on router A might be a local Ethernet interface, while interface 8 on router B might be an upstream T1 interface. You can filter data by exporter IP address, but this creates the need for an extra layer of filtering.

I'll use the previous interface list in the upcoming examples. Interfaces 1 and 2 are local Ethernet ports, interfaces 7 and 8 are T1 circuits to two different Internet service providers, and interface 9 is a VPN tunnel. The other interfaces should never see traffic.

Interface Number Primitive

Filtering by interface passes only the traffic that traversed that interface. Use the `ifindex` primitive for this purpose.

```
filter-primitive vpnInterface
    type ifindex
    permit 9
```

Interface 9 is the VPN interface. Filtering on it shows you only traffic that goes over the VPN.

(You can list multiple interfaces on one line.)

```
filter-primitive localEthernet
    type ifindex
    permit 1,2
```

Filtering by interface lets you focus on how traffic flows between particular network segments.

Autonomous System Primitives

The Autonomous System (AS) is the core of BGP routing, and routers with BGP peers include AS number information in their flow exports. You can pull out traffic from particular AS numbers with the as primitive as follows:

```
filter-primitive uunet
    type as
    permit 701
```

You can list multiple AS numbers separated by commas on a single line, or you can even list a range of AS numbers. Of course, you can also add multiple AS numbers on separate lines. (ARIN, RIPE, and other AS registrars frequently issue AS numbers to large organizations in blocks, so you might need to create such a filter.)

```
filter-primitive uunet
    type as
    permit 701-705
```

You can also write filters for route announcement prefix length using the `ip-address-prefix-len` primitive. I haven't found a use for a filter that says "Show me all the routes we're getting that are /25 or longer," but carriers and transit providers might find it useful to identify clients that are trying to announce tiny networks.[1]

Filter Match Statements

To assemble primitives into filters, use `match` statements. `flow-nfilter` compares each flow against every `match` statement in a filter, and if a flow fits every `match` statement, the flow passes through. If the flow does not fit every `match` statement, the flow is removed from the data stream.

Many match types have names that are similar to their associated primitives. For example, the `ip-protocol` primitive has a corresponding `ip-protocol` match. Other primitives have no single matching condition. For example, the `ip-port` primitive can match either the `ip-source-port` primitive or the `ip-destination-port` primitive. If you use an incorrect `match` statement in your configuration, `flow-nfilter` exits with an error.

Filter definitions support many different types of match condition. The `flow-nfilter` manual page has the complete list, but the ones I find useful are described here.

Protocols, Ports, and Control Bits

Matching protocols and ports is very common. Control bits and ICMP type and code are less common but powerful in a different way.

Network Protocol Filters

Use the `ip-protocol` match type to check each flow against an `ip-protocol` primitive.

I previously defined a primitive for OSPF. Here I'm using that primitive to pass only OSPF traffic:

```
filter-definition OSPF
  match ip-protocol OSPF
```

Listing multiple protocol primitives in a filter will cause no packets to match. After all, very few single flows are both TCP and UDP.

Source or Destination Port Filters

`flow-nfilter` has separate matches for source ports (`ip-source-port`) and destination ports (`ip-destination-port`). These match against the `ip-port`

---

1. If you're not a transit provider but are trying to announce tiny networks, the lesson you should learn here is this: Tiny route announcements won't work, and if they do, they *can* find you.

primitive. Here I'm using the `port80` primitive defined earlier to filter traffic to a web server:

```
filter-definition port80
    match ip-destination-port port80
```

To match multiple ports for one service, define a primitive that includes all the ports for that service. For example, earlier I defined a `webTraffic` primitive for ports 80 and 443.

```
filter-definition webTraffic
    match ip-destination-port webTraffic
```

Use the `ip-source-port` similarly. For example, to capture traffic leaving your web server, filter the flows leaving ports 80 and 443. (You'll see how to write reports that match both arriving and departing traffic in "Logical Operators in Filter Definitions" on page 76.)

```
filter-definition webTraffic
    match ip-source-port webTraffic
```

TCP Control Bit Filters

Use the `ip-tcp-flags` keyword to match TCP control bit primitives. For example, I previously defined a `rst-only` primitive that matched flows that contained TCP resets only.

```
filter-definition resets
    match ip-tcp-flags rst-only
```

This filter displays only the flows that match the `rst-only` primitive. You don't need to specify a protocol, because flow records contain control bits only for TCP flows. You could use very similar filters for the other TCP control bit primitives.

ICMP Type and Code Filters

Remember that flows record the ICMP type and code in the destination port field of ICMP flows. However, unlike TCP control bits, which appear only in the records of TCP flows, destination ports appear in TCP, UDP, and ICMP flows. To specifically match ICMP type and code, your filter must include the destination port and the protocol as follows:

```
    filter-definition redirects
❶      match ip-destination-port redirects
❷      match ip-protocol ICMP
```

I previously defined a `redirects` primitive at ❶ that matched both codes within the ICMP redirect type. Here, I'm adding a match (❷) for the ICMP protocol primitive as well. This filter passes only the flows that contain ICMP redirects.

Addresses and Subnets

`flow-nfilter` supports two match types for IP addresses: source (`ip-source-address`) or destination address (`ip-destination-address`). These match types can work on any of the three IP address primitives: `ip-address`, `ip-address-mask`, or `ip-address-prefix`.

You can match the source address on one line and the destination address on another line. For example, suppose you have an `ip-address-prefix` primitive for your client's network and another for your web servers. The following definition passes traffic from your client to your web server:

```
filter-definition clientsToWeb
    match ip-destination-address webServers
    match ip-source-address clientNetwork
```

You cannot list multiple matches of the same type in a single filter because a single flow cannot have multiple source or destination addresses! To pass traffic from several source or destination addresses, use a primitive that contains all the desired addresses.

The next filter captures data coming into the server from web clients. You need a corresponding report to catch traffic from your web servers to the client network (or a slightly more complicated filter to capture traffic moving in both directions, as you'll see in "Logical Operators in Filter Definitions" on page 76). Because you want to see only web traffic, you also filter with primitives for web traffic and TCP.

```
filter-definition clientsToWebHttpTraffic
    match ip-port webTraffic
    match ip-protocol TCP
    match ip-destination-address webServers
    match ip-source-address clientNetwork
```

You'll see other ways to achieve this same effect in "Using Multiple Filters" on page 75.

Filtering by Sensor or Exporter

Multiple flow sensors can export to a single collector, but at times you'll want to see only the flows that came from a particular sensor. You can use the `ip-exporter-address` match with any IP address primitive to create a filter that passes flows from a particular sensor, as follows:

```
filter-primitive router1
    type ip-address
    permit 192.0.2.1

filter-definition router1-exports
    match ip-exporter-address router1
```

This particular filter passes only the flows exported from the router at 192.0.2.1.

Time Filters

The start-time and end-time match types let you filter on when flows begin and end, using the time primitive. For example, the following sample captures all flows that take place entirely within a particular minute, using the 0803 time primitive defined earlier:

```
filter-definition 0803
    match start-time 0803
    match end-time 0803
```

You can define a filter to match flows starting or ending at any time that you can express with a primitive.

In most cases, you won't have accurate time information about problems. Human beings have a notoriously fuzzy time sense: "A few minutes ago" might be anything from 30 seconds to an hour, and after a few days even that is unreliable. Remember that each flow file covers a five-minute period. Most of the time you're better off searching entire flow files for issues rather than trying to filter on times. I find that filtering on times is useful only on very large flow files and then only when you have precise timing information from the flow files themselves. A human saying that the website broke at 8:15 AM is not reliable. If your flow records say that you had unusual traffic at 8:15 AM, however, you might want to see what else happened during that minute. Filtering on times can be useful in that instance.

Clipping Levels

A *clipping level* is the point at which you start ignoring data. For example, you might not care about flows that contain tiny amounts of data, or perhaps you want to see only tiny flows. To clip data, you can set clipping levels on the amount of traffic transmitted, the connection speed, and the duration of connections.

Octets, Packets, and Duration Filters

Use counter primitives to filter based on the number of octets per flow, the packets per flow, or the duration of flows. For example, earlier I defined a primitive for 1KB or larger. Let's use that primitive now to remove the tiny connections from the flow data.

```
filter-definition 1kBplus
    match octets 1kB
```

Similarly, you created a primitive for anything that totaled 1,000 or more, called 1second. You can write a filter that uses this primitive to allow only flows of 1,000 milliseconds (1 second) or longer.

```
filter-definition over1second
    match duration 1second
```

Counters are arbitrary numbers and can apply to octets, packets, or duration. For example, if you want a filter that includes only flows with 1,024 or more packets, you could easily reuse the 1kB primitive for that.

```
filter-definition 1024plusPackets
    match packets 1kB
```

Even though you can, I try not to reuse primitives in this way. You never hear of a kilobyte of packets! Such filters confuse me. Being confused while trying to identify network problems is not good.[2]

Packets or Bits per Second Filters

Perhaps you're interested in how quickly connections move or you're interested only in the really fast or really slow connections. If so, you can use double primitives to filter based on packets per second or bits per second.

For example, earlier you defined a double primitive for less than 100. You can use this for either packets per second or bits per second.

```
filter-definition lessThan100pps
    match pps lessThan100

filter-definition lessThan100bps
    match bps lessThan100
```

In this particular case, I don't mind reusing the lessThan100 primitive, because the name isn't so closely tied to a particular data type.

BGP and Routing Filters

You can filter flows based on the routing information included in the flow records. (If you are not using BGP, you can skip this section.)

Autonomous System Number Filters

The source-as and destination-as match types let you match based on AS numbers. For example, this filter lets you see what traffic you're receiving (from what was the UUnet network) using the uunet AS primitive defined earlier:

```
filter-definition uunet
    match source-as uunet
```

You could also turn this around to create a filter to permit the traffic you're sending to UUnet systems.

---

2. I don't need to waste my time calling myself an idiot because I gave a filter an ambiguous name. Many other people are delighted to call me an idiot for all sorts of reasons.

Next-Hop Address Filters

The *next hop* is the IP address where a router sends a flow. This is usually the IP address on the remote end of an ISP circuit (for outgoing flows) or the external address of your firewall (for inbound flows). Routers include the next hop in flow records. However, software flow sensors like `softflowd` know nothing of interfaces on remote hosts or how packets are routed, so flows exported from software flow sensors do not contain next-hop addresses.

Now suppose that the next-hop IP address for one of your Internet providers is 61.118.12.45. To filter all traffic leaving your network via that ISP, you could use a primitive and a definition like this:

```
filter-primitive ispA
    type ip-address
    permit 61.118.12.45

filter-definition ispA
    match ip-nexthop-address ispA
```

The `ip-nexthop-address` match type works with the primitives `ip-address`, `ip-address-mask`, and `ip-address-prefix`.

Interface Filters

Another way to filter by provider or network segment is to filter by the router interface. The match types `input-interface` and `output-interface` let you filter by traffic arriving or leaving your router.

You defined a primitive for router interface 9 earlier. Here I'm using it in a filter:

```
filter-definition vpn
    match input-interface vpnInterface
```

This shows traffic entering the router on this interface.

Using Multiple Filters

Suppose you want to identify all traffic between two machines. You could define primitives for those two hosts and then write a filter that specifically defines those hosts. However, this common situation will keep you very busy writing new filters. Instead, I find it much easier to define smaller filters and tie them together on the command line.

You can invoke `flow-nfilter` repeatedly in a single command. Find the flow files for the times you're interested in, filter them for the first host, and then filter them a second time for the second host.

```
# flow-cat ft-* | ❶ flow-nfilter -F host1 | ❷ flow-nfilter -F host2 | flow-print | less
```

The first `flow-nfilter` invocation at ❶ passes only flows that include traffic from `host1`. The second at ❷ passes only flows that include traffic from `host2`.

Similarly, you can write separate filters for certain protocols, like all web traffic. You previously created a filter for all HTTP and HTTPS traffic, called `webTraffic`.

```
# flow-cat ft-* | ❶ flow-nfilter -F host1 | ❷ flow-nfilter -F webTraffic | flow-print | less
```

The first filter at ❶ passes only traffic for the interesting host, and the second (❷) passes only HTTP and HTTPS traffic.

You can create simple filters for important hosts and subnets on your network. For example, if you have a customer who reports problems reaching your website, you could write one flow filter for your site and one for the customer's addresses and use them both to see what traffic passed between your networks. You could then look for SYN-only or RST-only flows that would indicate problems. Or you might find that traffic from the customer's network never reaches you at all. In any case, these two filters will tell you exactly what traffic appeared on your network and how it behaved.

By combining filters on the command line, you will write fewer filters and get more use out of the filters you create.

Logical Operators in Filter Definitions

When you put multiple match conditions in a filter definition, `flow-nfilter` places a logical "and" between them. For example, the following filter shows all traffic that runs over TCP and has a source port of 25. This passes an email server's responses to a connection.

```
filter-definition TCPport25
    match ip-protocol TCP
    match ip-source-port port25
```

You can use other logical operators to build very complicated filters.

Logical "or"

When I try to analyze a connection problem, I usually want to see both sides of the conversation. I want a filter that will show connections to port 25 as well as from port 25. For this, use the or operator as follows:

```
filter-definition email
    match ip-protocol TCP
    match ip-source-port port25
❶   or
❷   match ip-protocol TCP
❸   match ip-destination-port port25
```

After the or statement at ❶, a whole new filter definition begins. Although I listed TCP in the first filter, if you're interested in TCP in the second filter, you must repeat the match on TCP at ❷, after which you can add the new match statement at ❸ to catch flows that end on port 25. Now, if you apply this filter to your flow data, you'll see something like this:

```
# flow-cat ft-v05.2011-12-20.12* | flow-nfilter -F email | flow-print | less
   srcIP              dstIP               prot  srcPort  dstPort  octets   packets
❶ 217.199.0.33       192.0.2.37          6     5673     25       192726   298
❷ 192.0.2.37         217.199.0.33        6     25       5673     8558     181
   206.165.246.249    192.0.2.37          6     38904    25       13283    22
   192.0.2.37         206.165.246.249     6     25       38904    1484     16
   ...
```

The first flow at ❶ is from a remote IP to the address of the local email server, with a destination port of 25. This is an incoming mail transmission. The second flow at ❷ is from the mail server to the same remote IP address; it's coming from port 25. This is the response to the first flow.

I could use more sophisticated flow-print formats to view this in more detail, run flow-report on this data to check for errors, or add another filter to specifically point out TCP errors in the email stream. This simple check shows me that the mail server is exchanging substantial amounts of traffic on TCP port 25, however. I would tell my mail administrator to check the logs for errors or provide more information.

Filter Inversion

Sometimes it's easier to write a filter for the traffic you're *not* interested in. For example, suppose you want to see all the traffic to or from your email servers that isn't email. Although you could write primitives that included all port numbers except those for email, that's annoying and tedious.

Instead, use the invert keyword to reverse the meaning of a filter, like so:

```
filter-definition not-email
❶     invert
      match ip-protocol TCP
      match ip-source-port port25
      or
      match ip-protocol TCP
      match ip-destination-port port25
```

By adding invert to the report at ❶, you pass everything that doesn't match the defined filters. In this example, I'm passing every network transaction that doesn't involve TCP port 25.

But there's a problem with this filter: It will match all nonemail traffic on all the hosts for which you're capturing data. You, however, need to view only traffic for your email hosts.

To solve this problem, you could add your email servers into the `not-email` filter, but the email servers both send and receive email. You would need a definition section for remote servers connecting to your mail servers, a section for your servers' response to those remote servers, a third section for your mail servers connecting to remote mail servers, and a fourth for the remote servers' responses to your servers' requests. That's pretty ugly.

It's much simpler to define a separate filter that strips the flow data down to just the email servers and then to concatenate the two, as follows:

```
❶    filter-primitive emailServers
     type ip-address
     permit 192.0.2.37
     permit 192.0.2.36

❷    filter-definition emailServers
     match ip-source-address emailServers
     or
     match ip-destination-address emailServers
```

The `emailServers` primitive at ❶ includes the IP addresses of all the mail servers. Next, at ❷ I create a filter definition to match all traffic leaving or going to those servers. Then, to see all nonemail traffic to or from my email servers, I do this:

```
# flow-cat * | ❶ flow-nfilter -F emailServers | ❷ flow-nfilter -F not-email | flow-print | less
```

The `emailServers` filter at ❶ passes only the flows that involve my email servers. The `not-email` filter at ❷ passes only flows that are not SMTP. By combining these two filters, I see only interesting traffic. I'll probably need to adjust the filter further to remove other uninteresting traffic, such as DNS queries to the DNS server, but I'm almost there.

Of course, after reviewing the filtered traffic, I can go ask my email administrator why he's running his own DNS server on the mail server instead of using the corporate name servers and why he browses the Web from those machines instead of using the proxy server and its adult content filters.[3]

Filters and Variables

Flow-tools also includes filters that can be configured on the command line, which can be useful for very simple filters, such as identifying traffic from a particular IP address. The default filters that use these are fairly limited, but they'll suffice for simple traffic analysis. It's also easy to write your own variable-driven reports.

---

3. Yes, I could take this straight to human resources, but HR won't wash and wax my car.

Using Variable-Driven Filters

The filters that are configurable on the command line use three variables: ADDR (address), PORT (port), and PROT (protocol). These support five reports, letting you filter by protocol as well as by source and destination address and port: ip-src-addr, ip-dst-addr, ip-src-port, ip-dest-port, and ip-prot.

Suppose your boss calls. She's connecting from a random open wireless hotspot in some inconvenient city and can't get into the corporate VPN concentrator. You get her IP address, either by asking her for it or by accessing system logs to see where she's coming from. To see all the traffic coming to your network from her IP, without writing a custom filter, you could use a command-line variable on the flow files for that time window. For example, if she's at the IP address 192.0.2.8, you'd use a command like this:

```
# flow-cat * | flow-nfilter -F ip-src-addr ❶ -v ADDR=192.0.2.8 | flow-print
```

The -v argument at ❶ tells flow-nfilter that you're assigning a value to a variable. In this example, I've assigned the value 192.0.2.8 to the variable ADDR. You'll see all traffic originating from that IP address.

> **WHEN TO USE VARIABLE-DRIVEN FILTERS?**
>
> For simple filters on individual hosts and ports, use variable-driven filters. If you must filter on multiple hosts or ranges of ports, define primitives and filters in *filter.cfg*.

Defining Your Own Variable-Driven Filters

Variable-driven filters take advantage of the primitives VAR_ADDR (address), VAR_PORT (port), and VAR_PROT (protocol), as defined in *filter.cfg*. For example, the following is a default variable-driven filter that uses the ADDR variable. This looks exactly like a standard report, except that it uses the variable name instead of a primitive.

```
filter-definition ip-src-addr
    match ip-source-address VAR_ADDR
```

Use these variables to define your own variable-driven filters. For example, I like to see all traffic to *and* from a host of interest. Writing a command-line version of this report is easy.

```
filter-definition ip-addr
    match ip-destination-address VAR_ADDR
    or
    match ip-source-address VAR_ADDR
```

Similarly, I prefer to see all traffic to *and* from a port simultaneously.

```
filter-definition ip-port
    match ip-destination-address VAR_PORT
    or
    match ip-source-address VAR_PORT
```

With these reports, I can dynamically filter for any individual host or port on the fly.

Creating Your Own Variables

VAR_ADDR, VAR_PORT, and VAR_PROT are not magic variables hard-coded into flow-nfilter; they're defined in *filter.cfg*. Here's the definition of VAR_PORT:

```
filter-primitive VAR_PORT
    type ip-port
    permit ❶ @{PORT:-0}
```

Most of this primitive looks like any other primitive for a port number, but the permit statement (❶) is very different. This example takes the variable PORT as defined on the command line and turns it into a number. The specifics of how this works aren't important, but you can use this sample as a model for your own primitives.

Now here's another example. I frequently work with BGP, so I need an AS number primitive.

```
❶ filter-primitive VAR_AS
❷ type as
❸ permit @{AS:-0}
```

I've assigned this primitive the name VAR_AS at ❶ to correspond with the existing variable names, and I've assigned it the as type (❷). The permit statement at ❸ is copied from the VAR_PORT primitive, substituting the variable name AS for the port. Now I can create a filter using this variable.

```
   filter-definition AS
❶     match source-as VAR_AS
      or
❷     match destination-as VAR_AS
```

This closely resembles the earlier custom variable–based filters in that you pass traffic going to ❶ and from the specified AS (❷). Now you can use this filter to get the traffic to a particular autonomous system.

```
# flow-cat * | flow-nfilter -F as-traffic -v AS=701 | flow-print -f 4 | less
```

When you apply this filter, you'll see only the flows involving AS number 701.

At this point, you should be able to filter traffic in any way you like. Now let's run analysis on that data.

5

REPORTING AND FOLLOW-UP ANALYSIS

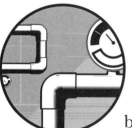 The ability to view exactly what traffic passed over your network is a powerful tool, but what can anyone do with this data in its entirety? After all, very few people can eyeball a list of 15,000 flows and identify the 10 most active hosts, identify the most commonly used ports, or even rank them by IP. Carefully choosing flow files to examine and then filtering their contents can reduce the number of flows you have to read, but this still leaves you with a huge data set to integrate, aggregate, and analyze even on a small network. You need a tool to aggregate flow data, sort it, and display the cumulative results.

The flow-report program reads flows and produces totals, rankings, per-second and per-interface counts, and other reports. You can create carefully customized reports to run over and over again, or you can use the built-in ones to perform ad hoc analysis. flow-report lets you quickly answer basic questions such as "Which web server sends the most traffic?" and "Which host is spewing viruses?" In this chapter, you'll see how to use flow-report's many options and how to quickly answer your most important questions about your network.

Default Report

Everything `flow-report` produces is configured in the file *stat.cfg*. The default configuration includes one generic report, with options to override many settings on the command line, much as `flow-nfilter` lets you configure filtering on the command line. You'll start with the default report and see how far you can stretch it.

First you'll use the default report without any configuration. This produces the *summary-detail report*, a generic statistical analysis of the flow data. The summary-detail report is rather lengthy, so I'll break it up into several chunks.

```
   #   flow-cat * | flow-report
   #    --- ---- ---- Report Information --- --- ---
   #   build-version:        flow-tools 0.68.4
❶  #   name:                 default
❷  #   type:                 summary-detail
❸  #   options:              +header,+xheader,+totals
❹  #   fields:               +other
❺  #   records:              0
   #   first-flow:           1322715601 Thu Dec  1 00:00:01 2011
   #   last-flow:            1322719199 Thu Dec  1 00:59:59 2011
   #   now:                  1325460205 Sun Jan  1 18:23:25 2012
   #
   #   mode:                 streaming
   #   compress:             off
   #   byte order:           little
   #   stream version:       3
❻  #   export version:       5
   #
❼  #   ['/usr/local/bin/flow-rptfmt', '-f', 'ascii']
```

Every line that starts with a hash mark is information about how the report was prepared or a comment about the actual flow files. This information includes the version of flow-tools used, the date and times of the first and last flows in the flow files, the current date and time, and so on.

At ❶ you see the report's name as defined in the report configuration file. I haven't created any custom reports yet, so I generated the default report.

Report types (❷) dictate how the flow data is arranged, searched, sorted, and presented. Report types include things such as "most common ports" and "most common addresses." I'll cover most of them in this chapter. This particular report is the summary-detail report.

Report options (❸) tell `flow-report` what to include in the report. For example, the +header and +xheader options tell `flow-report` to include the report meta-information you're looking at right now. You can override the default options on the command line or set them in a custom report.

The fields setting (❹) tells flow-report what information to include in the report. Fields are columns in the report, as you'll see later with other report types. Again, you can override the default fields on the command line or set them in a custom report.

The records field (❺) shows whether flow-report has limited its output to a certain number of lines. You can set a maximum number of lines on the command line or in a report definition. This feature is useful if you want to know, for example, the top 10 hosts generating a certain type of traffic.

Knowing the flow version (❻) in the flow files tells you what information the report includes. You won't get BGP information from NetFlow version 1, for example.

Finally, at ❼ you see the command used to format the report. The flow-report program produces comma-separated value (CSV) reports only and relies on an outside program (flow-rptfmt) to create formatted text or HTML.

Timing and Totals

The next section includes details about the data inside the flow records. The first six lines are presented only when the report definition includes the +totals option.

❶	Ignores:	0
	Total Flows:	54286
	Total Octets:	633669712
	Total Packets:	996238
❷	Total Duration (ms):	884588200
❸	Real Time:	1322719199
❹	Average Flow Time:	16294.000000
❺	Average Packets/Second:	636.000000
	Average Flows/Second:	11672.000000
	Average Packets/Flow:	18.000000
❻	Flows/Second:	0.042795
	Flows/Second (real):	0.000044

flow-report (❶) ignores flows with zero packets. Zero-packet flows are normally errors, but including them in other calculations will throw off your averages.

You then see the total number of flows, octets, and packets in these flows. I captured 54,286 flows, or 633Mb, in 996,238 packets.

The total duration (❷) is the sum of the total time that the flows lasted, in milliseconds. For example, 10 one-second flows would give a total duration of 10 seconds, or 10,000 milliseconds, even if the flows ran simultaneously.

The remaining information is all part of the default summary-detail report.

The Real Time header (❸) tells when the flow data ends in Unix epochal time. 1322719199 is Thursday, December 1, 2011, at 00:59:59 EST, or just short of 1 AM.

The average flow time (❹) is the average flow duration in milliseconds.
You then have averages at ❺ for packets per second, flows per second, and packets per flow.

The two Flows/Second values at ❻ can be confusing. The first, Flows/Second, gives the number of flows per second you would expect by dividing the number of flows by the number of seconds in the sample. The Flows/Second (real) value calculation is based on epochal time and is not useful for most network management purposes.

Packet Size Distribution

The next section of the summary-detail report, packet size distribution, shows the size of the packets in these flows as a fraction of all the packets.

❶ 1-32	❸64	96	128	160	192	224	256	288	320	352	384	416	448	480
❷ .000	❹.232	.443	.067	.157	.045	.008	.005	.004	.003	.011	.003	.002	.001	.002

512	544	576	1024	1536	2048	2560	3072	3584	4096	4608
.001	.001	.001	.006	.008	.000	.000	.000	.000	.000	.000

The first entry at ❶ shows what fraction of the packets in these flows has a size between 1 and 32 bytes; in this case, there are zero, as you can see at ❷.

A little less than a quarter of the packets in these flows (.232 as shown at ❹) are 64 bytes long (as shown at ❸). (I took these samples from a network segment with a heavily used DNS server, so I would expect many small flows.) Almost half of the packets are 96 bytes.

Packets per Flow

The next section of the summary-detail report is the packets per flow, formatted much like the packet size distribution table.

❶ 1	2	4	❸ 8	12	16	20	24	28	32	36	40	44	48	52
❷ .307	.051	.135	.235	.072	.041	.032	.023	.019	.013	.012	.006	.004	.004	.003

60	100	200	300	400	500	600	700	800	900	>900
.005	.013	.013	.003	.002	.001	.001	.000	.000	.000	.003

Here you see at ❷ that 0.307, or roughly 31 percent, of the flows include only one packet (as shown at ❶). As you saw earlier, one-packet flows are generally ICMP requests or UDP such as simple DNS queries. Almost a quarter of the flows contain five to eight packets per flow (as shown at ❸). The remaining flows are scattered widely among the packets per flow.

Octets in Each Flow

The next section of the summary-detail report tells you how many octets are in each flow.

❶ 32	64	128	256	512	1280	2048	2816	3584	4352	5120	5888	6656	7424	8192
❷ .000	.070	.173	.129	.097	.208	.115	.029	.028	.016	.017	.023	.011	.009	.005

8960	9728	10496	11264	12032	12800	13568	14336	15104	15872	❹ >15872
.004	.004	.003	.003	.003	.002	.002	.002	.002	.001	❸ .043

As you can see at ❷, none of the flows in this file contains only 32 octets (shown at ❶). (Remember, even a ping packet is usually 64 bytes.) The most common size for a flow is 513 to 1280 octets, with 0.208 representing roughly 20 percent of the flows. Although large flows are rare, you can see at ❸ that 0.043, or about 4 percent of the flows, are larger than 15,872 octets (as shown at ❹).

Flow Time Distribution

The last part of the summary-detail report, flow time distribution, tells you how long flows last in milliseconds.

❷ 10	50	100	200	500	1000	2000	3000	4000	5000	6000	7000	8000	9000	10000
❶ .158	.100	.088	.084	.157	.085	.036	.019	.017	.010	.009	.007	.007	.010	.009

12000	14000	16000	18000	20000	22000	24000	26000	28000	30000	>30000
.014	.008	.006	.008	.007	.005	.003	.003	.004	.004	❸ .141

As you can see at ❶, 0.158, or roughly 16 percent of the flows, lasted 10 milliseconds or less (as shown at ❷). A look at the data shows that this is the most common flow duration. As a general rule on this network, short flows are more common than longer ones: The long-running flows at the end (shown at ❸) stand out.

HOW DO YOU USE THE SUMMARY-DETAIL REPORT?

If you get complaints that your network is behaving oddly, compare today's packets with last week's or last year's to quickly see anomalies. If you see that your traffic has changed in size, duration, or quantity during a network problem, you know something has changed. Filter on these characteristics to identify the host or connection that's changed.

Modifying the Default Report

Much like with flow-nfilter, you can modify flow-report's behavior from the command line. The program supports five variables: TYPE, SORT, FIELDS, OPTIONS, and RPTOPT. I'll cover each with an example later in this chapter. For now, here's a brief look at each variable:

- TYPE tells flow-report which report to run. flow-report supports more than 70 report types. Much of this chapter is a discussion of the reports I find most useful. The flow-report manual page contains a complete list.

- SORT controls the data display order. You can sort most reports by any field in the report.
- FIELDS lets you adjust the fields that appear in a report.
- OPTIONS activates or deactivates various report-wide features.
- RPTOPT gives options to pass to the report formatting program, flow-rptfmt.

To set a variables, use -v and the variable name. For example, to set the TYPE variable, use the following:

```
# flow-cat * | flow-report -v TYPE=yourtype
```

I'll use variables throughout the rest of this section to modify reports and then explore the different report types.

Using Variables: Report Type

One question you might hear from an interested manager[1] is "What computer talks the most?" The report type ip-source-address displays how much traffic each host puts on the network.

```
# flow-cat * | flow-report -v TYPE=ip-source-address
...
#  ['/usr/local/bin/flow-rptfmt', '-f', 'ascii']
ip-source-address flows octets     packets duration
192.0.2.37        12163 107898108 204514  159749392
158.43.128.72     16389 1962766   16711   49357139
192.0.2.4         54280 127877204 785592  831419980
198.6.1.1         7627  970898    7992    26371278
...
```

With this report you get a list of IP addresses and the number of flows, octets, and packets sent by that host, as well as the total duration of all flows to this host in milliseconds. The data in this report is presented, in no particular order, as a list of IP addresses and traffic measurements, which demonstrates that you must know exactly what you mean by "busiest host." Is it the host that sends the greatest amount of traffic (octets)? Is it the host involved in the greatest number of connections (flows)? Or is it the host that sends the greatest number of individual packets?

Using Variables: SORT

Scrolling through a long report in search of the host that sends the most traffic isn't terribly effective. Instead, use the SORT variable to tell flow-report how to order the data.

You can assign SORT the value of the name of any field in a report. However, the fields are not necessarily the same as the names of the columns. The report header contains the fields entry, which lists the valid fields in the

---

1. The quickest way to make your manager lose interest is to answer this question in appalling detail. This might seem cruel, but it's best for everyone involved.

report type in the order they appear in the report. Here's the header information on fields from the ip-source-address report:

```
# fields:                +key,+flows,+octets,+packets,+duration,+other
```

The actual report includes the columns ip-source-address, flows, octets, packets, and duration, as shown here:

```
ip-source-address flows octets    packets duration
192.0.2.4         54280 127877204 785592  831419980
...
```

Note that the list of fields starts with an entry named key and follows that with entries called flows, octets, packets, duration, and other. The actual report starts with a column called ip-source-address and follows that with the fields flows, octets, packets, and duration. flow-report calls the field it's reporting on the *key*. I ran the ip-source-address report, so the key is the ip-source-address field. (This report has no other column, despite its presence in the list of fields.)

To sort by a column in descending order, assign the SORT variable the field name with a leading plus sign. To sort by a column in ascending order, assign the SORT variable the field name with a leading minus sign.

I'm interested in the host that creates the greatest number of connections, or flows, so I'll assign SORT the value +flows to sort the data by flows in descending order, like so:

```
# flow-cat * | flow-report -v TYPE=ip-source-address -v SORT=+flows
...
# ['/usr/local/bin/flow-rptfmt', '-f', 'ascii']
  ip-source-address flows octets    packets duration
❶ 192.0.2.4         54280 127877204 785592  831419980
  158.43.128.72     16389 1962766   16711   49357139
  192.0.2.37        12163 107898108 204514  159749392
  198.6.1.5         8826  1425518   11339   24124445
  192.0.2.36        8786  21773315  38616   44443605
  198.6.1.1         7627  970898    7992    26371278
...
```

The host 192.0.2.4 (❶) has sent 54,280 flows, almost four times as many as the next highest host.

At first glance, it might appear that sorting by flows also sorts by bytes (octets) to a certain degree, but that's illusionary. Here I report on the same data sorted by octets:

```
# flow-cat * | flow-report -v TYPE=ip-source-address -v SORT=+octets
...
# ['/usr/local/bin/flow-rptfmt', '-f', 'ascii']
ip-source-address flows octets    packets duration
207.46.209.247    25    131391013 90275   2967322
192.0.2.4         54280 127877204 785592  831419980
```

```
192.0.2.37         12163  107898108  204514  159749392
192.0.2.7          116    72083511   55415   15057488
192.0.2.130        145    49604492   74852   36232749
192.0.2.8          88     48766466   36166   7181558
...
```

When you compare the list of hosts that send the greatest number of octets to the list of hosts that send the greatest number of flows, notice that four of the top six hosts on each list don't even appear in the other list!

Analyzing Individual Flows from Reports

Look back at the `ip-source-address` report from in "Using Variables: SORT" on page 86. Notice how the host 207.46.209.247 used the most bandwidth, 131,391,013 octets. That's 131,391,013 divided by 1,024, which is about 128,312KB, or 125MB. The obvious question is "What did that host send in all those octets with but so few flows?"

To find out, use `flow-nfilter` to answer that question. Because this is a one-off query that probably won't be repeated, just configure the filter on the command line.

```
# flow-cat * | flow-nfilter -F ip-src-addr -v ADDR=207.46.209.247 | flow-print
srcIP           dstIP            prot  srcPort  dstPort  octets     packets
207.46.209.247  192.0.2.4     ❶ 6   ❷ 80       51538    16499752   11018
207.46.209.247  192.0.2.4       6     80       51540    16104523   10756
207.46.209.247  192.0.2.4       6     80       53410    20798      17
...
```

Thanks to this report, you can see that this connection ran over TCP (❶) and that it came from port 80 to a high-numbered port (❷). This is obviously a response from a web server. In this case, the destination IP happens to be my main proxy server. I can search my proxy logs and probably identify this traffic more exactly.

Unfortunately, web traffic isn't quite that simple. People frequently browse and click through many pages on a website, perhaps downloading data from many different places on the site or maybe downloading a single large file. How can you know whether this data represents a single large download or a bunch of smaller requests? There's no way to be certain, but one way to check is to compare the connections coming from that address to the connections going to that address.

To do so, you can change the filter to check for flows going to 207.46.209.247. You'll need the start and stop times for each flow to see whether new connections are starting or whether each flow is an independent request. `flow-print` format 5 displays timing information with each flow, so I use that to display my filtered data. (I've removed several irrelevant fields, such as the protocol, interface, packets, and octets, from this example to make the output fit on the page.)

```
# flow-cat * | flow-nfilter -F ip-dst-addr -v ADDR=207.46.209.247 | flow-print -f 5
  Start            End                 SrcIPaddress  SrcP   DstIPaddress    DstP
❶ 1201.11:58:00.409 1201.12:01:55.917 192.0.2.4     51538  207.46.209.247  80
❷ 1201.11:58:00.451 1201.12:02:05.769 192.0.2.4     51540  207.46.209.247  80
❸ 1201.12:03:00.506 1201.12:04:10.916 192.0.2.4     53410  207.46.209.247  80
  1201.12:03:00.505 1201.12:04:16.805 192.0.2.4     53409  207.46.209.247  80
❹ 1201.12:08:00.457 1201.12:09:25.912 192.0.2.4     55190  207.46.209.247  80
  1201.12:08:00.457 1201.12:09:26.775 192.0.2.4     55191  207.46.209.247  80
❺ 1201.12:13:00.519 1201.12:14:11.891 192.0.2.4     57581  207.46.209.247  80
  1201.12:13:00.520 1201.12:16:30.907 192.0.2.4     57580  207.46.209.247  80
...
```

The first flow (❶) starts at 1201.11:58:00.409, or 11:58 AM and .409 seconds, on December 1, and ends at 12:05:55.917. A second request at ❷ begins milliseconds later and ends at about the same time. These are clearly two separate HTTP requests.

What makes this output interesting is the timing of the other requests. Two more requests begin at ❸ exactly five minutes after the first two, and two more begin at ❹ five minutes after that. By viewing the requests rather than the responses to the requests, it becomes very obvious that something on your network is accessing this site (❺) every five minutes. People do not behave in such a mechanistic manner. The sensible assumption is that a piece of software is responsible for this traffic.

This report gives exact timestamps for when these repeating, high-bandwidth HTTP requests begin and end, which is all you need in order to find the site in your proxy logs. (In this particular case, this turned out to be clients downloading patches from Microsoft instead of using the corporate update server.)

NOTE   *If you have no proxy server, you aren't logging Internet usage. You can do flow analysis on your internal network to identify the specific workstations that were making these requests and see what those workstations have in common, but that's all. If the activity is ongoing, use your packet sniffer to identify what site the workstations are trying to reach.*

Other Report Customizations

Just as the SORT variable adjusts data display, other variables further change a report's format, allowing you to create a report that contains exactly the information you need, presented in the most usable manner. I'll modify the ip-source-address report I ran earlier this chapter to demonstrate exactly how each of these variables changes a report.

Choosing Fields

Perhaps you specifically want to know the number of bytes (or packets) sent by a host, and you don't care about the other information provided by a report. The FIELDS variable lets you select the columns to include in a report.

For example, the ip-source-address report includes five fields: address, flows, octets, packets, and duration. Say you want to remove the duration column from your report. To do so, give the FIELDS variable the value of the field you want to remove, with a leading minus sign, as shown here with -duration:

```
# flow-cat * | flow-report -v TYPE=ip-source-address -v SORT=+octets -v
FIELDS=-duration
...
ip-source-address flows octets     packets
207.46.209.247     25    131391013 90275
192.0.2.4               54280 127877204 785592
192.0.2.37              12163 107898108 204514
...
```

To remove multiple FIELDS values, separate each with commas. Here I've removed everything except the IP address and the number of octets:

```
# flow-cat * | flow-report -v TYPE=ip-source-address -v SORT=+octets -v
FIELDS=-duration,-packets,-flows
...
ip-source-address octets
207.46.209.247     131391013
192.0.2.4          127877204
192.0.2.37         107898108
...
```

If extraneous data confuses your audience, consider trimming unneeded fields.

Displaying Headers, Hostnames, and Percentages

The OPTIONS variable controls miscellaneous report settings. flow-report supports five options, but not all report types support all options, and not all options make sense for every report type. The effect of different options varies with the type of report being run. The report header shows the options used in a report.

```
# options:              +percent-total,+header
```

- The header option tells flow-report to include the generic informational header consisting of the name of the report type, the time of the last flow in the data, and so on. You saw an example of a flow report header in "Default Report" on page 82.

- The xheader option tells flow-report to provide extra header information. Not all report types have extra header information. In some reports, the extra header information is identical to the regular header information. Try this option to see what it does with a given report type.

- With the totals option, flow-report includes the total values of the information being reported on. Not all reports include this, because not all information can be totaled. (You cannot sensibly add IP addresses together, for example!)

- The `percent-total` option provides the information as a percentage of the total rather than an absolute amount. For example, in the `source-ip-address` report, the flows from a particular host would appear as a percentage of the total number of flows rather than the actual number of flows.

- Finally, the `names` option tells `flow-report` to use names rather than numbers. This option makes `flow-report` perform a DNS query for each IP address in the report, which makes reports with IP addresses run extremely slowly. Reports with a limited number of hosts can run reasonably quickly, however, and pulling information from static files such as */etc/protocols* and */etc/services* is very quick.

To remove options from an existing report, put a minus sign (-) before the option name in the OPTIONS variable. In the following example, I've removed all header information from the `ip-source-address` report and am presenting only the report data:

```
# flow-cat * | flow-report -v TYPE=ip-source-address -v SORT=+octets -v ❶ OPTIONS=-header
```

The minus sign before `header` at ❶ tells `flow-report` to remove this value from the list of options.

Adding options is a little more complicated. Once you start adding options, `flow-report` assumes that you will list all desired options. The default report includes the options `header`, `xheader`, and `totals`. To retain all of these and add the `percent-total` option, list them all on the command line, separated by commas, as shown here:

```
# flow-cat * | flow-report -v TYPE=ip-source-address -v SORT=+octets -v
OPTIONS=+percent-total,+header,+xheader,+totals
```

NOTE *If I were to include only the +percent-total option, flow-report would not use any other options even though they are the default.*

Presenting Reports in HTML

`flow-report` formats its output through an external program, `flow-rptfmt`. Most of `flow-rptfmt`'s features overlap `flow-report` functions, such as setting sorting order or choosing fields to display, but you can have `flow-rptfmt` create HTML with the `-f html` flag. Use the RPTOPT variable to pass commands to `flow-rptfmt`.

```
# flow-cat * | flow-report -v TYPE=ip-source-address -v RPTOPT=-fhtml
```

You'll consider `flow-rptfmt` further when I show how to create customized reports.

Useful Report Types

`flow-report` supports more than 70 types of reports and lets you analyze your traffic in more ways than you may have thought possible. In this section, I'll demonstrate the most commonly useful report types. Read the `flow-report` man page for the complete list.

NOTE *Many of these reports are most useful when presented in graphical format or when prepared on a filtered subset of data. You'll look at how to do both of these later in this chapter.*

IP Address Reports

Many traffic analysis problems focus on individual IP addresses. You've already spent some quality time with the `ip-source-address` report. These reports work similarly, but they have their own unique characteristics.

Highest Data Exchange: ip-address

To report on all flows by host, use the `ip-address` report. This totals both the flows sent and the flows received by the host. Here, you look for the host that processed the largest number of octets on the network. You lose the data's bidirectional nature, but this report quickly identifies your most network-intensive host.

```
# flow-cat * | flow-report -v TYPE=ip-address -v SORT=+octets
ip-address      flows  octets     packets duration
192.0.2.4       107785 995021734 1656178 1659809423
192.0.2.37      24294  347444011 456952  322712670
207.46.209.247  50     134705214 151227  5934644
...
```

Flows by Recipient: ip-destination-address

This is the opposite of the `ip-source-address` report I used as an example report throughout the beginning of this chapter. It reports on traffic by destination address.

```
# flow-cat * | flow-report -v TYPE=ip-destination-address
ip-destination-address flows octets     packets duration
158.43.128.72          16478 1090268    16816   49357139
192.0.2.37             12131 239545903  252438  162963278
198.6.1.1              7630  588990     7997    26371278
...
```

In this example, the host 158.43.128.72 has received 16,478 flows in 1,090,268 octets. Lots of people transmitted data to this host. You don't know whether this data is the result of connections initiated by this host or whether many hosts are connecting to this host. To answer that, you have to look at the actual connections. Use `flow-nfilter` to trim your data down to show only the flows involving this host, and use `flow-print` to see the data.

Most Connected Source: ip-source-address-destination-count

Many worms scan networks trying to find vulnerable hosts. If you have a worm infection, you'll want to know which host sends traffic to the greatest number of other hosts on the network. The ip-source-address-destination-count report shows exactly this.

```
# flow-cat * | flow-report -v TYPE=ip-source-address-destination-count
ip-source-address ip-destination-address-count flows octets    packets duration
❶ 192.0.2.37     ❷ 1298                       12163 107898108 204514  159749392
  158.43.128.72    5                           16389 1962766   16711   49357139
  192.0.2.4        2016                        54280 127877204 785592  831419980
...
```

This report shows you that the host 192.0.2.37 (❶) sent flows to 1,298 (❷) other hosts, as well as the number of flows, octets, and packets of these connections.

Most Connected Destination: ip-destination-address-source-count

You can also count the number of sources that connect to each destination. This is similar to the previous report but will contain slightly different data. Some flows (such as broadcasts and some ICMP) go in only one direction, so you must consider destinations separately from sources.

```
# flow-cat * | flow-report -v TYPE=ip-destination-address-source-count
ip-destination-address ip-source-address-count flows octets    packets duration
  158.43.128.72         5                      16478 1090268   16816   49357139
  192.0.2.37            1303                   12131 239545903 252438  162963278
  198.6.1.1             2                      7630  588990    7997    26371278
...
```

The ip-source-address-destination-count and ip-destination-address-source-count reports give additional insight into the key servers, resources, and users on your network, even when you don't have problems.

REPORTS THAT DON'T SORT BY EVERYTHING

Some reports don't offer the opportunity to sort by every field. For example, the two interconnectedness reports cannot sort by the number of hosts an address connects to. This is annoying, especially because this is precisely what you're interested in if you're running this report! On most flavors of Unix you can sort by a column by piping the output through sort -rnk columnnumber, as shown here:

```
flow-cat | flow-report | sort -rnk 2
```

Network Protocol and Port Reports

These reports identify the network ports used by TCP and UDP flows or, on a larger scale, just how much traffic is TCP, UDP, and other protocols.

Ports Used: ip-port

Forget about source and destination addresses. What TCP and UDP protocols are the most heavily used on your network? The ip-port report tells you.

```
# flow-cat * | flow-report -v TYPE=ip-port -v SORT=+octets
  ip-port flows octets    packets duration
❶   80 ❹ 63344 877141857 1298560 1444603541
❷   25    8903   361725472 475912   139074162
❸   443  10379 136012764 346935   324609472
...
```

This looks suspiciously like assorted Internet services. Port 80 (❶) is regular web traffic; port 25 (❷) is email; and port 443 (❸) is encrypted web traffic. You can see how much traffic involves each of these ports, but it's a combination of inbound and outbound traffic. For example, you know that 63,344 (❹) flows either started or finished on port 80. These could be to a web server on the network or web client requests to servers off the network. To narrow this down, you really must filter the flows you examine, run a more specific report, or both. Still, this offers a fairly realistic answer to the question "How much of the traffic is web browsing or email?" especially if you use the +percent-total option.

Flow Origination: ip-source-port

To see the originating port of a flow, use the ip-source-port report. Here I'm sorting the ports in ascending order:

```
# flow-cat * | flow-report -v TYPE=ip-source-port -v SORT=-key
  ip-source-port flows octets    packets duration
❶ 0             215   4053775   23056   21289759
  22            111   1281556   15044   4816416
  25            4437  10489387  181655  69456345
  49            19    3922      79      5135
  ...
```

Flows with a source port of zero (❶) are probably ICMP and certainly not TCP or UDP. It's best to filter your data to only TCP and UDP before running this report. Although ICMP flows use a destination port to represent the ICMP type and code, ICMP flows have no source port.

Source ports with low numbers, such as those in the previously shown report snippet, are almost certainly responses to services running on those ports. In a normal network, port 22 is SSH, port 25 is SMTP, and port 49 is TACACS.

Flow Termination: ip-destination-port

The report ip-destination-port identifies flow termination ports.

```
# flow-cat * | flow-report -v TYPE=ip-destination-port -v SORT=-key
ip-destination-port flows octets     packets duration
0                    91    3993212    22259   14707048
22                   231   26563846   22155   5421745
25                   4466  351236085  294257  69617817
49                   19    6785       101     5135
...
```

These look an awful lot like the source ports. What gives? Because a flow is half of a TCP/IP connection, the destination port might be the destination for the data flowing from the server to the client. A report on the same data should show just roughly as many flows starting on a port as you terminate on that port. Sorting the report by port makes this very obvious.

Individual Connections: ip-source/destination-port

Part of the identifying information for a single TCP/IP connection is the source port and a destination port. The ip-source/destination-port report groups flows by common source and destination ports. Here, I'm reporting on port pairs and sorting them by the number of octets:

```
# flow-cat * | flow-report -v TYPE=ip-source/destination-port -v SORT=+octets
   ip-source-port ip-destination-port flows octets    packets duration
❶  80             15193               3     62721604  43920   620243
❷  4500           4500                115   57272960  101806  30176444
❸  14592          25                  2     28556024  19054   480319
   ...
```

The first connection at ❶ appears to be responses to a web request, coming from port 80 to a high-numbered port. Three separate flows used this combination of ports. Then at ❷ there is IPSec NAT-T traffic on port 4500 and then transmissions to the email server at ❸.

I find this report most useful after I prefilter the data to include only a pair of hosts, which gives me an idea of the traffic being exchanged between the two. You might also use this report to identify high-bandwidth connections and filter on those ports to identify the hosts involved, but if you're interested in the hosts exchanging the most traffic, the ip-address report is more suitable.

Network Protocols: ip-protocol

How much of your traffic is TCP, and how much is UDP? Do you have other protocols running on your network? The ip-protocol report breaks down the protocols that appear on your network. In this example, I'm using the +names option to have flow-report print the protocol name from */etc/protocols* rather than using the protocol number. Looking up names in a static file is much faster than DNS resolution.

```
# flow-cat * | flow-report -v TYPE=ip-protocol -v OPTIONS=+names
ip-protocol flows octets      packets duration
icmp        158   75123       965     6719987
tcp         83639 1516003823  2298691 1989109659
udp         76554 69321656    217741  296940177
esp         34    3820688     18720   8880078
vrrp        12    151708      3298    3491379
```

As you can see, clearly TCP and UDP are our most common protocols, but there is also an interesting amount of ESP traffic. ESP is one of the protocols used for IPSec VPNs.

> ## REPORTS COMBINING ADDRESSES AND PORTS
>
> flow-report also supports reports that provide source and destination addresses and ports together, in almost any combination. Read the flow-report manual page for the specific names of these reports. I find flow-print more useful for that type of analysis.

Traffic Size Reports

Has the number of large data transfers increased on your network over the past few days? If so, flow-report lets you dissect your traffic records and identify trends. These reports are most useful when graphed and compared to historical traffic patterns.

Packet Size: packet-size

How large are the packets crossing your network? You're probably familiar with the 1,500-byte limit on packet size, but how many packets actually reach that size? The packet-size report counts the packets of each size. Here I'm running this report and sorting the results by packet size:

```
# flow-cat * | flow-report -v TYPE=packet-size -v SORT=+key
packet size/flow flows octets    packets duration
1500             ❶ 5   ❷ 2776500 ❸1851  1406780
1499             2     14717980  9816    390603
1498             5     60253559  40207   999167
...
```

As you can see at ❶, 1,500-byte packets have been seen in five flows, containing a total of 2.7 million bytes (❷). You've seen 1851, (❸) of these 1,500-byte packets. Sorting by packets would identify the most and least common packet size.

Bytes per Flow: octets

How large are your individual flows? Do you have more large network trans-actions or small ones? To answer this, report on the bytes per flow with the octets report.

```
# flow-cat * | flow-report -v TYPE=octets -v SORT=-key
octets/flow flows octets     packets duration
46          ❶ 367 ❷16882    367     1214778
48          ❸ 59   2832  ❹ 59      272782
...
168         ❺ 496   83328 ❻ 1311   5819361
...
```

This network had 367 46-octet flows (❶), for a total of 16,882 (❷) octets.

In a small flow, the number of flows (❸) probably equals the number of packets (❹), and each of these tiny flows has only one packet. When flows contain more data, each flow (❺) contains multiple packets (❻).

Packets per Flow: packets

The number of packets in a flow offers an idea of what kind of transactions is most common on your network. The sample DNS queries you looked at in Chapter 1 had only one packet in each flow, while long-running FTP sessions might have thousands or millions of packets. The packets per flow report packets tells you how many flows have each number of packets, as shown here:

```
# flow-cat * | flow-report -v TYPE=packets -v SORT=-key
packets/flow flows octets     packets duration
1            ❶ 74213 6978064  74213   19224735
2              3411  551388   6822    190544194
3              4764  2033952  14292   37130046
...
```

As you can see at ❶, this data contains 74,213 one-packet flows, carrying almost 7 million octets. (That sounds so much more impressive than 6.5MB, doesn't it?)

Traffic Speed Reports

I've had managers ask "How fast is the network?" so often that I've given up telling them that the question is meaningless. Saying that you have a gigabit Ethernet backbone sounds good, but it's like saying that your car's speedom-eter goes up to 120 miles per hour without mentioning that the engine starts making a sickly ratcheting cough at 40 miles per hour. Here are some ways to take a stab at answering that question in something approaching a meaning-ful way.

Counting Packets: pps

Another critical measure of network throughput is packets per second (pps). Many network vendors describe the limits of their equipment in packets per second. The pps report, much like the bps report, shows how many flows travel at the given number of packets per second.

```
# flow-cat * | flow-report -v TYPE=pps -v SORT=+key
pps/flow flows octets     packets duration
❶ 3000    1     231    ❷ 3   ❸ 1
  1000   70    4192      70    70
  833     1     403       5     6
...
```

Wow! One flow went at 3,000 packets per second (❶)? Yes, technically, but note that it contained only three packets (❷) and lasted for one millisecond (❸). Multiplying anything by a thousand exaggerates its impact.

Again, this report isn't terribly useful to the naked eye but can be interesting when graphed.

Traffic at a Given Time: linear-interpolated-flows-octets-packets

The linear-interpolated-flows-octets-packets report averages all the flows fed into it and lists how many flows, octets, and packets passed each second. I find this the most useful "speed" report.

```
# flow-cat * | flow-report -v TYPE=linear-interpolated-flows-octets-packets
unix-secs  flows       octets        packets
1334981479 35.605553   35334.016293  96.820015
1334981480 63.780553   62865.828793  184.570015
1334981481 38.702116   69297.703533  192.235604
...
```

The first column gives the time, in Unix epochal seconds: 1334981479 is equivalent to Saturday, April 21, 2012, at 11 minutes and 19 seconds after midnight, EDT. Each row that follows is one second later. In this second, I passed 35.6 flows, 35334 octets, and 96.8 packets.

This report is ideal for answering many frequently asked questions, such as "How much traffic goes between our desktops and the domain controllers at remote sites?" Take the flow data from your internal connection, run it through `flow-nfilter` once to reduce it to traffic from your desktop address ranges, and then run it through again to trim that down to traffic with your remote domain controllers. Finally, feed the results into `flow-report`, and use the resulting report to generate graphable data.

A little creativity will give you data on things you never expected you could see. For example, TCP resets are a sign of something being not quite right; either a client is misconfigured, a server daemon has stopped working, or a TCP connection has become so scrambled that one side or the other says "Hang up, I'm done."

You can use `flow-nfilter` to strip your flows down to TCP resets. (One TCP reset is one packet.) Run this report with `-v FIELDS=-octets,-flows` to display only the number of TCP resets in a given second, and you'll then have graphable data on TCP resets on your network.

NOTE   *Although the quality of a network administrator's work is difficult to measure, I suggest offering "before" and "after" pictures of TCP reset activity during your performance reviews.*[2]

Routing, Interfaces, and Next Hops

Flow records include information on which interfaces a packet uses. In simple cases, this information isn't terribly useful: If you have a router with one Internet connection and one Ethernet interface, you have a really good idea how packets flowed without any fancy network analysis. A router using BGP, with multiple Internet providers, will distribute outgoing traffic to all Internet providers based on its routing information. Most people use `traceroute` to identify which path the router takes to a particular destination. BGP routing is dynamic, however; the path a packet takes now might not be the path it took five minutes ago or during an outage. Routers that support NetFlow version 5 or newer include interface information with each flow, however, so you can retroactively identify the route a flow used. (Remember, software flow sensors, such as `softflowd`, do not have access to interface information.)

Interfaces and Flow Data

In Chapter 4, you filtered on router interfaces. Reporting on interfaces is the natural extension.

---

2. Remember that a certain level of TCP reset activity is normal, and much of it is caused by buggy or graceless software. Do *not* let your boss give you a goal of "zero TCP resets" during your performance review.

Remember, each router represents its interfaces with numbers. You might think of a router interface as Serial 0, but the router might call it Interface 8. A Cisco router might renumber its interfaces after a reboot, unless you use the snmp ifIndex persist option.

I'm using the router from Chapter 4 as a source of flow information. On this router, interfaces 1 and 2 are local Ethernet ports, and interfaces 7 and 8 are T1 circuits to two different Internet service providers.

The First Interface: input-interface

To see which interface a flow entered a router on, use the input-interface report. Here, I'm adding a filter to report on data only for a single router:

```
# flow-cat * | flow-nfilter -F router1-exports | flow-report -v TYPE=input-
interface
input-interface flows octets      packets duration
1               22976 136933632 306843  58766984
2               320   182048      1307    3214392
7               4934  59690118  165408  46161632
8               1316  7386629   11142   7592624
```

Most of these flows start on interface 1, with the fewest on interface 2.

The Last Interface: output-interface

To show the interfaces that are being used to leave a router, use the output-interface report.

```
# flow-cat * | flow-nfilter -F router1-exports | flow-report -v TYPE=output-
interface
   output-interface flows octets      packets duration
❶ 0                1765  447958    5043    3599588
   1                5057  66979701 175073  52900988
   2                17545 20507633 56531   9440036
   7                111   43079633 34710   8266712
   8                5068  73177502 213343  41528308
```

The first thing I notice in this output is the sudden appearance of interface 0 at ❶. This is a list of valid router interfaces, and 0 isn't one of them. What gives?

These are flows that arrived at the router and never left. The appearance of interface 0 prompted me to more closely scrutinize my flow data, and I found flows that appeared to come from IP addresses reserved for internal, private use. Closer inspection of the firewall revealed several rules that allowed internal traffic to reach the Internet-facing network segment without address translation, but the router dropped all traffic from these internal-only RFC1918 addresses. I also found quite a few traffic streams from the public Internet that were sourced from these private IP addresses, but the router dropped them too, as I would expect.

The lesson to learn is, of course, that proper reporting will do nothing but make more work for you. But at least you'll be able to identify and fix problems before an outsider can use those problems against you.

The Throughput Matrix: input/output-interface

Putting the input/output-interface reports together into a matrix showing which traffic arrived on which interface can be illuminating. Use the input/output-interface report for this. Here, I'm sorting the output by the number of flows so you can easily tell which pairs of interfaces see the greatest number of connections.

```
# flow-cat * | flow-nfilter -F router1-exports | flow-report -v TYPE=input/
output-interface -v SORT=+flows
input-interface output-interface flows octets    packets duration
❶ 1             ❷ 2             17539 20507195 56522   9438220
❸ 1               8             4801  73147574 212806  41001424
  7               1             3888  59604956 164102  45390152
  8               1             1169  7374745  10971   7510836
  7               0             1040  84724    1297    769664
  1               0             525   199230   2805    60628
  2               8             267   29928    537     526884
  8               0             147   11884    171     81788
  1               7             111  ❹43079633 34710   8266712
  2               0             53    152120   770     2687508
  7               2             6     438      9       1816
```

The busiest connection is between interface 1 (FastEthernet0/0) and interface 2 (FastEthernet0/1), shown at ❶ and ❷. This might or might not make sense, depending on your network topology. In mine, it's expected. You then route traffic out one of the Internet circuits at ❸.

This report clearly indicates the difference between flows and bytes. As you can see at ❹, one of the connections with a relatively few flows is actually pushing a comparatively large amount of traffic.

Note the absence of flows between interfaces 7 and 8. This indicates traffic entering on one of the Internet circuits and leaving by the other. You would have become a transit provider, carrying Internet traffic from one network to another. This would happen if, say, you sold a T1 to a third party and they sent their traffic through you to the Internet. If you're not an Internet backbone, this would be a serious problem.

The Next Address: ip-next-hop-address

Reporting by interface gives you a good general idea of where traffic is going, and reporting by IP address offers a detailed view. For an intermediate view, use the ip-next-hop-address report. You do not need to filter this report by the router offering the flows, because the report doesn't confuse the results with interface numbers. This report effectively tells you where the network traffic is going, both for your local hosts and for your upstream providers. I've sorted this report by octets so that the highest-bandwidth next hops appear first.

```
# flow-cat * | flow-report -v TYPE=ip-next-hop-address | -v SORT=+octets
ip-next-hop-address flows octets    packets duration
❶ 192.0.2.4          2490  154742050 174836  31131852
❷ 95.116.11.45       5068  73177502  213343  41528308
  192.0.2.37         5944  65552868  73357   13692932
❸ 12.119.119.161     111   43079633  34710   8266712
  192.0.2.13         2370  21382159  21595   4996548
  192.0.2.194        17545 20507633  56531   9440036
❹ 66.125.104.149     17534 20506982  56521   9447180
...
```

As you can see in this report at ❶, the most heavily used next hop is the proxy server. This isn't a great surprise.

The second most heavily used next hop isn't even an address on my network. It's the ISP's side of one of my T1 circuits, as shown at ❷. This hop represents traffic leaving my network. I also have IP addresses for the second (❸) and third ISPs (❹).

Where Traffic Comes from and How It Gets There: ip-source-address/output-interface

flow-report includes reports based on IP addresses and interfaces. Because these reports are so similar, I'll cover two in detail, and I'll let you figure out the rest.

The ip-source-address/output-interface report shows the source address of a flow and the interface the flow left the router on. If you filter your underlying flow data by an individual host of interest and run that data through this report, you'll get information on how much traffic this one host sent to each of your Internet circuits as well as information on how much data that host received from each remote host. In the following report, I'm filtering by the router exporting the flows to avoid interface number confusion and by the IP address of my main external NAT address:

```
# flow-cat * | flow-nfilter -F router1-exports | flow-nfilter -F ip-addr
-v ADDR=192.0.2.4 | flow-report -v TYPE=ip-source-address/output-interface
ip-source-address output-interface flows octets   packets duration
❶ 192.0.2.4        2                3553  422428  5849    1881348
❷ 192.0.2.4        8                324   3826147 69225   2851980
❸ 198.22.63.8      1                137   56475   762     915472
  ...
❹ 192.0.2.4        7                2     124     2       0
  ...
```

The first entry at ❶ gives the proxy server itself as a source address and shows that I sent many flows out interface 2. That's an Ethernet to another local network segment. You also see at ❷ that the proxy sent large amounts of traffic out interface 8, one of the Internet connections.

You'll see entries at ❸ for remote IP addresses that send a comparatively small number of flows.

The surprising entry here is at ❹ where the proxy server sends a really small amount of traffic out interface 7, the other Internet circuit. Measurements show that this other circuit is consistently heavily used. Whatever is using this circuit isn't the main proxy server, however. I could identify the traffic going out over this circuit by removing the filter on the main proxy server and adding a filter for interface 7. I'll do that with a different report.

Where Traffic Goes, and How It Gets There: ip-destination-address/input-interface

After viewing the results of the previous report, I'm curious about what hosts exchange traffic over interface 7. In Chapter 4, I created a filter that passed all traffic crossing interface 7. You'll use that filter on traffic from this router together with a flow report to see what's happening. Rather than reporting on the source address and the output interface, you'll use ip-destination-address/input-interface to see where traffic arriving on a particular interface is going. The resulting command line might be long enough to scare small children, but it will answer the question.

```
# flow-cat * | flow-nfilter -F router1-exports | flow-nfilter -F interface7 |
flow-report -v TYPE=ip-destination-address/input-interface -v SORT=+octets
ip-source-address input-interface flows octets    packets duration
192.0.2.7         7              2     27347244 22122   3601016
69.147.97.45      1              2     19246168 12853   232400
192.0.2.8         7              2     15442834 11779   3600988
76.122.146.90     1              2     14113638 56214   3601884
...
```

Remember, I designed the filter interface7 so that it matched traffic either entering or leaving over interface 7. That's why this report includes both output interfaces 1 and 7.

Two local hosts, both web servers, receive most of the traffic sent to you over this router interface. More investigation shows that the Internet provider for this line has good connectivity to home Internet providers, such as Comcast and AT&T. The other provider has better connectivity to business customers. (How do you know what kind of connectivity your providers have? You can extract this information from the BGP information in flow records.)

Other Address and Interface Reports

Flow-report includes two more reports for interfaces and addresses, ip-source-address/input-interface and ip-destination-address/output-interface. After the previous two examples, you should have no trouble using or interpreting these reports.

Reporting Sensor Output

If you have multiple sensors feeding a single collector, you might want to know how much data each sensor transmits. Use the `ip-exporter-address` report to find that out.

```
# flow-cat * | flow-report -v TYPE=ip-exporter-address
ip-exporter-address flows octets     packets duration
192.0.2.3            29546 204192427 484700  115735632
192.0.2.12           36750 202920788 231118  39230288
```

As you can see in this report, records from the first router included fewer flows but more octets than those from the second router. Your results will vary depending on the throughput of each of your routers, the kind of traffic they carry, and their sampling rate.

BGP Reports

Flow records exported from BGP-speaking hardware include Autonomous System (AS) information. Reporting on this information tells you which remote networks you are communicating with and even how you reached those networks. If your network does not use BGP, these report types are of no use to you, and you can skip the rest of this chapter.

Flow-tools includes many reports and tools of interest to transit providers, but few if any readers of this book are transit providers. BGP-using readnsers are probably clients of multiple ISPs and use multiple providers for redundancy. I'll cover flow BGP information from the BGP user's perspective. Transit providers reading this book[3] are encouraged to read the `flow-report` manual page for a complete list of reports involving AS numbers.

Using AS Information

What possible use can this type of AS information be for a network engineer? Knowing who you exchange traffic with might have little impact on day-to-day troubleshooting, but it has a great impact on who you purchase bandwidth from.

When the time comes to choose Internet providers, run reports to see who you consistently exchange the most traffic with. If you know that you consistently need good connectivity to three particular remote networks, use them as bullet points in your negotiations with providers. If you don't make bandwidth purchasing decisions, provide the decision maker with this information. The statement "40 percent of our Internet traffic goes to these three companies" is much more authoritative than "I worked with company X before, and they were pretty good."

Traffic's Network of Origin: source-as

The `source-as` report identifies the AS where flows originated. I'll sort this report by octets, because that's how I pay for bandwidth.

---

3. Both of you.

```
# flow-cat * | flow-nfilter -F router1-exports | flow-report -v TYPE=source-as
-v SORT=+octets
  source-as flows octets      packets duration
❶ 0         23024 137077373   307572  61361020
❷ 14779     2     19246168    12853   232400
  33668     136   15664027    64345   14486504
  21502     2     5087464     3450    47692
  ...
```

The invalid AS 0 appears first at ❶. When traffic originates or terminates locally, flow sensors do not record an AS number for the local end of that traffic, which means that your local AS number will never appear in a flow report. The source AS of traffic you transmit shows up as 0, and the destination address of traffic you receive is also shown as 0. The only time you will see both a source and a destination AS number in a flow record is if the exporter is a transit provider, such as an Internet backbone. Traffic coming from AS 0 is the total of all traffic sourced by your network and transmitted to other networks. You might want to filter out all flows with a source AS of 0 from your data before running the report to remove the information about the data that your network transmits.

In the hour shown in the earlier report, the largest amount of traffic originated from AS 14779 (Inktomi/Yahoo!, shown at ❷), but it included only two flows. I suspect that if you were to filter this same data on AS 14779 and run flow-print against it, you'd see that someone had downloaded a file, and I would further guess that the proxy logs would show that someone needed printer software. You can repeat this exercise for each of the AS numbers in the list.

Destination Network: destination-as

To see where you're sending traffic to, use the destination-as report. For a slightly different view of traffic, sort by the number of flows.

```
# flow-cat * | flow-nfilter -F router1-exports | flow-report
-v TYPE=destination-as -v SORT=+flows
  destination-as flows octets    packets duration
❶ 702           11834 767610    11869   23248
❷ 0             6828  67428097  180125  56502392
❸ 701           4154  459973    6372    1893152
  3209          397   553003    9751    1220164
  ...
```

As you can see at ❶, you sent more flows to AS 702 than you received from everybody else combined (shown at ❷). Also note at ❸ that AS 701 belongs to the same organization as AS 702, but flow-report does not aggregate them. Different autonomous systems within one organization almost certainly have slightly different routing policies, despite the best efforts of their owner to coordinate their technical teams.

BGP Reports and Friendly Names

The BGP reports can use friendly names, which will save you the trouble of looking up the owner of interesting AS numbers. Although whois is a fast command-line tool for checking the ownership of AS numbers and you can look up AS information on any number of registry websites, none of these interfaces is suitable for automation. flow-tools gets around this by keeping a static list of AS assignments in the file *asn.sym*. Registries are continuously assigning and revoking AS numbers, however, so the list included with flow-tools will quickly become obsolete. To get the best information on AS names, you must update flow-tools' list of AS numbers.

To update the list of AS numbers, first download the latest list of ARIN assignments from *ftp://ftp.arin.net/info/asn.txt*, and save it on your analysis server.

Flow-tools includes *gasn*, a small script to strip out all of ARIN's comments and instructions and convert ARIN's list to a format it understands. The standard flow-tools installation process doesn't install this rarely used program in one of the regular system program directories, but you can probably find it under */usr/local/flow-tools/share/flow-tools* if you installed from source. Use locate gasn to find the program if you installed from an operating system package.

Here, you feed ARIN's *asn.txt* in the current directory to the *gasn* script located in */usr/local/flow-tools/share/gasn* and produce a new file, *newasn.sym*:

```
# cat asn.txt | perl /usr/local/share/flow-tools/gasn > newasn.sym
```

Take a look at your *newasn.sym* file. The contents should resemble these:

```
0 IANA-RSVD-0
1 LVLT-1
2 DCN-AS
3 MIT-GATEWAYS
...
```

As of this writing, this file contains more than 64,000 AS numbers, each on its own line.

Your system should already have an existing *asn.sym* file, possibly in */usr/local/etc/flow-tools/* or */usr/local/flow-tools/etc/sym/*. Replace that file with your new file. When you add the +names option to flow-report, you should see the current AS names.

```
# flow-cat * | flow-nfilter -F router1-exports | flow-report -v TYPE=source-as
-v SORT=+octets -v OPTIONS=+names
source-as                     flows octets     packets duration
IANA-RSVD-0                   23024 137077373 307572  61361020
INKTOMI-LAWSON                2     19246168  12853   232400
MICROSOFT-CORP---MSN-AS-BLOCK 64    4669359   3259    106792
GOOGLE                        130   4052114   3184    616152
...
```

Not all AS numbers have sensible names, especially those that are acronyms or words in foreign languages, but you can easily pick out some of the obvious ones and identify the others with whois.

Customizing Reports

I use command-line reports for occasional analysis on an ad hoc basis, such as when I'm trying to find patterns in problematic traffic. If you're going to regularly use a report with a long command line, I recommend creating a customized report. Writing truly custom detailed reports of the type I've been demonstrating requires programming, but flow-report lets you highly customize existing reports.

The *stat.cfg* file contains flow report definitions. You'll probably find this file in */usr/local/flow-tools/etc/cfg* or */usr/local/etc/flow-tools*, depending on how you installed flow-tools. The only report that comes in *stat.cfg* is the default report. Don't touch it; it's what makes the various command-line reports function. Add your custom changes below it.

Setting variables on the command line does not work in customized reports because the reason to customize a report is to avoid typing all those command-line variables. You can create a report that will accept command-line modifications, but to do so, you'll need to understand how to write basic reports first. To create such a report, study the default report in *stat.cfg*.

Custom Report: Reset-Only Flows

I frequently use flow-report to create graphable data on flows that contain only TCP resets. These flows can indicate misconfigured software, network equipment, or general system cussedness. Some of the best graphable data comes from the liner-interpolated-flow-octets-packets report. Let's create such a report. My goal is to be able to run the report very simply, like this:

```
# flow-cat * | flow-report -S resets-only
```

Use -S to tell flow-report that you're running a customized report. The new report will be named resets-only.

A minimal report in *stat.cfg* looks like this:

```
❶ stat-report packets
❷     type linear-interpolated-flows-octets-packets
❸     output

❹ stat-definition resets-only
      report packets
```

Much like a flow-nfilter filter, a customized flow report has two main components: the stat-report and the stat-definition. The stat-report at ❶ is somewhat like a filtering primitive. This customized stat-report is called packets, for reasons that will become clear later.

The stat-report needs to know what type of flow-report it is based on, as shown at ❷. The resets-only report starts life as the linear-interpolated-flows-octets-packets report. At ❸ we tell the resets-only report to produce output.

The stat-definition at ❹ lets you aggregate multiple stat-reports into a single report. This definition includes only a single report, named resets. Even with this minimal definition, you can already run the resets-only report. The resulting numbers will be identical to setting TYPE=linear-interpolated-flows-octets-packets on the command line even though it appears slightly different.

```
# flow-cat * | flow-report -S resets-only
# recn: unix-secs*,flows,octets,packets
1228150499,35.605553,35334.016293,96.820015
1228150500,63.780553,62865.828793,184.570015
1228150501,38.702116,69297.703533,192.235604
...
```

The first thing you'll notice in the previous report is that flow-report creates comma-separated value (CSV) reports by default. This is perfectly fine if you're going to feed the results to a graphing program, but CSV data gives me a headache when I have to read it. A graphing program can read tab-delimited data just as easily as CSV, so let's make the report produce human-friendly output.

Report Format and Output

flow-report uses the external program flow-rptfmt to improve the output's appearance. Let's direct the output into flow-rptfmt.

```
stat-report packets
  type linear-interpolated-flows-octets-packets
  output
❶ path |/usr/local/bin/flow-rptfmt
```

The path variable at ❶ tells flow-report where to send the output. By using a path that starts with a pipe symbol (|), you tell flow-report to feed its output to a program, just like a pipe on the command line. Everything after the pipe is run as a command. Here I'm using the standard report formatting software, flow-rptfmt. Adding a formatting program to the report produces this output:

```
#  ['/usr/local/bin/flow-rptfmt']
unix-secs  flows      octets       packets
1228150499 35.605553  35334.016293 96.820015
1228150500 63.780553  62865.828793 184.570015
1228150501 38.702116  69297.703533 192.235604
...
```

You'll learn more about using `flow-rptfmt` and other output options in "Customizing Report Appearance" on page 112.

Removing Columns

You're interested in counting the number of TCP resets that occur over time. (One TCP reset is one packet.) The octets and packets columns are irrelevant, so remove them.

```
stat-report packets
  type linear-interpolated-flows-octets-packets
  output
❶ fields -octets,-flows
    path |/usr/local/bin/flow-rptfmt
```

This works exactly like removing fields on the command line. The `fields` header at ❶ tells `flow-report` which columns to remove. Removing the octets and flows fields from this report gives you output much like the output shown next, and you now see only the data of interest:

```
# ['/usr/local/bin/flow-rptfmt']
unix-secs  packets
1228150499 96.820015
1228150500 184.570015
1228150501 192.235604
...
```

Applying Filters to Reports

The report lists times and the number of packets, so you're headed in the right direction. But it's listing the total number of packets in the flow file, not just the TCP resets. You need to add a filter to strip away everything except the data you're interested in. You could use a filter on the command line, of course, but the purpose of a customized report is to reduce the amount of typing you do.

`flow-report` lets you add a filter in either the `stat-report` or the `stat-definition`. I define my filter in the `stat-definition`. Recall from Chapter 4 that you configured the `rst-only` filter to pass only TCP resets.

```
stat-definition reset-only
  filter rst-only
  report packets
```

The report output now looks like this:

```
unix-secs  packets
1228150595 0.068702
1228150596 0.068702
1228150597 0.068702
...
```

This network has a low number of TCP resets, but if you page through the results, you'll see peaks and valleys of reset-only flows. You'll use this data, among others, to create graphs in Chapter 8.

Combining stat-reports and stat-definitions

If you can use filters in either a stat-report or a stat-definition, why did I put the filter in my stat-definition?

Look at the packets stat-report. I wrote it to display reset-only TCP flows, but it is really just a linearly interpolated packet count. You can use this same stat-report elsewhere to create customized reports on data filtered differently. For example, if you had a filter to show all your SYN-only flows, you could use the packets stat-report to create data for both.

```
stat-definition reset-only
  filter rst-only
  report packets

stat-definition syn-only
  filter syn-only
  report packets
```

Both the reset-only and syn-only reports format and present their results identically. The only difference is the filter applied to create each report.

More Report Customizations

Any customization you can perform on the command line will also work in a customized report, but the configuration file supports additional features as well.

Reversing Sampling

Some flow sensors sample flows only, sending just a fraction of their data to the flow collector (see Chapter 2). This is better than having no flow data but can confuse reporting. To improve this situation, you can tell flow-report to scale up its output to compensate for sampling. For example, if your router samples at a rate of 1:10, you can scale up the output by a factor of 10 to get traffic volumes roughly comparable to the original. The report here scales the source and destination IP addresses:

```
 stat-report subnets
 type ip-source/destination-address
❶ scale 10
 output
   path |/usr/local/bin/flow-rptfmt

stat-definition subnets
 report subnets
```

The scale keyword at ❶ defines a scaling multiplier. Take a look at the output from this report:

```
# flow-cat * | flow-report -S subnets
# ['/usr/local/bin/flow-rptfmt']
ip-source-address ip-destination-address flows octets    packets duration
192.0.2.37        158.43.128.72          8702  5760730    88840   30096122
158.43.128.72     192.0.2.37             8649  10405130   88280   30096122
192.0.2.4         198.6.1.1              7625  5886410    79920   26370707
...
```

I've copied this report to subnets-unscaled and removed the scale command. Let's compare the output.

```
# flow-cat * | flow-report -S subnets-unscaled
# ['/usr/local/bin/flow-rptfmt']
ip-source-address ip-destination-address flows octets   packets duration
192.0.2.37        158.43.128.72          8702  576073    8884    30096122
158.43.128.72     192.0.2.37             8649  1040513   8828    30096122
192.0.2.4         198.6.1.1              7625  588641    7992    26370707
...
```

The source and destination addresses are unchanged, as is the number of flows, but the octet and packet counts have increased tenfold in the scaled report. This gives you a mostly accurate view of the amount of traffic passing through your network. Although you're still entirely missing data on some flows, this is about as close to reality as you can get from sampled data.

Filters in stat-report Statements

To use a filter in a stat-report statement, you must place it before the output definition. For example, the following filter statement applies the specified filter to your data before reporting:

```
stat-report subnets
  type ip-source/destination-address
  filter web-traffic
  output
    path |/usr/local/bin/flow-rptfmt
```

Reporting by BGP Routing

Perhaps you're interested in internetwork connectivity rather than connectivity between individual IP addresses. If your flow records include BGP information, you can have flow-report generate reports using network block data. To do so, set the ip-source-address-format and ip-destination-address-format options to prefix-len, and flow-report will print the netmask with each entry.

```
stat-report subnets
  type ip-source/destination-address
❶ ip-source-address-format prefix-len
❷ ip-destination-address-format prefix-len
  output
    path |/usr/local/bin/flow-rptfmt
```

Here you've told `flow-report` to include the netmask in the source (❶) and destination (❷) addresses. The report now looks like this:

ip-source-address	ip-destination-address	flows	octets	packets	duration
63.125.104.150/12	87.169.213.77/10	9	1008	18	23760
❶ 192.0.2.37/25	158.43.128.72/16	8233	537169	8233	4
192.0.2.4/25	❷ 198.6.1.1/16	6634	485854	6658	168412
...					

You can see at ❶ that 192.0.2.37 is routed as a /25 network. Although a /25 is too small to be announced on the public Internet, these addresses are local. The router had better know the netmask of directly attached networks! You also see that, for example, the address 198.6.1.1 at ❷ is announced as a /16.

To have `flow-report` aggregate data by network, set the address format to `prefix-mask`. Here's the same report on the same data, using the `prefix-mask` format:

ip-source-address	ip-destination-address	flows	octets	packets	duration
❶ 63.112/12	87.128/10	15	1792	32	58384
❷ 192.0.2/25	158.43/16	23663	1532256	23707	17372
192.0.2/25	198.6/16	8299	915307	12698	3711276
...					

Now you no longer see individual IP addresses. Instead, you see source address blocks as they are routed. You're sending traffic from some addresses inside the 63.112/12 range (❶) to addresses inside 87.128/10. `flow-report` has aggregated all the individual connections from one block to another.

Look at the second line of each of these reports. The first report shows that you sent 8,233 flows from the address 192.0.2.37 to the address 158.43.128.72. The report with the address mask set says that you sent 23,663 flows (❷) from addresses inside the block 192.0.2/25 to addresses inside 158.43/16. This line on the second report includes all the flows from the entry you checked in the first report, plus other flows that fit within those address blocks. They've been aggregated.

Customizing Report Appearance

`flow-report` supports many options for customizing presentation. Use these options in the `stat-report` definition only beneath the word `output`. Using them earlier will generate an error.

flow-rptfmt Options

Remember, setting path to a pipe followed by a program name tells flow-report to feed its output into that program. Everything after the pipe is executed as a regular shell command. This means you can do things such as redirect the output to a file.

```
path |/usr/local/bin/flow-rptfmt > /tmp/resets.txt
```

The previous line would have the report appear in the file */tmp/resets.txt* rather than on the screen.

If you prefer, flow-rptfmt can produce a very simple HTML table of its output by adding the -f html arguments to activate this function, as shown next. (You'll probably want to redirect the output to a file under your web server's root directory.)

```
path |/usr/local/bin/flow-rptfmt -f html > /var/www/resets/today.html
```

Of course, dumping regularly produced reports to a single file probably isn't useful. What you really need is a way to send the output to a file based on timing information.

Dump CSV to a File

Although flow-rptfmt is the standard tool for formatting reports, you might decide that the plain-text CSV works better for some purposes, such as for automated graph creation. If you set path to a filename, flow-report will dump raw CSV text straight to that file, which is most useful if you automatically process the data.

```
path /tmp/reset.csv
```

Using Time to Direct Output

A stat-report definition can create and use timing information when saving CSV files using the time option and special characters in the path setting.

Before using this definition, decide which time you want flow-report to use. Do you want to use the current time or the time in the flow files? If the time in the flow files, do you want the time when the flows begin or end? Control this with the time option using one of four different time values: now (the time when the report is run), start (the time the first flow begins), end (the time the last flow ends), or mid (the average of the start and end times, the default). For most uses, the default is fine.

The path value can accept variables from the strftime library. Table 5-1 lists the most common ones. If you need a time representation that isn't listed in this table, such as the day of the year, the day of the week as a numerical value, or the current time zone as expressed as minutes offset from universal time, read the manual page.

Table 5-1: Some strftime Variables for flow-report

Variable	Replaced with
%a	Abbreviated day name (Mon, Tue, and so on)
%b	Abbreviated month name (Jan, Feb, and so on)
%d	Day of the month as a number (1–31)
%H	Hour as per 24-hour clock (00–23)
%M	Minutes (0–59)
%m	Month (1–12)
%Y	Four-digit year (0–9999)
%y	Two-digit year (00–99)

flow-report can use the strftime variable values to direct output. For example, suppose you want to have the report output directed into a file with a name based on the time, in a directory hierarchy based on the year, month, and day. Use the strftime variables to name the file and to choose a directory to place the file, as shown here:

```
stat-report subnets
   type ip-source/destination-address
   output
❶    time end
❷    path /tmp/%Y/%m/%d/%H/%M-report.csv
```

This report uses the time the last flow ends (❶). As shown at ❷, the results will appear in a file under a directory named for the year, month, day, and hour, and they use the last time in the file for the filename. For example, if I'm reporting on flow data from December 1, 2011, between 8 AM and 8:59 AM, the results would appear in the directory */tmp/2011/12/01/08*.

NOTE *Although flow-report will expand strftime variables and hand the correct numbers to flow-rptfmt, flow-rptfmt cannot create missing directories.*

The following report places HTML reports in a directory under the web root, using filenames based on the year, month, day, and hour of the data you're reporting on:

```
stat-report subnets
   type ip-source/destination-address
   output
     time mid
     path |flow-rptfmt -f html > /var/www/reports/report-%Y-%m-%d-%H-report.html
```

Set Sorting Order

Use the sort output option to control which column the report sorts on. This works the same as if you changed sorting on the command line. Use any column name in the report as the value for sort. A leading plus sign says start with the largest value and go down; a leading minus sign means start with the smallest and go up. The following example stat-report tells you what remote address ranges your network communicates with most because you list the highest traffic networks first by sorting on octets.

```
stat-report subnets
  type ip-source/destination-address
  ip-source-address-format prefix-len
  ip-destination-address-format prefix-len
  output
  sort +octets
    path |flow-rptfmt
```

Cropping Output

Flow reports can run to hundreds or thousands of lines. Often you don't want the entire report and instead want merely the first entries, whether that's the first five or the first 500, but there's no sense in creating the 50,000-line report just to get those few entries. The records option gives the maximum number of results to show. Here, I'm adding a records entry to the previous report:

```
output
records 5
  sort +octets
  path |flow-rptfmt
```

The report is no longer a list of all the networks you communicate with. Instead, it's the top five networks you communicate with.

Other Output Options

You might or might not want header information, percentages, and so on, in your customized report. Control these with the options keyword. (I discussed these options in "Displaying Headers, Hostnames, and Percentages" on page 90.) Here I'm turning off the informational headers:

```
output
  options +header
  path |flow-rptfmt
```

Alternate Configuration Files

As you proceed, you might find yourself with an increasing number of customized reports used by more and more people. Reports, like filters, will not work if the configuration file is not parseable. As more people and processes run reports, you might find it difficult to develop new reports without annoying other system users or interrupting scheduled jobs. If so, tell flow-report to use a different configuration file than the default with the -s flag.

```
# flow-report -s test-stat.cfg -S newreport
```

Create, edit, and remove reports on a copy of the configuration file. When your changes are working the way you want, just copy your new configuration over the old one. Users won't notice unless you change a report that they're using.

Now that you can report on your traffic any way you like, you'll create graphical reports and even write your own flow analysis software in Chapter 6.

6

PERL, FLOWSCAN, AND CFLOW.PM

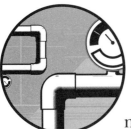 Welcome to the most troublesome part of a flow-tools implementation: the Perl module. Perl is popular for quickly creating reporting tools and web interfaces. One of the most user-friendly flow-reporting tools, FlowScan, is built on Perl, but unfortunately, the Perl module for working with flow files, *Cflow.pm*, is difficult to install correctly. This isn't because of Perl but because flow collectors all have different on-disk storage formats. Your *Cflow.pm* installation must know how to read flow-tools flow files.

Cflow.pm is named after the obsolete flow collector cflowd. When the cflowd project shut down, cflowd's authors recommended migrating to flow-tools. *Cflow.pm* was modified to include optional support for flow-tools. Many mailing list archive messages and lots of documentation refer to cflowd and *Cflow.pm* and don't necessarily differentiate between the two. You need *Cflow.pm*, not cflowd.

Installing Cflow.pm

Historically, correctly installing *Cflow.pm* has been the most difficult and annoying part of any flow analysis implementation. Internet searches will uncover all sorts of articles and mailing list archives discussing *Cflow.pm* installation issues, including a series of articles by this author. The new flow-tools release has a specific process for installing *Cflow.pm*. Use the recommended process, and test your *Cflow.pm* immediately after installation. Do not proceed if your *Cflow.pm* install does not give sensible results.

Testing Cflow.pm

The *Cflow.pm* kit includes a command-line tool for accessing flow files, flowdumper. It's not as powerful or as flexible as the tools included in flowtools, but it does test *Cflow.pm*. If flowdumper prints the contents of your flow files correctly, your *Cflow.pm* install is working. Just run **flowdumper -s**, and give it the name of a flow file.

```
# flowdumper -s ft-v05.2011-12-14*
2011/12/16 23:59:42 69.134.229.81.51459 -> 192.0.2.37.443 6(PUSH|ACK) 1 81
2011/12/16 23:59:43 192.0.2.4.10690 -> 198.6.1.1.53 17 1 81
2011/12/16 23:59:43 192.0.2.37.443 -> 69.134.229.81.51459 6(ACK) 1 40
...
```

The -s tells flowdumper to print a summary of each flow on one line. Each line represents a flow. You'll see the source and destination addresses and ports, the protocol number, the TCP flags, the number of packets, and the number of octets.

If your *Cflow.pm* install is faulty, flowdumper returns either silently or with an error. You cannot proceed with Perl modules or FlowScan until you resolve any error.

> **FAILURE LURKS HERE**
>
> Correct *Cflow.pm* installation seems to be the single most common reason flow management projects fail. Test *Cflow.pm* immediately upon installation. Do *not* proceed with any software that uses *Cflow.pm* until flowdumper gives correct answers. You have been warned.

Install from Operating System Package

Some operating system vendors include *Cflow.pm* packages that may include flow-tools support. Install the package, and test flowdumper. If it doesn't work, uninstall the package before proceeding.

Install from Source

Get the *Cflow.pm* source code, *Cflow-1.053.tar.gz*, from *http://net.doit.wisc.edu/~plonka/Cflow/* and extract it. Do not follow the building instructions included with the *Cflow.pm* source, however. Flow-tools has changed since Cflow.pm was released, and to build it use the instructions in flow-tools' *contrib/README* file.

Go into the extracted *Cflow.pm* source and run

```
# perl Makefile.PL CCFLAGS='-DOSU' LIBS='-lft'
# make
# make install
```

Test `flowdumper` right now. If it doesn't work, proceed to the next section.

Installing from Source with a Big Hammer

If your installation from default source fails, this should work. (Unix and Perl purists will scream in moral outrage, and they're welcome to fix the real problem.)

In the *Cflow-1.053* source directory, open *Makefile.PL* in a text editor. Find this section of code:

```
sub find_flow_tools {
  my($ver, $dir);
  my($libdir, $incdir);
❶ if (-f '../../lib/libft.a') {
  ...
```

The ❶ reference to *libft.a* is the source of all the trouble. If all else fails, hard-code the path to *libft.a*. My test system has */usr/local/lib/libft.a*, so I would change this source code to read as follows:

```
    if (-f '/usr/local/lib/libft.a') {
```

Then build and install *Cflow.pm* as shown in the earlier "Install from Source" section. `flowdumper` will now show data.

If none of these methods work for you, contact the flow-tools mailing list with a full description of your problem, including output from the failed builds.

flowdumper and Full Flow Information

Although `flowdumper` is generally less useful than `flow-print`, it has some unique features. You've already used the summary feature (`-s`) to test *Cflow.pm*. (`flowdumper` can also accept Perl instructions on the command line, but if you're sufficiently skilled in Perl to do that, you can read the `flowdumper` manual page.)

If you don't use the summary feature, `flowdumper` prints all the information the flow file includes for every flow.

```
# flowdumper ft-*
FLOW
      index:          0xc7ffff
❶    router:         192.0.2.12
❷    src IP:         158.43.128.72
      dst IP:         192.0.2.37
      input ifIndex:  9
      output ifIndex: 1
      src port:       53
      dst port:       34095
      pkts:           1
      bytes:          130
❸    IP nexthop:     192.0.2.37
      start time:     Sat Dec 31 23:54:42 2011
      end time:       Sat Dec 31 23:54:42 2011
      protocol:       17
      tos:            0x0
❹    src AS:         702
      dst AS:         0
      src masklen:    16
      dst masklen:    25
      TCP flags:      0x0
      engine type:    0
      engine id:      0
...
```

You've seen most of this flow information previously, but the interesting thing here is that flowdumper shows everything in the flow record, including data fields that are irrelevant in most environments. You'll see the sensor address (❶), the source and destination addresses (❷), and so on. You'll also see that the sensor is exporting information such as next-hop data (❸), BGP routing data (❹), and such. Although you usually wouldn't want to try to use complete flowdumper output for day-to-day management, it lets you verify that your system is collecting all the data you think it should. A more useful system for day-to-day reporting, however, is FlowScan.

FlowScan and CUFlow

Although the text-based flow reports demonstrated in Chapter 5 are clearly useful, even nontechnical people easily understand visual representations of traffic. Chapters 7 and 8 demonstrate graphing arbitrary data, but much of the time graphing nonarbitrary data is sufficient. Every network administrator already has a pretty good idea of what constitutes the most common traffic on their network. For example, if you run a web farm, you probably care more about HTTP and HTTPS traffic than you do that of other services. If you manage an office network, you might care a lot about CIFS and printer traffic. Much of the time you can get adequate results by graphing the stuff you know about and lumping what you don't know about into an "other" category. That's what FlowScan is for.

FlowScan is an engine for extracting and aggregating flow data. It provides a web interface that displays graphs depicting network traffic that the network administrator previously deemed interesting. These graphs are suitable for display to users, staff, and customers who would be confused by the more detailed flow reports.

FlowScan is built on *Cflow.pm* and uses the Round Robin Database (RRD), just like MRTG and Cacti. RRD is a fixed-size database that retains data over the long term by compressing and averaging older entries. In other words, RRD gives a pretty good view of recent traffic, a decent view of traffic a few months past, and only a high-level view of last year's traffic. This suffices more often than you'd think, however. Most users want to know why the Internet was slow for the last hour or perhaps how today's traffic compares to last year's traffic. FlowScan will answer these questions, though it cannot explain exactly why the Internet was slow on the afternoon of October 3 a year ago.

FlowScan's modular framework lets network administrators choose from a variety of reporting methods. Of those, I'll cover the popular CUFlow module.

FlowScan Prerequisites

FlowScan has the following requirements:

- Web server, such as any recent version of Apache
- Perl
- Korn shell or pdksh (*http://www.cs.mun.ca/~michael/pdksh/*)
- RRDtool (*http://oss.oetiker.ch/rrdtool/*) with Perl shared module support
- The Boulder::Stream Perl module
- The ConfigReader::DirectiveStyle Perl module
- The HTML::Table Perl module
- The Net::Patricia Perl module
- *Cflow.pm*

You can install most of these from operating system packages. Although the FlowScan documentation includes warnings about installing the RRDtool Perl module RRDs.pm, RRDTool has included this module for some time now.

NOTE   *Be sure to test your* Cflow.pm *install before starting on FlowScan.*

Installing FlowScan and CUFlow

FlowScan was originally written to work with the obsolete cflowd collector. If you install FlowScan from an operating system package, the package will probably want to install cflowd and its obsolete compiler libraries, as well as other clutter as dependencies. Other times, the operating system providers have edited the FlowScan software to make the most common use case easier but more unusual uses much more difficult. For these reasons, I recommend installing FlowScan by hand. To do so, follow these steps:

1. Download FlowScan from its author's website at *http://net.doit.wisc.edu/~plonka/FlowScan/*.

2. Download a copy of version 1.6 or newer of the FlowScan Perl module from *http://net.doit.wisc.edu/~plonka/list/flowscan/archive/att-0848/01-FlowScan.pm* or by searching Google for *flowscan.pm 1.6*. (You can also check the Links section of this book's website.)

3. Extract the FlowScan tarball, and go into the build directory.

4. The FlowScan author recommends installing FlowScan in the directory where you keep your flow files. Use this directory as the prefix in the configure command. (If you do not choose a location, FlowScan will install directories, configuration files, and Perl modules in /usr/local/bin, which is less than desirable.)

```
# cd FlowScan-1.006
# ./configure --prefix=/var/db/flows/test
# make install
```

The directory */var/db/flows/test/bin* should now contain your FlowScan software.

5. You'll also need FlowScan's tiny configuration file, *flowscan.cf*, which isn't automatically installed. It's in the unpacked FlowScan source in the *cf* directory. Copy this template to the FlowScan *bin* directory.

6. Finally, upgrade the existing *FlowScan.pm* file. Version 1.5, which ships with FlowScan, supports cflow only, but version 1.6 and newer can read flow-capture files. Copy version 1.6 right over *bin/FlowScan.pm*.

FlowScan User, Group, and Data Directories

With FlowScan installed, create a user called *flowscan* just for FlowScan, and give that user ownership of the FlowScan *bin* directory. Also give the group permissions on the directory so that network administrators can edit FlowScan configuration files without have to enter the root password.

FlowScan needs two directories at the same level as the *bin* directory: one, called *flowscandata*, for incoming flow data files, and the other, *flowscanrrd*, for flow RRD records. Set the sticky bit on these directories so that incoming files are owned by the flowscan user as follows:

```
# chown -R flowscan:flowscan bin
# chmod g+w bin
# chmod g+ws flowscandata
# chown flowscan:flowscan flowscandata flowscanrrd
# chmod g+ws flowscandata/ flowscanrrd/
```

Now add your network administrators to the `flowscan` group so that they can configure FlowScan without the need for root access.

FlowScan Startup Script

Your operating system might include its own startup scripts for FlowScan. If so, check the script's instructions to learn how to configure it. If not, FlowScan includes startup scripts for Linux and Solaris in the *rc* directory. In this section, I'll show how to configure the Linux script. (The Solaris script is very similar, and these scripts should work with minor modifications on any modern operating system.) The top of the file includes four variables that you'll need to set.

```
❶ bindir=/var/db/flows/test/bin
❷ scandir=/var/db/flows/flowscandata
❸ logfile=/var/log/flowscan.log
❹ user=flowscan
```

The *bindir* directory (❶) contains the FlowScan files and *flowscan.cf*.

The *scandir* directory (❷) is where FlowScan checks for new data files.

Put the *logfile* directory (❸) anywhere you like. I prefer to have all my logs in */var/log*. You must touch the logfile before running FlowScan and give the flowscan user permission to change the file,

Finally, tell FlowScan what user (❹) will run flowscan.

The second section of this file contains paths to a variety of standard commands. These should be correct for most Unix-like systems, but if you have trouble, verify each separately.

Once you've made your changes, have your system startup script run the FlowScan startup script as an argument to `/bin/sh`. (Depending on your system startup process, you might have to add the line `#!/bin/sh` to the top of the script.)

Configuring FlowScan

The *flowscan.cf* file has only four configuration values: `FlowFileGlob`, `ReportClasses`, `WaitSeconds`, and `Verbose`.

`FlowFileGlob` tells FlowScan which files to process. Use it to tell FlowScan the directory to examine and the type of file to try to process. Here, I'm examining any `flow-capture` files in the directory */var/db/flows/test/flowscandata*:

```
FlowFileGlob /var/db/flows/test/flowscandata/ft-v*[0-9]
```

`ReportClasses` lists all the report modules you're using. FlowScan comes with two modules, CampusIO and SubNetIO. These are not very configurable and do not really represent modern traffic patterns, so you'll use CUFlow.

```
ReportClasses CUFlow
```

Now you tell FlowScan how often to check the directory for files. The CUFlow module assumes that FlowScan runs every five minutes. Don't change this; just use the default.

```
WaitSeconds 300
```

Finally, verbose logging can help during setup. Set this to 0 once you have FlowScan running. For now, set it to 1.

```
Verbose 1
```

You've finished configuring FlowScan, but it won't do anything until you set up a reporting module. Let's set up CUFlow and then return to FlowScan.

Configuring CUFlow: CUFlow.cf

CUFlow is more configurable than FlowScan's default modules, but it assumes that all traffic it processes is either entering or leaving your network. This makes FlowScan suitable for use on border routers, site MPLS routers, and so on, but not as useful for monitoring traffic that begins and terminates on your network. Transit carriers will have limited use for CUFlow, but even a big ISP has some local networks.

To install CUFlow, download it from *http://www.columbia.edu/acis/ networks/advanced/CUFlow/CUFlow.html*, and then extract and copy the files *CUFlow.cf* and *CUFLow.pm* to your FlowScan *bin* directory.

CUFlow.cf includes a variety of statements to tell FlowScan what data to look for and how to process it. Edit these to match your network, as follows.

Subnet

The Subnet statement tells CUFlow the addresses on your local network. CUFlow uses this to determine whether traffic is inbound or outbound. Flows with a source on this network are considered outbound, while flows with a destination on this network are inbound.

```
Subnet 192.0.2.0/24
```

You can have multiple Subnet statements, as needed.

Network

Network statements include hosts and ranges that you want to track separately. You can have any number of Network statements, and one address can appear in multiple Network statements. List either individual hosts or networks with a slash to indicate netmask. Be sure to give each network a one-word name.

```
Network 192.0.2.4              proxy
Network 192.0.2.128/26         dmz
Network 192.0.2.36,192.0.2.37  mailservers
```

OutputDir

The OutputDir directive tells CUFlow where to store its RRD data files. Do not store your records in a web-accessible location or in your flow-capture log directory. Instead, store them in the *flowscanrrd* directory next to the *bin* directory that you created for these records.

```
OutputDir /var/db/flows/test/flowscanrrd
```

Each FlowScan module must have its own output directory. If you choose to run multiple FlowScan modules, create additional RRD directories as necessary.

Scoreboard

CUFlow can also compute the most active sites within a flow file and present a scoreboard of the host addresses that have passed the greatest number of flows, octets, and packets. The Scoreboard option takes three arguments: the number of addresses in your "most active" list, a directory to store those lists in, and the filename of the most current list, as shown here:

```
Scoreboard ❶ 10 ❷ /var/www/flowscan/topten ❸ /var/www/flowscan/topten/topten.html
```

Here the scoreboard computes the top 10 hosts (❶), storing the old data in the directory */var/www/flowscan/topten/* (❷), and puts the most recent data in the file */var/www/flowscan/topten/topten.html* (❸). You must create the *Scoreboard* directory, give your flowscan user ownership of the directory, and configure your web server to permit access to the current and historical pages.

NOTE   *Do not put your scoreboard files in the same directory as your flow files. Your flow files should be nowhere near files served by a web server.*

AggregateScore

CUFlow can also track the most active hosts over time using AggregateScore. Configure the AggregateScore option much the same as the Scoreboard option with the number of hosts to present, a file to store long-term totals, and a web page for the results, as shown here. (Be sure to put the aggregated data file someplace inaccessible to your web server, such as your RRD data directory.)

```
AggregateScore ❶ 10 ❷ /var/db/flows/test/flowscanrrd/agg.dat ❸ /var/www/flowscan/overall.html
```

Here I'm presenting the top 10 busiest hosts (❶) in the flow history, storing the long-term data in the directory */var/db/flows/test/flowscanrrd/ agg.dat* (❷), and presenting an HTML page of the top 10 in */var/www/ flowscan/overall.html* (❸).

Again, you must create the directories beforehand, and FlowScan must have permission to write files in them.

Router

If you have multiple flow sensors sending data to the same collector (such as two routers in a BGP/HSRP cluster), identify different sensors with Router statements as shown here. CUFlow can separate data from different sensors so that you can see how much traffic each handles.

```
Router 192.0.2.2    rocky
Router 192.0.2.3    bullwinkle
```

Here you identify each router by IP address and give it a human-friendly name. The friendly name will appear in the web interface.

Service

Service statements define TCP/IP ports that you want to track separately. CUFlow will generate a separate RRD file for each port or set of ports tracked by a Service statement, with each appearing in a separate color in the web interface.

NOTE   *Increasing the number of Service statements increases the processing power and disk I/O CUFlow consumes, so don't just copy /etc/services here!*

CUFlow.cf includes some examples that you can edit to fit your needs. For example, users on my network are not allowed to use Gnutella or eDonkey, so I comment them out of the file. Here are some example Service statements:

```
Service 20-21/tcp ftp
Service 22/tcp ssh
Service 53/udp,53/tcp dns
```

The first Service statement, FTP, uses two TCP ports. The second is much simpler and uses only a single TCP port. The third runs on both TCP and UDP.

If you're not sure which ports to track, run some command-line reports to identify the most heavily used ports on your network.

Protocol

The Protocol statement is very similar to Service, except for Layer 3 instead of Layer 4.

```
Protocol 1 icmp
Protocol 6 tcp
Protocol 17 udp
```

If you have IPSec VPNs, you might want to track protocols 50–51 (ESP and AH). PPTP users are probably interested in protocol 47 (GRE).

AS

BGP-based sites might be interested in tracking traffic to or from particular networks by AS number. Again, each AS entry here takes processing time. Don't just dump the complete list of AS assignments here!

AS 7853,13385,36377,16748,33542,36196,14668	Comcast
AS 65535	Lucas
AS 701-705	UUnetLegacy

Software flow sensors such as softflowd do not export BGP information, so don't bother with AS analysis when using a software sensor.

Now that you've configured CUFlow, let's get some data to it.

Rotation Programs and flow-capture

FlowScan checks a single directory for flow files: */var/db/flows/flowscandata*. If FlowScan doesn't find any files, it goes back to sleep for five minutes. This flow-capture system logs data to files stored in a directory hierarchy. For example, the files for February 17, 2011, are stored in the directory */var/db/flows/test/2011/2011-02/2011-02-17*. How can you get these files into your */var/db/flows/flowscandata* directory? You can use a flow-capture log rotation script.

flow-capture's -R option runs a script when a flow file is closed and a new temp file created. For example, to run the script /usr/local/bin/flow-rotate.sh on each new logfile, you would run flow-capture as follows:

```
# flow-capture -p /var/run/flow-capture.pid -R /usr/local/bin/flow-rotate.sh -n 287 \
-w /var/db/flows -S 5 10.10.10.10/172.16.16.16/5678
```

flow-capture gives the rotation program one argument: the name of the closed logfile relative to the flow directory. For example, as I write this, the flow-capture in my test lab is writing to the file *tmp-v05.2011-02-17.152001-0500* in today's directory. At 3:25 PM, flow-capture will close this temporary file, rename it *ft-v05.2011-02-17.152001-0500*, and create a new *tmp-*file. At this point, flow-capture will run any script specified by -R with the path to the current file. It's as if you ran this command on every logfile as soon as it was closed.

```
# flow-rotate.sh   2011/2011-02/2011-02-17/ft-v05.2011-02-17.152001-0500
```

Your script needs to take this name and perform any necessary post-processing on the flow data file. First, you want to copy the flow file to your data directory. Start with the following shell script:

```
#!/bin/sh

cp $1 /var/db/flows/test/flowscandata/
```

Second, once you have the filename, copying the file to the *flowscan* data directory is simple.

Now give this script as an argument to flow-capture -R, and then verify that the flow file is copied to the FlowScan data directory.

NOTE *Make your rotation scripts very simple. Remember that this script will run every five minutes, and if it generates extensive logs or sends email, you'll get those messages 288 times a day.*

Running FlowScan

Now it's time to start FlowScan by running its startup script. The FlowScan logfile should have an entry like this:

```
2011/02/17 17:29:07 working on file ❶ /var/db/flows/test/flowscandata/ft-
v05.2011-02-17.172501-0400...
2011/02/17 17:29:10 flowscan-1.020 CUFlow: Cflow::find took ❷ 3 wallclock
secs (3.36 usr +  0.00 sys =  3.36 CPU) for ❸ 615816 flow file bytes, ❹ flow
hit ratio: 31593/31599
2011/02/17 17:29:12 flowscan-1.020 CUFlow: report took ❺ 1 wallclock secs
(0.00 usr  0.00 sys +  0.12 cusr  0.04 csys =  0.16 CPU)
❻ Sleep 300...
```

In this output, FlowScan started (❶) processing the file your log rotation program copied to the data directory. You can see at ❷ how long FlowScan searched the file for data and at ❸ the file size.

The most interesting thing here, though, is the flow hit ratio at ❹. This ratio tells you how many flows in the file matched your Subnet statement. You should have an overwhelming number of matches. Here, I'm matching 31,593 out of 31,599 flows in the file, which is acceptable. (Broadcast traffic and misconfigured hosts probably account for the small number of non-matching flows.) You can also see at ❺ how long FlowScan took to write the RRD files.

Finally, at ❻ FlowScan runs out of files to process, and it goes to sleep for five minutes. When it awakens, it will process any files it finds in the data directory.

NOTE *If your log messages do not look like this, you have made an error. Check your permissions, and then google for the error. Someone has almost certainly made the same mistake before. They always have.*

FlowScan File Handling

FlowScan deletes flow files when it finishes processing them. This is desirable behavior when you've copied the file to a FlowScan-specific data directory, because although disk space is cheap these days, saving two copies of every flow file is a bit much!

If you don't want FlowScan to delete processed files, create a *saved* directory in the FlowScan data directory, and FlowScan will move processed files to this directory. This retention is not hierarchical, however: You'll add 288 files to this directory daily, 2,016 files weekly, and 104,832 in a year. After a while, a simple `ls` command will take surprisingly long to complete. I recommend that you let FlowScan discard processed files and rely on your originals instead.

Displaying CUFlow Graphs

CUFlow includes a CGI script to display graphs called *CUGrapher.pl*. This script converts the RRD data into graphs. To use this script, copy it to your web server's CGI directory, and then set two variables near the top of the script to generate your graphs as follows:

1. Set the `$rrddir` variable to the directory where you have stored your FlowScan RRD files.

    ```
    my $rrddir = "/var/db/flows/test/flowscanrrd";
    ```

2. Set the site or company name name with the `$organization` variable.

    ```
    my $organization = "Obey Lucas in All Things";
    ```

3. Now point your web browser at the CGI script, and you should see something like Figure 6-1.

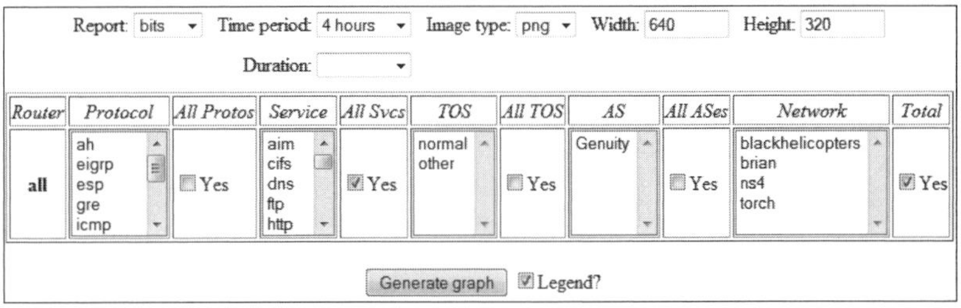

Figure 6-1: Initial CUFlow menu

Check the checkbox beneath All Svcs, and check the Total checkbox on the far right, as shown in Figure 6-1. This will display a FlowScan graph of all the TCP/IP services used on this network, somewhat like Figure 6-2.

Each protocol you defined in *CUFlow.cf* has its own color, as shown in the legend at the bottom of the screen. The legend in the example in Figure 6-2 shows the colors assigned to RTSP, HTTP, SMTP, and so on. Whitespace indicates traffic that isn't listed as a service in *CUFlow.cf*. Next to each color you'll see the total amount of traffic for that protocol.

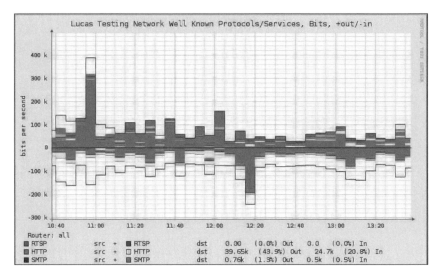

Figure 6-2: Services in CUFlow

Further, positive numbers show traffic leaving your network, and negative numbers show traffic entering the network. For example, at the start of this graph (at the far left), you have 140Kbps leaving the network and 80Kbps entering. Most of the outgoing traffic consists of known services. The large amount of whitespace in the incoming traffic includes traffic that CUFlow hasn't been told to categorize. To identify the traffic in this whitespace, examine the flow files themselves.

CUFlow lets you generate graphs for protocols, networks, and services over various time periods, but it will report on only one protocol, network, or service at a time. Also, CUFlow adds all your selections together. For example, if you select TCP from the Protocol column, HTTP from the Service column, and your web server from the Network column, the result will be a meaningless graph that includes all TCP traffic, all HTTP traffic, and all of your web server's traffic, combined. To create a more specific graph, such as all the HTTP traffic to a particular server, you must use a more flexible tool such as FlowViewer (Chapter 7). Alternatively, if you will need to check this graph repeatedly, split your flow records, and run multiple FlowScan and CUFlow instances.

Flow Record Splitting and CUFlow

CUFlow is a useful tool for graphing the most common network situations, but it has its limitations. For example, you cannot select from multiple columns to, say, see how much HTTP traffic your web servers have sent; you can see only the total amount of HTTP traffic or the total amount of web server traffic. Also, you cannot perform true ad hoc reporting with CUFlow, but you can configure it to represent the most common questions about your network.

CUFlow's limitations hit home in certain environments. At one time I ran a data center that provided services to remote sites over a private MPLS network. Each plant had a T1 or E1, while the data center had a DS3. Every site got all of its services from the main data center. I had flow exports and CUFlow on the headquarters DS3, which reported on traffic going to the central mail servers, file servers, proxy servers, and so on, and I wanted to offer management access to graphs that showed how much traffic each plant used and what that traffic was. Most of the plants did not have equipment capable of exporting flow data, however.

I provided useful (but imperfect) results by splitting plant flow information out of the DS3 flow records and running a separate FlowScan instance for each plant. I say "imperfect" because these results wouldn't display plant-to-plant traffic, for example. However, because the overwhelming majority of each plant's offsite traffic went to the central data center, it provided a good guess at what traffic was on the circuit.

Splitting flow records is applicable to many environments. For example, web farms don't have remote sites, but they probably have major customers who would each like their own FlowScan pages. You can deliver those separate pages by first splitting the flows into multiple data sets and then setting up a separate FlowScan instance for each data set.

Splitting Flows

To split your flow data into smaller data sets, use `flow-nfilter`. You probably already have a filter for each subset of data, but you'll need to be sure that the filter covers both incoming and outgoing traffic. For example, to pull only flow data that includes the addresses 192.0.2.0/24, you could use this primitive filter:

```
filter-primitive site1
    type ip-address-prefix
    permit 192.0.2.0/24

filter-definition site1
    match ip-source-address site1
    or
    match ip-destination-address site1
```

Next, use `flow-print` to verify that the filter passes flows for only these addresses, and use `flow-cat` and `flow-nfilter` to create a flow file that contains this data only.

```
# flow-cat ft-v05.2011-02-18.112001-0500 | flow-nfilter -F ❶ site1 > ❷ ft-v05.site1
```

The file *ft-v05.site1* (❷) is a flow file that contains only the flows permitted by the site1 filter (❶). Verify this with `flow-print`.

Scripting Flow Record Splitting

FlowScan expects a steady supply of flow files. You should not manually run `flow-cat` and `flow-nfilter` for every new flow file. Instead, use a flow rotation script to filter each new flow file into the smaller data set, as in this example:

```
#!/bin/sh
PATH=/bin:/usr/bin:/usr/local/bin

#for our primary flowscan instance
cp $1 /var/db/flows/test/flowscandata

#for flowscan on a data subset
flow-cat /var/db/flows/test/$1 | \
    flow-nfilter ❶ -f /usr/local/etc/flow-tools/site1-filter.cfg -F site1 > \
❷   /var/db/flows/site1/flowscandata/
```

The beginning of this script is the same as the flow rotation script you used to copy the flow file to your existing FlowScan instance. (You don't want to break what already works!) The last command splits out the flows for one particular site and creates a flow file of that data in a separate directory. Use `flow-nfilter`'s `-f` argument (❶) to use a nonstandard flow filter definition file, remembering that if your flow filter file has an incomplete or invalid rule, `flow-nfilter` will not run.

NOTE   *If you happen to be editing your filter rules when the rotation script runs, the script will fail. It's best to have a separate filter definition file just for splitting out these flows.*

Each instance of FlowScan needs its own incoming data directory (❷), as discussed at length in the next section. Add lines to this script for each FlowScan instance on a subset of your data, and be sure to restart `flow-capture` each time you change the rotation script.

Filtered CUFlow and Directory Setup

Give each FlowScan instance its own directory. The main flows are collected in */var/db/flows/test*, so use a directory like */var/db/flows/site1*. This directory needs three subdirectories: *flowscandata* (for incoming filtered flow files), *flowscanrrd* (for RRD files created from processed flow files), and *bin* (for this FlowScan instance). Be sure that the flowscan user can write to these directories.

Copy everything in your original FlowScan *bin* directory into the *bin* directory for this FlowScan instance in order to get all of the updated modules. Then, to set up your new instance, edit *flowscan.cf* by changing `FlowFileGlob` to give the path to the data directory for your new instance.

Now, because each FlowScan instance needs a separate directory under your web server in order to store its scoreboard and top hosts lists, create that directory, and then edit *CUFlow.cf* to change the *OutputDir, Scoreboard,* and *AggregateScore* directories and files to point to that directory. Finally, give each FlowScan instance its own startup script by copying the existing startup script, editing it to match your new instance, and assigning a new logfile to it. (Remember that the logfile must exist, and the flowscan user must be able to write to it before you start FlowScan.) Now start your second FlowScan instance. If there's a problem, you should see it in the logfile.

Although it may be tempting to create separate FlowScan instances for every group of servers or even every host on your network, doing so increases system load and maintenance overhead. FlowScan runs every five minutes, and if your server needs more than five minutes to completely process hundreds of FlowScan instances, your system will become unusable.

TREADING INTO PERL

FlowScan and CUFlow don't cut it for everyone. For those of you who would rather roll your own, the rest of this chapter discusses how to write your own Perl modules to read flow records. The following code fragments assume that you have a basic, working knowledge of Perl, but not many people are network engineers, systems administrators, *and* Perl programmers. If you're not comfortable reading line noise and couldn't care less about exporting variables or functions, skip to the next chapter.

Using Cflow.pm

Perl is a popular language for systems administration and web development. The *Cflow.pm* module lets you write Perl that reads flow files directly.

A Sample Cflow.pm Script

Here's a simple *Cflow.pm* Perl script that prints out all UDP port 500 (Checkpoint ISAKMP, used in IPSec VPNs) flows, stripped down from the script provided in the *Cflow.pm* documentation. This script takes the name of one or more flow files as arguments.

```
#!/usr/bin/perl

❶ use Cflow qw(:flowvars find);
❷ find (\&wanted, @ARGV);

❸ sub wanted {
      return unless (($srcport == 500 && $dstport == 500 ) && $udp == $protocol);
      printf("%s %15.15s.%-5hu %15.15s.%-5hu %2hu %10u %10u\n",
             $localtime, $srcip, $srcport, $dstip,
             $dstport, $protocol, $pkts, $bytes)
}
```

This script first includes *Cflow.pm* (❶), and then it exports the flow variable names and the find() function from that module. The meat of *Cflow.pm* (❷) consists of the find() and wanted() functions. When you feed a flow file to the script, find() sends each flow in the file to the wanted() function. In the wanted() function (❸), the script performs whatever functions you program in for each individual flow.

Cflow.pm offers many variables to access flow data. Although the meaning of many of these variables is easy to guess, such as $srcport, $dstport, $protocol, and so on, I list them in Table 6-1.

Find() and wanted() allow you to use *Cflow.pm* as the engine to feed flow data into a database, RRD, or hash file; flag interesting flows that fit patterns unique to your environment (that you can't easily filter for); and so on.

Cflow.pm Variables

Table 6-1 shows the variables for evaluating flows offered by *Cflow.pm*.

Table 6-1: *Cflow.pm* Variables

Variable	Meaning	Sample Output
$unix_secs	Epochal seconds of the flow start time	1229490004
$exporter	Sensor IP address as a long (decimal)	1430200323
$exporterip	Sensor IP address as a dotted quad	192.0.2.3
$localtime	Epoch time converted to local time	2011/12/16 23:59:43
$srcaddr	Source IP address as a long (decimal)	1430200341
$srcip	Source IP address as a dotted quad	192.0.2.27
$dstaddr	Destination IP address as a long (decimal)	1166468433
$dstip	Destination IP address as a dotted quad	69.134.229.81
$input_if	Input interface index	2
$output_if	Output interface index	9
$srcport	TCP or UDP source port number or equivalent	53
$dstport	TCP or UDP destination port number or equivalent	46819
$ICMPType	ICMP type (high byte of $dstport, for ICMP flows only)	3
$ICMPCode	ICMP code (low byte of $dstport, for ICMP flows only)	1
$ICMPTypeCode	Human-friendly name for ICMP type and code	HOST_UNREACH
$pkts	Packets in flow	5
$bytes	Octets sent in duration	138
$nexthop	Next-hop router's IP address as a long (decimal)	1398215405
$nexthopip	Next-hop router's IP address as a dotted quad	12.61.8.12
$starttime	Epoch seconds in local time at start of flow	1229489984

Table 6-1: *Cflow.pm* Variables (continued)

Variable	Meaning	Sample Output
$start_msecs	Milliseconds portion of start time	131
$endtime	Epoch seconds in local time at end of flow	1229489985
$end_msecs	Milliseconds portion of end time	871
$protocol	TCP/IP protocol number	17
$tos	Type of service	0
$tcp_flags	Bitwise OR of all TCP flags, or 0x10 for non-TCP flows	16
$TCPFlags	Human-friendly representation of tcp_flags	ACK
$raw	The entire original raw flow format	*binary*
$reraw	The modified raw flow file format, for writing to a new file	*binary*
$Bps	Minimum bytes per second for this flow	40
$pps	Minimum packets per second for this flow	5
$src_as	BGP source AS of the current flow	701
$dst_as	BGP destination AS of the current flow	11512
$src_mask	Source address prefix mask bits	/23
$dst_mask	Destination address prefix mask bits	/16
$engine_type	Type of flow switching engine (vendor-specific)	1
$engine_id	Engine ID of the flow switching engine (vendor-specific)	0

To use these variables, you must first preface them with Cflow:: or export them from *Cflow.pm* as I did at the top of the sample script.

Other Cflow.pm Exports

Cflow.pm also exports the symbolic names for TCP flags and ICMP types and codes. You might find these names, shown in Table 6-2, easier to work with than raw numbers, especially in complicated scripts.

Table 6-2: Exported TCP Flag Symbolic Names

Variable	Meaning	Value
$TH_FIN	FIN	1
$TH_SYN	SYN	2
$TH_RST	RST	4
$TH_PUSH	PUSH	8
$TH_ACK	ACK	16
$TH_URG	URG	32

Make the TCP flags accessible by exporting `tcpflags`. Similarly, export `icmptypes` and `icmpcodes` to use their symbolic names, as shown in Table 6-3.

Table 6-3: Exported ICMP Type Symbolic Names

Variable	Meaning	Value
$ICMP_ECHOREPLY	Echo reply	0
$ICMP_DEST_UNREACH	Destination unreachable	3
$ICMP_SOURCE_QUENCH	Source quench	4
$ICMP_REDIRECT	Redirect	5
$ICMP_ECHO	Echo request	8
$ICMP_TIME_EXCEEDED	Time exceeded	11
$ICMP_PARAMETERPROB	Error not covered by other ICMP types	12
$ICMP_TIMESTAMP	Timestamp request	13
$ICMP_TIMESTAMPREPLY	Timestamp response	14
$ICMP_INFO_REQUEST	Network info request (obsolete)	15
$ICMP_INFO_REPLY	Network info reply (obsolete)	16
$ICMP_ADDRESS	Netmask request	17
$ICMP_ADDRESSREPLY	Netmask request response	18

Symbolic names are included for ICMP codes for ICMP types 3 (unreachable, Table 6-4), 5 (redirects, Table 6-5), and 11 (time exceeded, Table 6-6).

Table 6-4: Exported ICMP Type 3 Code Symbolic Names

Variable	Meaning	Value
$ICMP_NET_UNREACH	Network unreachable	0
$ICMP_HOST_UNREACH	Host unreachable	1
$ICMP_PROT_UNREACH	Protocol unreachable	2
$ICMP_PORT_UNREACH	UDP port unreachable	3
$ICMP_FRAG_NEEDED	fragmentation needed	4
$ICMP_SR_FAILED	Source routing failed	5
$ICMP_NET_UNKNOWN	Network not known	6
$ICMP_HOST_UNKNOWN	Host not known	7
$ICMP_HOST_ISOLATED	Source host isolated	8
$ICMP_NET_ANO	Network administratively prohibited	9
$ICMP_HOST_ANO	Host administratively prohibited	10
$ICMP_NET_UNR_TOS	Network unreachable at this type of service	11
$ICMP_HOST_UNR_TOS	Host unreachable at this type of service	12
$ICMP_PKT_FILTERED	Communication prohibited by filtering	13
$ICMP_PREC_VIOLATION	Host precedence violation	14
$ICMP_PREC_CUTOFF	Precedence cutoff in effect	15

Table 6-5: Exported ICMP Type 5 Code Symbolic Names

Variable	Meaning	Value
$ICMP_REDIRECT_NET	Redirect for network	0
$ICMP_REDIRECT_HOST	Redirect for host	1
$ICMP_REDIRECT_NETTOS	Redirect for network and type of service	2
$ICMP_REDIRECT_HOSTTOS	Redirect for host and type of service	3

Table 6-6: Exported ICMP Type 11 Code Symbolic Names

Variable	Meaning	Value
$ICMP_EXC_TTL	Time to live exceeded in transit	0
$ICMP_EXC_FRAGTIME	Fragment reassembly time exceeded	1

NOTE   *Between the values available for every flow, TCP flags, and ICMP types and codes, you can add code to perform flow analysis.*

Acting on Every File

Cflow.pm supports actions after processing a flow file, such as freeing memory, reinitializing variables, or perhaps moving a file to an archive directory. If you include it in your script, *Cflow.pm* will call the perfile() function once per flow file. Include the reference to perfile in your find() function immediately after your wanted reference.

```
#!/usr/bin/perl
use Cflow qw(:flowvars find );
find (\&wanted, \&perfile, @ARGV);

sub wanted {
}

sub perfile {
    print "working on \"$_[0]\"...\n";
}
```

This code example prints the filename once per file.

Return Value

The find() function returns the ratio of the number of flows that matched the wanted() function. For example, here I'm returning the number of ICMP flows in the flow file:

```
#!/usr/bin/perl
use Cflow qw(find :flowvars );
$hitrate = find (\&wanted, @ARGV);
```

```
sub wanted {
    return unless (1 == $protocol);
    $icmp++;
}

print "hitrate is $hitrate\n";
```

Running this generates output such as the following:

```
hitrate is 34/4140
```

Thirty-four of the 4,140 flows in the input file were ICMP flows.

Verbose Mode

Cflow.pm generates error messages by default. To disable this, set verbose to 0 as follows:

```
use Cflow qw(find :flowvars );
verbose(0);
...
```

Every time I set this, I usually end up wishing that I hadn't because it generates lots and lots of output, obscuring useful data. Still, it's useful for debugging.

Now that you understand how to do simple web-based reports, you'll learn how to do hard ones.

7

FLOWVIEWER

Almost everybody likes pretty pictures of network traffic. FlowScan and CUFlow graph common, expected traffic types in a user-friendly manner. Your network is anything but common or expected, however. In addition to CUFlow, you'll also need a more customizable analysis tool, whether because you need a one-time report, insight into traffic that you never expected to see, or a close-up view of last year's traffic. As you'll learn in this chapter, the FlowViewer suite (*http://ensight.eos.nasa.gov/ FlowViewer/*) is one such customizable tool that can quickly create and access web-based reports.

FlowViewer includes three separate components: FlowViewer, FlowTracker, and FlowGrapher. *FlowViewer* is a web interface for `flow-print` and `flow-nfilter` that, once you've defined filters in a web form, will print out the matching flows. *FlowGrapher* lets you graph subsets of data on an ad hoc basis. *FlowTracker* is a simple way to build and view RRDs, much like CUFlow, but it lets you filter graphed traffic very specifically. If you want to continuously track HTTPS and telnet traffic to and from your enterprise resource planning (ERP) system, FlowTracker is your friend. As a whole, these three tools offer a great deal of visibility into the network.

NOTE *FlowViewer has an extensive manual that includes more detail than I've been able to fit into one chapter. See the FlowViewer manual for more in-depth information.*

FlowTracker and FlowGrapher vs. CUFlow

If FlowTracker, FlowGrapher, and CUFlow have similar functions, why not use only one or the other? Primarily for reasons of ease of use.

CUFlow is easily understood. You can give your customers access to a CUFlow graph, and with minimal explanation they can interpret the results fairly accurately. Your most feeble-brained co-worker can understand CUFlow output. But at the same time, this ease of understanding costs you flexibility. The user gets only the features and reports configured by the network administrator, and older reports suffer from RRD database compression, as discussed in Chapter 6.

On the other hand, FlowViewer's graphing and tracking functions are more powerful than those of CUFlow but also more confusing. Reports are almost infinitely customizable, adjustable, and configurable, and this broad feature set means that you really need to know what you're doing in order to get useful information. Also, FlowViewer has no concept of a read-only user: Anyone who can access your FlowViewer website gets full access to all of its features. FlowViewer is meant for network administrators, not general users.

FlowViewer Security

As mentioned, anyone who can access FlowViewer can see everything about your internal network. A skilled intruder would find this irresistible. Others will just annoy you: Unskilled visitors, such as your help-desk staff, will probably misinterpret FlowViewer's results and make you spend time explaining why they're wrong. For this reason, I strongly recommend password protecting the FlowViewer website and restricting the IP addresses permitted to access the server. Using HTTPS, even with a self-signed certificate, will protect your user credentials and data in transit.

FlowViewer's default install also uses a world-writable directory to store reports. This is a security risk, particularly on a multiuser system. If you're using a shared system as your analysis workstation, you must restrict permissions more tightly than FlowViewer's defaults.

Installing FlowViewer

If possible, install FlowViewer from a package provided by your OS vendor. If your vendor doesn't provide a FlowViewer package, you'll need to install by hand, of course.

Prerequisites

Install the following software packages before installing FlowViewer, all of which should be available as packages for most operating systems:

- Web server, such as any recent Apache
- Perl
- RRDtool (*http://oss.oetiker.ch/rrdtool/*) with Perl shared module support
- GD Graphics Library (*http://www.boutell.com/gd/*)
- The gd::graph Perl module
- The GDBM Perl module (might be packaged as GDBM_File)

You'll also need to know the system user who runs your web pages. This is probably a user named *www*, *http*, or *www-data*. If your web server is running, enter `ps -axe` or `ps -axj` to get the name of the user running the server.

FlowViewer Installation Process

To install FlowViewer, first download the latest version of FlowViewer from *http://ensight.eos.nasa.gov/FlowViewer/*. The compressed installation file includes a FlowViewer directory with several files containing the entire package. Untar it in a directory under your web server.

Now configure your web server to permit CGI execution in that directory. For example, here's how to configure Apache to support FlowViewer in the directory */usr/local/www/flowviewer*:

```
❶ Alias /FlowViewer/ /usr/local/www/flowviewer/
❷ <Directory /usr/local/www/flowviewer/>
      Options +ExecCGI
      AddHandler cgi-script .cgi
      Order allow,deny
      Allow from all
  </Directory>
```

The alias definition at ❶ maps the web location *http://servername/FlowViewer/* to the local directory */usr/local/www/flowviewer/*. Then, at ❷ you assign specific permissions to the FlowViewer directory, permitting CGI execution and client access. Finally, restart Apache.

That's it for installation. The more difficult part of FlowViewer is configuration.

Configuring FlowViewer

All the tools in the FlowViewer suite use the *FlowViewer_Configuration.pm* configuration file. Although this file contains many settings, only a few are required for proper operation; the others allow you to tweak the application's appearance and the behavior of FlowTracker's RRD files. If you're interested in settings not discussed here, see FlowViewer's extensive manual.

I'll cover only the settings needed to make FlowViewer work. (Some operating system packages set these for you as part of their install process.) Without further ado, here are the settings that you'll need to make:

- The $ENV{PATH} variable includes only the paths for system commands that FlowViewer requires. On almost all systems, you should leave this alone. You do not need to have flow-tools and RRDtool in these directories; they have their own path variables that you'll set later.

- The $FlowViewer_server variable tells FlowViewer the hostname of your website. For example, to make my test collector visible at *https://netflow .blackhelicopters.org/*, I set $FlowViewer_server to netflow.blackhelicopters.org.

- The $FlowViewer_service variable helps FlowViewer construct web pages. Set this to either http or https, as appropriate for your website.

Directories and Site Paths

FlowViewer stores files on the web server, and all file storage directories must be writable by the web server user. Create these directories, and change their ownership to the web server user. (Unwritable directories are a common cause of FlowViewer problems.)

Most directory variables also have a "short" version that defines where a web browser can find that directory on the server. FlowViewer uses this short name to create links to generated content. I'll walk you through examples when you set the first few variables.

> **SEARCH-AND-REPLACE CONFIGURATION**
>
> The default *FlowViewer_Configuration.pm* assumes that Apache's *DocumentRoot* directory is */htp/htdocs* and that the CGI directory where FlowViewer is installed is */htp/cgi-bin*. You might do a simple search and replace on these values, replacing them with the correct *DocumentRoot* and *FlowViewer* installation directories for your environment. In all of the following examples, my website root directory is */var/ www/ssl*, and FlowViewer is installed in */usr/local/www/flowviewer*. You must create all the directories you tell FlowViewer to use.

$reports_directory tells FlowViewer where to store reports, and $reports_short gives the location on the website where a client would find the *$reports* directory. The report directory must be under Apache's *DocumentRoot* or another directory accessible to Apache. Here, I've created a *FlowViewer* directory in my *DocumentRoot*:

```
$reports_directory      = "/var/www/ssl/FlowViewer";
$reports_short          = "/FlowViewer";
```

FlowViewer stores generated graphs in *$graphs_directory*, and $graphs_short defines the location on the website where a client would find *$graphs_directory*. Like *$reports_directory*, *$graphs_directory* must be accessible on the website. I use the directory */var/www/ssl/FlowGrapher*.

```
$graphs_directory = "/var/www/ssl/FlowGrapher";
$graphs_short = "/FlowGrapher";
```

The FlowTracker tool stores files in *$tracker_directory*, which is accessible on the website as *$tracker_short*. I use the directory */var/www/ssl/FlowTracker*.

```
$tracker_directory = "/var/www/ssl/FlowTracker";
$tracker_short = "/FlowTracker";
```

The $cgi_bin_directory variable points to the directory that contains the FlowViewer software. You could choose to copy this to your web server's regular CGI executable directory, but I suggest installing FlowViewer in its own directory and then configuring your web server to run CGI scripts in that directory. For example, as you can see here, my FlowViewer install is in */usr/local/www/flowviewer*, and I configured the web server to offer this as *http://servername/flowviewer*.

```
$cgi_bin_directory = "/usr/local/www/flowviewer";
$cgi_bin_short = "/flowviewer";
```

FlowViewer saves temporary files in *$work_directory*, which is accessible on the web server as *$work_short*. Here I'm using */var/www/ssl/FlowWorking*:

```
$work_directory = "/var/www/ssl/FlowWorking";
$work_short = "/FlowWorking";
```

Reports and filters saved for later are stored in *$save_directory*, which is accessible to web clients as *$save_short*. Create */var/www/ssl/FlowViewer_Saves* for this.

```
$save_directory = "/var/www/ssl/FlowViewer";
$save_short = "/FlowViewer_Saves";
```

The remaining directories do not have "short" variables for their path on the website. FlowViewer uses them for internal tracking or to find key software, and the client should never access them directly.

- When a user asks FlowViewer to resolve the names of IP addresses, it caches the results in *$names_directory*. For example, I put my names cache in */usr/local/www/flowviewer/names*. Remember, any cached DNS data slowly becomes obsolete as hosts change IP addresses.

- FlowTracker stores the filters it uses to create trackers in *$filter_directory* and stores the RRD files in *$rrdtool_directory*.

- The *$flow_bin_directory* directory is where flow-tools is installed. This is usually something like */usr/local/bin* or */usr/local/flow-tools/bin*.

- Similarly, *rrdtool_bin_directory* is where RRDtool is installed, which is usually */usr/local/bin* or */usr/local/rrdtool/bin*.

Here's how they look in the configuration:

```
$names_directory         = "/usr/local/www/flowviewer/names";
$filter_directory        = "/usr/local/www/flowviewer/FlowTracker_Files/FlowTracker_Filters";
$rrdtool_directory       = "/usr/local/www/flowviewer/FlowTracker_Files/FlowTracker_RRDtool";
$flow_bin_directory      = "/usr/local/bin";
$rrdtool_bin_directory   = "/usr/local/bin";
```

Website Setup

The next four values set some basic properties in FlowViewer's web interface:

- FlowTracker automatically generates a web page listing all trackers currently running. The default file is *index.html* in *$tracker_directory*. Change this by setting $actives_webpage to the desired filename.

- The autogenerated tracker page lists your organization name as the value of $trackings_title.

- To put your company logo next to the FlowViewer graphic at the top of each page, create a logo file 86 pixels high, and copy it to *$reports_directory*.

- Then assign $user_logo the filename. The logo will link to a website defined in $user_hyperlink.

They'll look like this in the configuration:

```
$actives_webpage    = "index.html";
$trackings_title    = "Lucas LLC";
$user_logo          = "myfirm.jpg";
$user_hyperlink     = "http://www.michaelwlucas.com/";
```

Devices and Exporters

In Chapter 2, you decided to use either a single collector that accepted flow records from all your sensors or a separate collector for each sensor. Flow-Viewer can support either configuration, but you must tell it which one it's using.

The simplest scenario is a single sensor and a single collector when you expect to never have more, but I don't recommend making this assumption. Networks change over time, and your FlowViewer install should accommodate that change. If you insist that you'll have only one collector and one sensor, though, see the FlowViewer manual for information on changing $no_devices_or_exporters.

One Collector per Sensor

In Chapter 2, I recommended setting up one collector per sensor. Your flow data would go into a directory such as */var/db/flows*, with a subdirectory for each device. You'd wind up with directories such as */var/db/flows/router1* for the sensor router1, */var/db/flows/router2* for the sensor router2, and so on.

For this setup, assign the flow data root directory to $flow_data_directory. In my setup, $flow_data_directory is */var/db/flows*. Now assign the variable @devices the list of directory names that represent sensors. For example, my network has the sensors router1, router2, and router3. I would assign the following values to @devices. (FlowViewer offers everything in @devices as an option in a drop-down menu.)

```
$flow_data_directory    = "/var/db/flows";
@devices=("router1","router2","router3");
```

One Collector for All Sensors

If all your sensors send their data to a single collector, don't set @devices or $flow_data_directory. Instead, set $exporter_directory to the location of your consolidated flow data. If you ran a single collector and all your data went into */var/db/flows*, set $exporter_directory to */var/db/flows*. Also, uncomment @exporters, and set it to the list of sensors in the collector, listing exporters by IP address and hostname, as shown here:

```
$exporter_directory    = "/var/db/flows";
@exporters = ("192.0.2.1:router1","192.0.2.2:router2","192.0.2.3:router3");
```

FlowViewer is now configured and ready for use. Point your web browser to *FlowViewer.cgi* to see its initial screen.

Troubleshooting the FlowViewer Suite

FlowViewer has many setup options, and you'll probably make mistakes during your first install. I strongly recommend keeping a terminal window open and running tail -f on your web server error log to display errors as they occur. In my experience, the most common errors are incorrect directory variables and directory permissions.

Watch the error log as you use FlowViewer, and correct errors as they appear. Follow these procedures, and within a few moments of testing, you should have a correctly working FlowViewer install.

Using FlowViewer

Once properly installed, FlowViewer should look something like Figure 7-1.

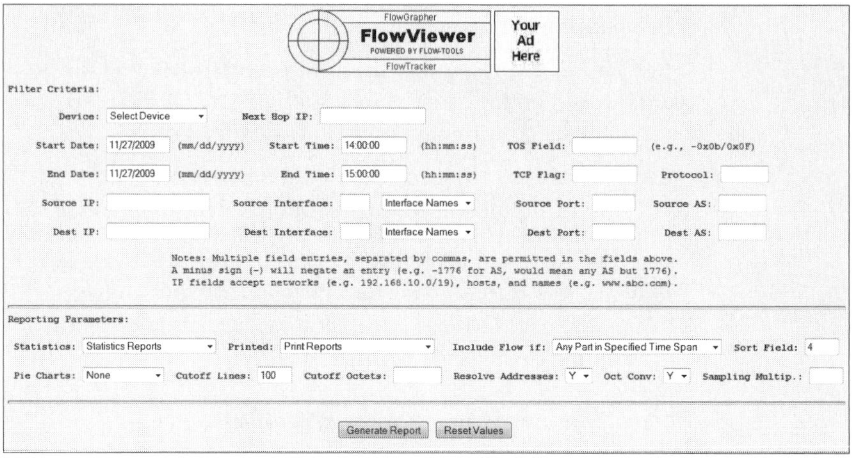

Figure 7-1: Default FlowViewer interface

The upper part of the screen, Filter Criteria, controls traffic selection. This is essentially an interface to `flow-nfilter` that lets you choose exactly which flows you want to examine. FlowGrapher and FlowTracker share most of FlowViewer's filter interface. The lower part of the screen, Reporting Parameters, controls the display of results. You can run reports on traffic or just view the matching flows.

In the following sections, I'll cover how to use the filtering interface first and then the viewing options.

Filtering Flows with FlowViewer

Each field you modify in the Filter Criteria section is fed to `flow-nfilter`. Most fields accept multiple entries, separated by commas. You can also negate an entry by prefixing it with a minus sign. (If you have general questions on filtering flows, see Chapter 4.)

Device

If you have multiple sensors, you must first select the device that provides the data you want to examine. This drop-down menu is taken directly from the devices or exporters list you configured for FlowViewer, and it's the only field that requires you to enter anything.

Next Hop IP

This is the IP address where the sensor sends traffic. Remember that only hardware flow sensors, such as routers and switches, include next-hop address information in flows. Software flow sensors do not have access to this information.

Start and End Date and Time

Here you set the time you're interested in. Times are in 24-hour-clock format. FlowViewer defaults to offering the most recent complete hour. See "Include Flow If" on page 148 for a discussion on how FlowViewer handles flows that cross the start or end times.

TOS Field, TCP Flag, and Protocol

FlowViewer's Type of Service (DSCP) and TCP flags filtering accepts both decimal values (16) and hexadecimals (0x10).

You can enter the IP protocol either by name (TCP, UDP, and so on) or by number (6, 17, and so on).

Source and Dest IP

You can report on either a single address, a hostname, multiple comma-separated addresses, or networks with a netmask in prefix length (slash) notation. For example, to report on traffic from the network 192.0.2.0 with a netmask of 255.255.255.128, you would enter **192.0.2.0/25**.

NOTE   *Be very careful when using hostnames for network analysis. Some hosts have multiple IP addresses. In this case, you're better off using actual IP addresses to reduce ambiguity.*

Source and Dest Interface

If you think you know how your traffic flowed, you can filter by source or destination interface. When you do, remember that interfaces are numbered by index number, which you can get from SNMP. You can add interface names to FlowViewer, as I'll discuss at the end of this chapter.

I most often use FlowViewer when analyzing problems and outages. When doing so, I recommend against filtering by interface because traffic flowing incorrectly is a common cause of problems and outages, and filtering by interface can filter away the problem traffic.

Source and Dest Port and AS

FlowViewer can filter by TCP or UDP port. You can also encode ICMP types and codes as a port, as discussed in "ICMP Types and Codes and Flow Records" on page 52, and use that to filter ICMP flows. Further, if your sensor exports BGP information, you can filter by source and destination AS number.

Reporting Parameters

FlowViewer can provide either statistical reports or printed reports. Both types of reports share the remaining optional settings. I'll cover the options first and then discuss the two types of reports. You can run one report at a time, but if you select both a statistics report and a printed report, FlowViewer will return an error.

Include Flow If

This setting determines how FlowViewer selects flows to report on. The default, Any Part in Specified Time Span, includes a flow record if any part of the flow is within the time you specify. For example, if you're interested in flow data from 9 to 10, your raw data might include a flow that starts at 8:59:30 and ends at 9:01:30 and also one that starts at 9:59:59 and ends at 10:05:59, with part of these flows trailing off either end of your chosen time window.

Most of the time, the default setting gives the best view of traffic during your chosen time. When using the default setting, these flows will be included in the filtered data. On the other hand, the End Time in Specified Time Span setting chops off anything that trails past the closing window. Specifically, in this example, the flow that starts at 9:59:59 and ends at 10:05:59 would not be included in the selected data. The Start Time in Specified Time Span setting slices off the flow that begins at 8:59:30, and the Entirely in Specified Time Span setting excludes both of those trailing flows.

Sort Field, Resolve Addresses, and Oct Conv, and Sampling Multip

Like `flow-report`, FlowViewer can sort its output on any field with the output columns numbered starting from 1. To sort by a particular field, give the number of the column you want to sort by in the Sort Field space.

Some reports can replace IP addresses with hostnames, but, by default, FlowViewer resolves names. To make FlowViewer show only IP addresses, change Resolve Addresses to **N**. Similarly, FlowViewer by default displays large octet counts as kilobytes, megabytes, or gigabytes instead of raw counts of millions or billions of bytes. To see raw byte counts, set Oct. Conv to **N**. (Displaying results as kilobytes, megabytes, or gigabytes won't affect sorting; FlowViewer is smart enough to sort different units correctly.)

If your sensors sample traffic, you know that the traffic levels shown in your reports are only a fraction of your real traffic. FlowViewer will multiply its results by the number you enter in Sampling Multip to approximate your real-world traffic.

Pie Charts

FlowViewer's statistical reports can generate pie charts of their results, but pie charts are not useful for FlowViewer reports; they're like making a pie chart of the phone book. For statistical reports, you can choose to include an "other" catchall category in your graph. Try both ways to see which generates the most useful graph in your environment.

Cutoffs

If you have a busy router, even a well-filtered report might include hundreds of thousands of flows. In such case, cutoffs prove useful because they tell FlowViewer when to stop printing results. You can cut off reports either by the number of lines of output or by the number of octets.

If you really want to have all that data, consider running the report from the command line and saving the results to a file for later analysis.

Printed Reports

FlowViewer's printed reports are a web interface of flow-print. Table 7-1 maps FlowViewer's printed reports to flow-print formats. Chapter 3 covers the various print formats in detail.

Table 7-1: Printed Reports and flow-print Formats

Printed Report	flow-print Format
Flow Times	-f 1
AS Numbers	-f 4
132 Columns	-f 5
1 Line with Tags	-f 9
AS Aggregation	-f 10
Protocol Port Aggregation	-f 11
Source Prefix Aggregation	-f 12
Destination Prefix Aggregation	-f 13
Prefix Aggregation	-f 14
Full (Catalyst)	-f 24

Note that not all reports will produce output. For example, if your flow data does not include BGP information and you run a BGP-based report, you'll get an empty report.

Statistics Reports

FlowViewer's statistics reports are based on flow-stat, the predecessor to flow-report. flow-stat is much less flexible than flow-report, but some of its reports are more suitable for a web application. Most flow-stat analyses are available as subsets of flow-report output formats, as listed in Table 7-2.

Table 7-2: FlowViewer Statistics Reports and Corresponding flow-reports

Statistics Report	flow-report
Summary	summary (default)
UDP/TCP Destination Port	ip-destination-port
UDP/TCP Source Port	ip-source-port
UDP/TCP Port	ip-port
Destination IP	ip-destination-address
Source IP	ip-source-address
Source/Destination IP	ip-source/destination-address
Source or Destination IP	ip-address
IP Protocol	ip-protocol
Input Interface	input-interface
Output Interface	output-interface
Input/Output Interface	input/output-interface

(continued)

Table 7-2: FlowViewer Statistics Reports and Corresponding flow-reports (continued)

Statistics Report	flow-report
Source AS	source-as
Destination AS	destination-as
Source/Destination AS	source/destination-as
IP ToS	ip-tos
Source Prefix	like ip-source-address with ip-source-address-format set to prefix-len
Destination Prefix	like ip-destination-address with ip-destination-address-format set to prefix-len
Source/Destination Prefix	like ip-source/destination-address with both ip-source-address-format and ip-destination-address-format set to prefix-len
Exporter IP	ip-exporter-address

NOTE   *If you need a report not offered here, use* flow-report *instead.*

FlowGrapher

FlowGrapher creates graphs of arbitrary flow data. Select the FlowGrapher text from the logo at the top of the FlowViewer page to get to FlowGrapher.

FlowGrapher Settings

The top part of the FlowGrapher page lets you define packet filters as narrowly as necessary. FlowGrapher filters are identical to the FlowViewer filter definitions listed in Figure 7-1, so I won't over them again, but the bottom of the FlowGrapher page offers new graphing options, as shown in Figure 7-2.

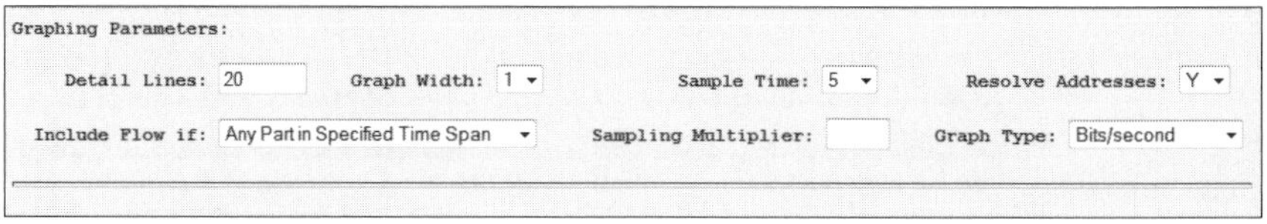

Figure 7-2: FlowGrapher options

Include Flow if, Resolve Addresses, and Sampling Multiplier work the same way as the equivalent fields in FlowViewer. The options unique to FlowGrapher—Detail Lines, Graph Width, and Sample Time—determine how your graph is charted, its appearance, and how any related data is presented.

Detail Lines

FlowGrapher prints the first few lines of flow-print output for the selected flow files beneath the graph. This list lets you verify that the graph includes the flows you think should be included by your filter.

Graph Width

The default FlowGrapher image is 600 pixels wide, but graphs that cover more than a couple of hours must be wider in order to show necessary detail. The Graph Width setting multiplies the width of a graph by the selected number. For example, choosing **3** creates a graph 1,800 pixels wide.

Sample Time

FlowGrapher computes bandwidth in "buckets" of time in order to smooth the data and present a more realistic graph. (You'll see why this is important in Chapter 8.) The default bucket size of five seconds is reasonable for almost all environments. A larger bucket size will decrease the size of bandwidth spikes and might be more realistic if most of your traffic consists of long-lived flows.

Graph Type

You can choose either Bits/second (the default), Flows/second, or Packet/second graphs. Most of the time you'll want Bits/second, but if your environment has large numbers of small packets, you might find the Packets/second graph useful. Flows/second is mostly useful to determine whether you have more or less activity than usual.

FlowGrapher Output

Figure 7-3 shows a traffic graph for my server, without the logo or the sample flow-print output.

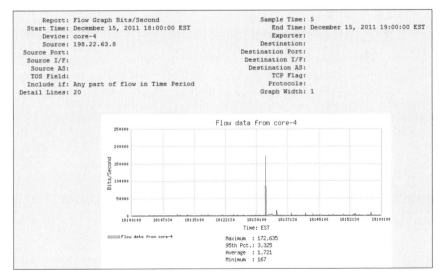

Figure 7-3: Sample traffic graph

Notice how FlowGrapher prints the selected filter criteria above the graph. This information lets you easily re-create the graph with slightly different conditions and reminds you what you tried to graph when you return to an image later.

NOTE *To create a traffic graph that's beyond FlowGrapher's capacity, see Chapter 8.*

FlowTracker

FlowTracker generates RRD-based graphs of flow data on an ongoing basis, much like FlowScan and CUFlow. Each graph you create is called a *tracker*. One tracker graphs either inbound or outbound traffic, but not both. FlowTracker is much more flexible than FlowScan, but that flexibility also makes it unsuitable for customers or management to access directly.

FlowTracker Processes

Like FlowScan, FlowTracker creates RRD files from flow-capture files as they're created. Rather than moving flow files, however, FlowTracker uses two processes to watch the flow-capture directories for changes and to read each new flow file as it's closed. If these processes stop, FlowTracker will not update RRDs for new flows or create new graphs.

Start the FlowTracker_Collector and FlowTracker_Grapher processes when the system boots. The included flowcap script might work for your operating system, but if not you can start them as shown here:

```
#!/bin/sh
PERL5LIB=/usr/local/www/flowviewer/ /usr/local/www/flowviewer/FlowTracker_Collector &
PERL5LIB=/usr/local/www/flowviewer/ /usr/local/www/flowviewer/FlowTracker_Grapher &
```

Start these processes after the network is initialized. Have your network management system monitor these processes and either send an alarm or automatically restart them if they fail.

FlowTracker Settings

FlowTracker offers the same filtering options as FlowViewer and FlowGrapher, without the option to select the time you want to cover. (FlowTracker continuously processes flow data, so time-based filtering doesn't make sense.) FlowTracker creates graphs based on the filters you define, just like FlowGrapher and FlowViewer.

Figure 7-4 shows the FlowTracker-specific configuration options.

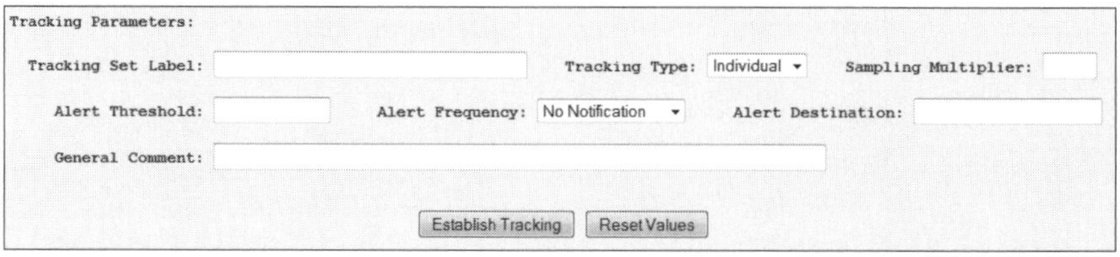

Figure 7-4: FlowTracker options

Once you've entered your desired settings, click **Establish Tracking** to start your tracker.

Tracking Set Label

Tracking Set Label is the tracker's name. You should name trackers by the host, network, or traffic name and by the direction the traffic is going, such as "Server 1 Web traffic inbound" or "Server 2 outbound." The text you enter here will appear as a link to the actual tracker on the main FlowTracker page.

Tracking Type

FlowTracker can aggregate individual trackers into a "group tracker." I'll cover group trackers later; for now, all of your trackers should be Individual.

Sampling Multiplier

Like other parts of FlowViewer, FlowTracker can apply a sampling multiplier to approximate correct traffic levels in your graph.

Alert Threshold

As a continuously running process, FlowTracker can monitor total traffic levels and send an alarm if traffic exceeds a certain level. To set an alarm at a number of bits per second, enter that number here. (Note that your server must have a properly configured mail system to send alarms.)

Alert Frequency

Generating an alarm every time the traffic exceeds your critical level can be annoying if your traffic load bounces back and forth across that level. Use Alert Frequency to tell FlowTracker to send an alarm each time traffic exceeds the critical limit, only once per day, or to disable emailed alerts entirely.

Alert Destination

This is the email address that receives alerts.

General Comment

Any notes or comments here will appear on the finished graph.

Viewing Trackers

Trackers that you've already created will appear at the bottom of the FlowTracker page. Figure 7-5 shows four trackers, inbound and outbound for two machines.

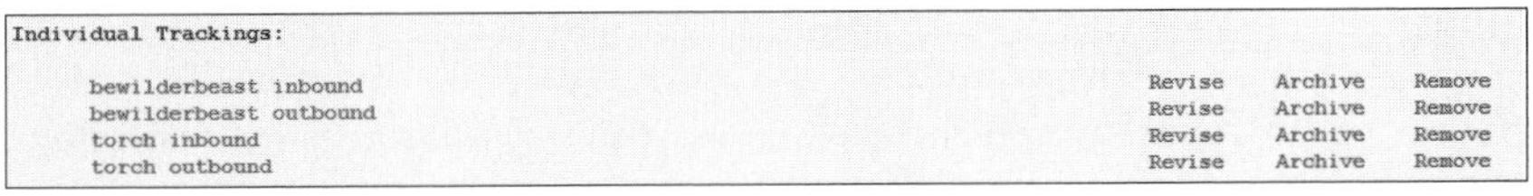

```
Individual Trackings:

    bewilderbeast inbound                                Revise    Archive    Remove
    bewilderbeast outbound                               Revise    Archive    Remove
    torch inbound                                        Revise    Archive    Remove
    torch outbound                                       Revise    Archive    Remove
```

Figure 7-5: FlowTracker individual trackings

To view a tracker, click its name. Trackers include views of the last 24 hours, 7 days, 4 weeks, 12 months, and 3 years. Each graph looks much like FlowGrapher output, so I won't reproduce those graphs here.

You can edit trackers to update filters or correct mistakes. To do so, click the **Revise** link next to a tracker in order to populate a FlowTracker page with the tracker's original settings, and then make the desired changes. You can also add a note to be displayed on the graphs to show when a tracker was changed.

Archiving a tracker tells FlowTracker to stop processing the current flows for this particular tracker, while continuing to update other trackers. It retains the archived tracker's configuration and graphs. Archiving lets you retain historical information without wasting computing power and lets you easily reactivate the tracker if needed.

Finally, you can also entirely remove a tracker by clicking the link. This deletes all graphs and the associated databases.

Group Trackers

FlowTracker lets you combine individual trackers into group trackers to give you a unified view of different types of traffic. For example, in Figure 7-5 you can see separate inbound and outbound trackers for two servers. To view a server's inbound and outbound traffic simultaneously, you need to use a group tracker.

To create a group tracker, name the tracker, and select a tracking type of **Group**. Next, when you click **Establish Tracking**, FlowTracker will open a separate page to define your group tracker, as shown in Figure 7-6.

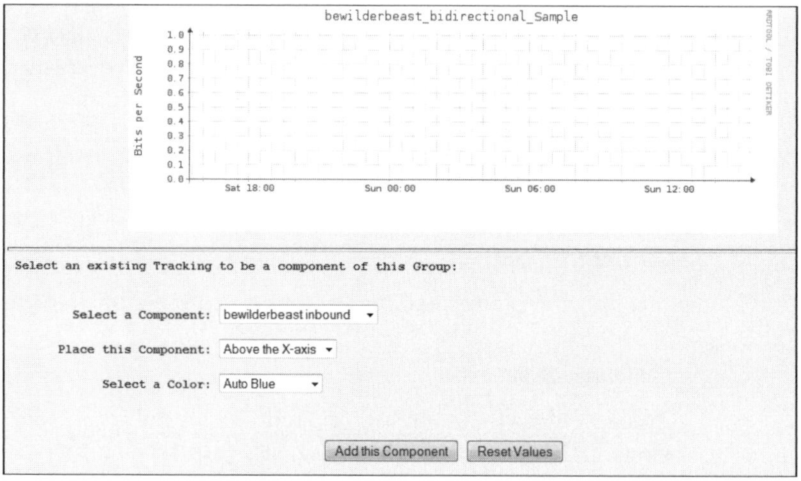

Figure 7-6: Basic FlowTracker setup

The sample graph shown at the top of Figure 7-6 is not based on actual data but will show you how your color choices will look on an actual graph.

Further down in the figure are the critical components. Here you can choose individual trackers to include in your group tracker or choose to have the tracker appear above or below the x-axis. I try to consistently put inbound trackers above the x-axis and outbound trackers below in order to minimize confusion. Switch these if you prefer; just pick a standard and stick with it.

You can assign colors to each tracker in your graph. The Auto choices choose colors in the same color family. I recommend using one Auto color for all inbound trackers and a different Auto color for all outbound trackers.

Once you've added an individual tracker to your group tracker, click **Add this Component**. Then, immediately beneath this option, you'll see a list of all the individual trackers in this group tracker. For example, Figure 7-7 displays this group tracker after I've added both the inbound and outbound trackers for both individual servers.

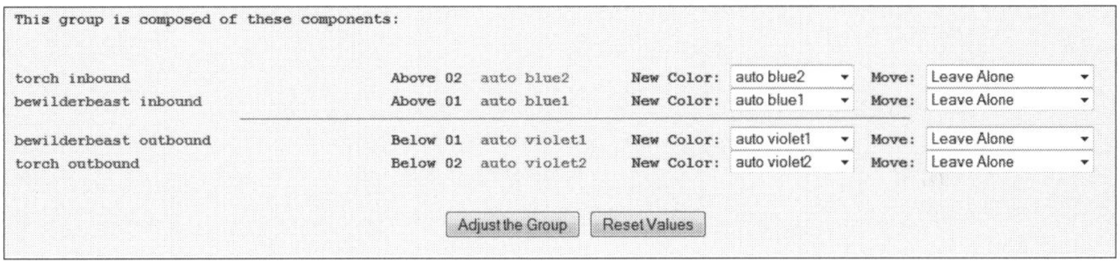

Figure 7-7: Group tracker components

Both the torch and bewilderbeast servers will now appear in this one tracker. The inbound trackers will appear above the x-axis, as shown by the long horizontal line. The color name appears in the chosen color (which doesn't appear in this black-and-white figure, of course). If you don't like the color, change it with the New Color drop-down.

Use the Move drop-down on the far right to rearrange the server order, and then click **Adjust the Group** to apply your changes. I recommend having servers in the same order on both the inbound and outbound sides of the tracker.

Once you've configured your group tracker, click **Done** at the bottom of the page to create the tracker. You can revise, archive, and remove your group tracker as with an individual tracker.

ADDITIONAL RRD SOFTWARE

Different tools have different presentations and focus. If you find that FlowTracker isn't quite right for your long-term tracking needs, take a look at Webview Netflow Reporter, at *http://wvnetflow.sourceforge.net/*.

Interface Names and FlowViewer

Flows manage interfaces by index number, but humans use the interface name. If you tell FlowViewer the name associated with each interface number, it'll offer those names as an option in the web interface. If you create the file *NamedInterfaces_Devices* in the *FlowViewer* directory, FlowViewer will populate the Interface Names drop-down in the filter section of all three tools with information from the file.

Each line in the *NamedInterfaces_Devices* file contains three entries:

```
exporter name:SNMP index:human-friendly name
```

For example, my main router's gigabit uplink is at SNMP index 5. The entry for this interface might look like this:

```
core-4:5:Gigabit Ethernet 1/0 - uplink
```

Entering interface information for all your exporters into FlowViewer will save you trouble in the future and simplify problem solving. Rather than having to look up the number for the interface you're interested in, you can just select it from the menu.

FlowTracker, FlowViewer, and FlowGrapher will let you visualize most common situations, but they don't solve everything. In the next chapter, you'll see how to graph data when FlowGrapher isn't powerful or flexible enough.

8

AD HOC FLOW VISUALIZATION

Although viewing the content of flows and running reports helps track down problems, some issues can be properly assessed through visualization only. The average human brain simply cannot assemble 6,000 lines of plain-text data into a coherent understanding of the situation. Transforming large quantities of data into visual form eases comprehension.

Perhaps the most common way to convert data to graphical form is through an office suite, such as Microsoft Office or OpenOffice.org. Office suites are not suited to automation, however. Once you have designed your graphs, regenerating them with new data should be trivial or even instantaneous. Tools such as CUFlow (Chapter 6) and FlowGrapher (Chapter 7) provide basic graphing, but they lack true ad hoc flexibility, such as the ability to choose the style of graph or whether to overlay one graph atop another. To provide truly unlimited flexibility in a manner that you can automate or quickly reproduce, you need gnuplot.

gnuplot 101

gnuplot (*http://www.gnuplot.info/*) has a notoriously steep learning curve and a reputation for complexity. The notoriety and reputation are not completely unwarranted. gnuplot's power and efficiency more than make up for its challenges, however. Although mastering gnuplot can take years, you can quickly learn enough to create impressive graphs of your network data. Almost every Unix-like operating system includes current gnuplot packages, and you can also find packages for Windows, DOS, VMS, and almost every other operating system used in the past 20 years.

Using gnuplot on the reporting server simplifies reporting and the development of graphs. To use gnuplot on your reporting server, you'll need an X server on your workstation. If you use a Unix workstation, you're all set. If not, you can find any number of X Windows servers for Microsoft Windows. Be sure to choose one that can forward X over SSH, rather than speaking raw X over the network. (On Windows, I use the PuTTY SSH client and Xming X server.)

If you don't want to use an X terminal on your desktop, install gnuplot on your workstation, and then run reports on the server and transfer them to your workstation. Develop your graphs on your workstation, save their configurations, and copy those configurations to your server to automatically create more graphs.

OTHER GRAPHING PROGRAMS

gnuplot's main advantage is that it's easily automated. To create graphs on the fly without worrying about reproducing them later, consider Grace (*http://plasma-gate .weizmann.ac.il/Grace/*).

Starting gnuplot

The best way to learn gnuplot is to use it. When gnuplot starts, it displays a message and offers its own command prompt.

```
# gnuplot
...
Terminal type set to 'x11'
gnuplot>
```

To leave gnuplot, enter either **exit** or **quit**.

Most gnuplot commands either alter a drawing's appearance or create a new drawing. For a taste for how gnuplot works, graph a sine wave. (For some reason, the sine plot is traditional in gnuplot tutorials.) On the gnuplot command line, enter the following:

```
gnuplot> plot sin(x)
```

You should see another window appear, displaying the classic sine wave, as shown in Figure 8-1.

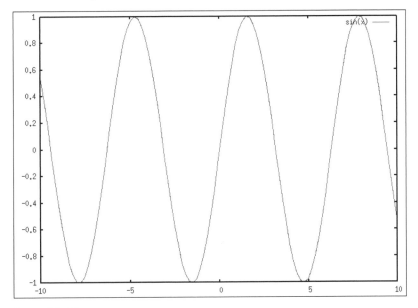

Figure 8-1: Sine wave

To modify your graphs, use the set command. You can set countless values, from the title of a graph to the labels on the x- and y-axes, colors used, and so on. Here I'm giving the graph the title of *test graph*:

```
gnuplot> set title "test graph"
```

The displayed graph doesn't change until you tell gnuplot to replot the data, like so:

```
gnuplot> plot sin(x)
```

Now your graph should have a title.

gnuplot Configuration Files

The test graph you created here took very little effort. You didn't read in any data or enter complicated formulas. Flow data is much more complicated than a sine wave, however, and in this chapter you'll work through several iterations of your graph to make it look "just right." You can save all the settings from a gnuplot session so that you can call up those same settings and use them to plot new data. Just tell gnuplot the name of the file you want to save your configuration in.

```
gnuplot> save "test.plt"
```

You'll find a gnuplot configuration file named *test.plt* in your current directory. This file contains all the gnuplot commands you entered, including the title and the plot sin(x) instruction. Exit gnuplot, and restart it. Then load this configuration file:

```
gnuplot> load "test.plt"
```

Your graph will reappear, with all the changes you specified.

Retyping two commands to re-create your graph wouldn't be difficult, but graphs based on flow reports might include dozens of instructions, some of them long and tedious. Being able to save your gnuplot configuration and reuse it to graph new data will save time and effort and reduce errors.

Now let's get some real data to graph.

Time-Series Example: Bandwidth

One common question network engineers get is "How much bandwidth does this application use?" I've worked in more than one global operation where management was concerned about how much internal bandwidth email consumed or where the Active Directory team needed to know how much bandwidth the interdomain controller communications used.

Flow reports can answer this question in many different ways. An average of bandwidth use through the day is useful but won't reveal intermittent performance bottlenecks. A connection that's completely idle most of the time but that has a massive throughput spike during each day's peak hours might have an average throughput of about 50Kbps. The one-day average is simultaneously accurate and useless. The best way to answer this question is with a graph.

You'll start by investigating how much bandwidth you use between your desktop DHCP range and the Active Directory domain controllers at remote sites on your internal network during a particular 24-hour period. This is a very specific example of a question network engineers get all the time, and you can use this technique to answer any bandwidth-related question. You'll begin with a look at the total inbound and outbound traffic in a total bandwidth report.

Total Bandwidth Report

Any time you want to create a graph of bandwidth, packets, or flows over time, the best way to get the data is with the linear-interpolated-flows-octets-packets report (discussed in Chapter 5). This report produces a good estimate of the number of octets, flows, and packets per second in a selection of flow data. You're specifically interested in bandwidth (octets) per second, so you can produce this information with this *stat.cfg* configuration:

```
stat-report octets
    type linear-interpolated-flows-octets-packets
    output
```

```
❶      fields -packets,-flows
        path |/usr/local/bin/flow-rptfmt
        sort -key

stat-definition octets
    report octets
```

Because you're interested in the number of bytes transmitted, you remove at ❶ the packet and flow counts from this report. The other settings are flow-report's defaults. Next, you need to decide what data to feed into the report.

Filtering Flows for Total Traffic

Say you want to graph the bandwidth usage between your desktop DHCP range and several remote hosts. To filter these hosts out of your flow data, you'll use primitives for these hosts.

```
filter-primitive localDesktops
    type ip-address-prefix
    permit 172.17.3/24
    permit 172.17.4/23

filter-primitive remoteDC
    type ip-address
    permit 172.18.0.10
    permit 172.18.0.11
...
```

You need one filter for the remote domain controllers and one for the desktops. (You could write a single filter that captured traffic from the desktops to the domain controllers and back, but two separate filters are generally more reusable.)

```
filter-definition desktops
    match src-ip-addr desktops
    or
    match dst-ip-addr desktops

filter-definition remoteDCs
    match src-ip-addr remoteDC
    or
    match dst-ip-addr remoteDC
```

Now run the flows for the day you've chosen through these filters and through your interpolated octets flow-report. You're reporting on all the flows for January 14, 2011.

```
# flow-cat ft-v05.2011-01-14.* | flow-nfilter -F desktops | flow-nfilter -F
remoteDCs | flow-report -S octets > desktop-DC-traffic.txt
```

The top of the file should look something like this:

```
#  ['/usr/local/bin/flow-rptfmt']
unix-secs  octets
1294981479 168.000000
1294981610 30.000000
...
1295066753 15.000000
1295066757 367.000000
```

The numbers on the left side are Unix epochal seconds. To double-check the report times, convert the first and last ones one with the date program.

```
# date -r 1294981479
Fri Jan 14 00:04:39 EST 2011
# date -r 1295066757
Fri Jan 14 23:45:57 EST 2011
```

The first matching flow began at four minutes after midnight, and the last one ended at almost 11:46 PM, both on January 14. The report covers the time you're interested in.

gnuplot will have problems with the column names of this file because unix-secs and octets are not graphable numbers. The simplest way to deal with this is to delete the first two lines either by hand or with sed. (Although editing the file by hand might be easier when creating graphs by hand, sed can be automated.)

```
# sed '1,2d' desktop-DC-traffic.txt > octets.txt
```

The Target Graph

What do you want a graph to look like? It should clearly show how much bandwidth is used. The axes should be labeled with times and the unit of bandwidth measurement, and the graph itself should have a label. If you want real human beings to care about your graphs, times should be local clock time, not in epochal seconds or Greenwich mean time (GMT). If the graph has different lines for different types of traffic, it should have an interpretation key. And this should all be automatically generated. Oh, and while you're at it, you'll make the data accurate and meaningful.

The First Graph: Missing the Target

Begin by creating a default gnuplot graph of your data and comparing this to your desired result.

```
gnuplot> plot "octets.txt"
```

The bandwidth at any given time is represented by a point, as shown in Figure 8-2. Bandwidth utilization on a second-by-second basis is too irregular for nice curving lines, but you'll learn how to make graphs using markers other than points later.

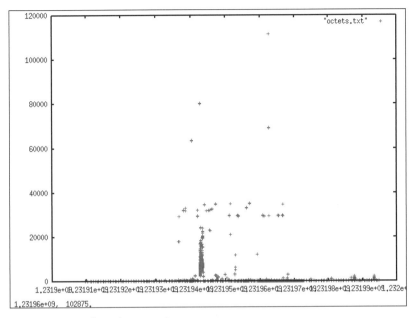

Figure 8-2: Raw throughput graph

Neither axis has a label; the default graph could represent apples vs. pomegranates for all you can tell. In addition, the times along the bottom appear as epochal seconds, such as 1.2319E+08, rather than useful times. Epochal seconds are accurate, strictly speaking, but not exactly what you want to hand to your co-workers. You'll iteratively improve the graph, first by setting labels on the two axes and then by telling gnuplot how to format the time.

```
❶ gnuplot> set xdata time
❷ gnuplot> set timefmt x "%s"
❸ gnuplot> set format x "%H"
❹ gnuplot> set xlabel "time"
❺ gnuplot> set ylabel "bytes"
❻ gnuplot> plot "octets.txt" using ($1):($2)
```

You first tell gnuplot at ❶ that the data along the x-axis represents time. Then at ❷ you tell gnuplot the format of the time data along the x-axis. The %s character is a gnuplot time format that represents epoch seconds, and it gives gnuplot the information it needs to convert epoch seconds to human-friendly times. gnuplot can print measures of time in the same strftime format used by flow-rptfmt (see Chapter 5). For a graph that covers 24 hours, printing the hour is a sensible choice, and you set that format at ❸. You then label the x- and y-axes at ❹ and ❺.

Now that you've started getting fancy, you tell gnuplot at ❻ exactly how to plot the data in your file. The dollar sign followed by a number indicates a column of data. ($1) means "column 1," and ($2) means "column 2." The statement plot "octets.txt" using ($1):($2) tells gnuplot to read octets.txt and plot the first column against the second column. The result looks like Figure 8-3.

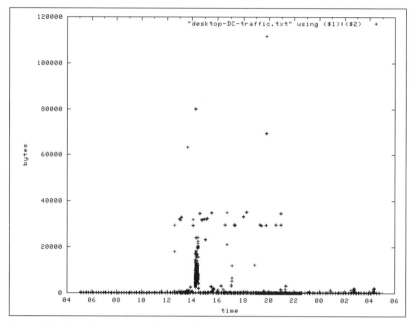

Figure 8-3: Flow diagram with basic labels

This graph is closer to the target graph described earlier. The x-axis is labeled in bytes, and the y-axis is labeled in human-readable times. Notice that the times along the bottom don't match the data in the report, however. The flow data started just after midnight and ended just before midnight, but this graph starts at about 5 AM and ends 24 hours later. This is a time zone problem. I'm in Eastern standard time (EST), and gnuplot produced a graph in Coordinated Universal Time (UTC). This graph needs to display the local time. Also, I buy bandwidth in kilobits rather than kilobytes. Although the kilobytes label is accurate, I want the graph to show kilobits.

To convert UTC to EST, you subtract five hours, shifting each value by $(5 \times 60 \times 60 =)$ 18,000 seconds. You need to reduce all times listed in the data by 18,000 seconds to have the graph display an accurate clock time. To convert bytes to kilobits, you divide by 125. (One byte has 8 bits, and one kilobit has 1,000 bits: 1000 / 8 = 125.) You can set both of these conversions as constants in gnuplot in order to transform the data as you graph it. (Don't forget to change the label on the y-axis when you change the measurement.)

❶ gnuplot> **edt = -18000**
❷ gnuplot> **kb = 125**
❸ gnuplot> **set ylabel "kb"**
    gnuplot> **plot "octets.txt" using ($1+edt)** ❹ **:($2/kb)** ❺

First, you define a constant for the number of seconds between EST and UTC (❶) and another for the number of octets per kilobit (❷).

Next, because you're changing the measurement on the y-axis from bytes to kilobits, you also change the y-axis label, as shown at ❸.

The tricky part is where you tell gnuplot to change the data as you're graphing it. Previously, you graphed the first column against the second. You're transforming the first column by adding the time zone offset to every value in that column (❹). You transform the second column by dividing every entry by the constant kb (❺). You don't change the numbers in the *octets.txt* file; you transform them on their way to the graph.

While you're here, you can make some other changes, such as assigning a title and giving the graph a grid.

```
gnuplot> set title "Traffic between desktops and remote DCs, 14 Jan"
gnuplot> set grid
gnuplot> replot
```

You'll get the graph shown in Figure 8-4, which at first glance is similar to the graph in Figure 8-2 but with more appropriate times and more useful bandwidth measurements, which make it more suitable for sharing with co-workers.

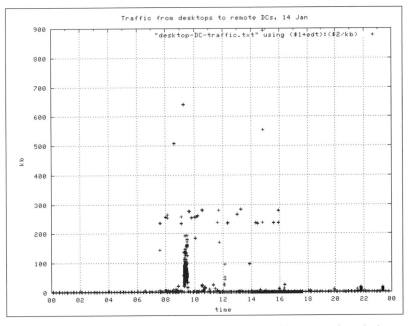

Figure 8-4: Network utilization with better times, bandwidth units, grid, and title

Changing How the Graph Is Drawn

Although I like graphs composed of individual points, many people prefer a different style of graph. gnuplot supports a nearly limitless number of graph styles. One popular style of bandwidth graph is one that uses a solid line, called an *impulse*, to represent the bandwidth used at any given time. Here, I'm creating exactly the same graph as before but using impulses:

```
gnuplot> plot "octets.txt" using ($1+edt):($2/kb) with impulses
```

Other than specifying impulses, this is exactly the same command.

You'll get a graph like Figure 8-5. Some people will find this style of graph easier to understand. Just use whatever format your brain is wired to accept.

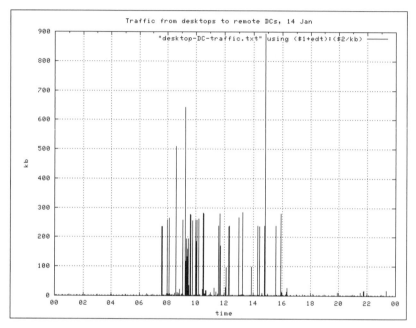

Figure 8-5: Network utilization with impulses

Clipping Levels

You've probably noticed in Figure 8-5 that a few data points vary greatly from the averages. If you examine the original data, you'll find that several connections are only three or four packets. Passing four octets in one millisecond is not the same as passing 4,000 octets in 1,000 milliseconds (or one second), but that's what a simple "average octets per second" calculation produces on a mostly idle network.

To eliminate these outliers, you can establish a sensible clipping level to create a more realistic graph. To do this, you'll use gnuplot's built-in logical operators, in the format shown here. (Perl and C aficionados should be familiar with this syntax.)

```
(a ? b : c )
```

This translates to "Is a true? If true, use b. If untrue, use c."

After assessing your first graph and the data underlying those peaks, you might decide that you want your graph to have a maximum value of, say, 300Kbps, and that if a value exceeds 300Kbps, it should be treated as 300. Translated into the previous syntax, you have the following:

```
( $2/kb>300 ? 300 : $2/kb)
```

$2/kb is the bandwidth in kilobits. With >300 ?, you check to see whether the bandwidth exceeds 300. If it does, you use the value 300. If not, you use the actual value of $2/kb.

To have gnuplot perform this check for you, enter it in the plot statement.

```
gnuplot> plot "octets.txt" using ($1+edt):($2/kb>300 ? 300 : $2/kb ) with
impulses
```

You'll get a result like the graph shown in Figure 8-6.

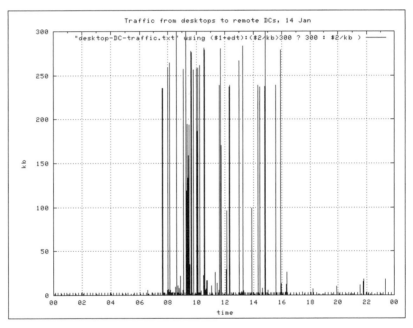

Figure 8-6: Network utilization with clipping levels

By setting a clipping level, you get a graph that offers a more realistic image of your actual bandwidth usage.

CLIPPING LEVELS AND MULTIPLE GRAPHS

When creating graphs for comparison, use the same clipping levels in all the graphs. Varying clipping levels will confuse the results.

Printing Graphs to Files

gnuplot supports a wide variety of graphics formats. To view the complete list your version supports, enter **set terminal** at the gnuplot> prompt. The three most commonly used formats for websites are GIF, JPEG, and PNG.

To have gnuplot print graphs to a file instead of to your screen, tell gnuplot the file type and name. Here, you save the graph to a JPEG file:

```
❶ gnuplot> set terminal jpeg
  Terminal type set to 'jpeg'
  Options are 'nocrop medium '
❷ gnuplot> set output "bandwidth.jpeg"
❸ gnuplot> replot
❹ gnuplot> set terminal x11
```

The set output statement at ❶ tells gnuplot the type of output to produce, and the one at ❷ says where to put any output. To actually create the file, you have gnuplot redraw the graph at ❸. Finally, at ❹ you set the terminal to display its output to the screen again.

Save Your Work!

You can use this configuration to easily generate very similar graphs. Save it as a basis for future reports.

```
gnuplot> save "totalBW.plt"
```

Unidirectional Bandwidth Reports

The graph in Figure 8-6 showed the total amount of bandwidth used for communication between the desktops and the domain controllers at remote sites. What if you want a report on the bandwidth used in one direction only, such as from servers to desktops or from desktops to servers?

The report you'd generate isn't very different from the total bandwidth report you generated in the previous section. To create the report, you'd use the flow-nfilter configuration to extract the data of interest, feed that to your octet's flow-report, and then feed that to a very similar gnuplot configuration.

Filtering Flows for Unidirectional Traffic

The filter configuration uses the same desktops and remoteDCs primitives you used for the total bandwidth report. As shown here, you create two new filters, one for each direction:

```
filter-definition DCtoDesktops
    match src-ip-addr remoteDC
    match dst-ip-addr desktops

filter-definition DesktopsToDC
    match src-ip-addr desktops
    match dst-ip-addr remoteDC
```

The first filter shows only the traffic the domain controllers send to the desktops; the second filter shows the traffic desktops send to the domain controllers. Now you run one of these new filters against the same flow files, beginning with the traffic from the domain controllers to the desktops.

```
# flow-cat ft-v05.2011-01-14.* | flow-nfilter -F DCtoDesktops | flow-report -S
octets > DCtoDesktop.txt
# sed '1,2d' DCtoDesktop.txt > octets.txt
```

You use the same sed command to remove the two extra lines at the top of the file. Finally, verify that the contents of the data file resembles that of your previous report: two columns containing epoch dates and bandwidth amounts.

Creating a Unidirectional Graph

The unidirectional traffic graph should look a lot like the total bandwidth graph. In fact, to produce the final graph, you can simply modify the existing gnuplot configuration and change the title.

```
❶ gnuplot> load "totalBW.plt"
❷ gnuplot> set title "DC to Desktop Traffic, 14 Jan 11"
❸ gnuplot> replot
```

You begin by loading at ❶ the configuration you used for the total bandwidth graph. This configuration gives you correct times, bits instead of octets, and so on. Next, at ❷ you change the title, and at ❸ you create a new plot with your new data. The result would look like Figure 8-7.

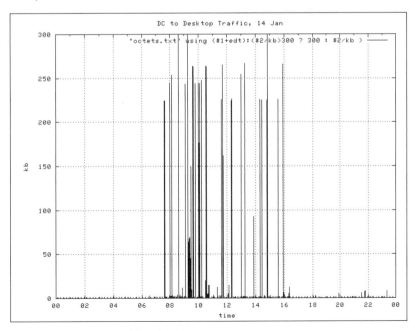

Figure 8-7: Unidirectional bandwidth usage

As you can see, reusing gnuplot configurations with different data is a very quick way to produce graphs with a consistent appearance but different data.

To create a graph for traffic going in the opposite direction, you would do almost the same thing; simply change the graph title and the flow filter.

Combined Inbound/Outbound Traffic

A graph showing both inbound and outbound traffic simultaneously is likely to be more useful than a graph showing traffic in one direction only. You already have the data; to produce a graph showing traffic in both directions, you just need a slightly different gnuplot configuration.

Preparing the Data Files

If you were to create two unidirectional graphs, you would already have the data files you need, and that's essentially what you'll do. You can't call both data files *octets.txt*; however, you need to give each a distinct name. Since you're measuring traffic between local and remote hosts, let's call one of them *inbound.txt* and the other *outbound.txt*. Trim the headers off the raw data files with sed, but otherwise leave the data unchanged.

```
# flow-cat ft-v05.2011-01-14.* | flow-nfilter -F DCtoDesktops | flow-report -S
octets > DCtoDesktop.txt
# flow-cat ft-v05.2011-01-14.* | flow-nfilter -F DesktopsToDC | flow-report -S
octets > DesktopToDC.txt
# sed '1,2d' DCtoDesktop.txt > inbound.txt
# sed '1,2d' DesktopToDC.txt > outbound.txt
```

Displaying Two Graphs Simultaneously

To display two graphs simultaneously, begin with your unidirectional graph configuration. You'll change the name of the files being plotted, but all the other configuration information such as time zone, kilobits instead of bytes, and so on, will work just as well for this new graph.

To plot two different data sets drawn from two different files on one graph, separate each with a comma in a single plot statement, as shown here:

```
gnuplot> plot "inbound.txt" using ($1+edt):($2/kb>300 ? 300 : $2/kb) ❶ \
    > ❷ title "inbound" ❸, \
    > "outbound.txt" using ($1+edt):($2/kb>300 ? 300 : $2/kb) title
"outbound"
```

This listing displays several new features here. The backslash (\) at ❶ tells gnuplot that a command continues on the next line. If you need to use a backslash to show a continued line, enter the backslash, and then just press ENTER. You'll be taken to the next line.

The `title` at ❷ within the `plot` statement labels the data. In this case, you have two types of data, labeled `inbound` and `outbound`. The comma (,) at ❸ separates the two data sources. The resulting graph looks something like Figure 8-8.

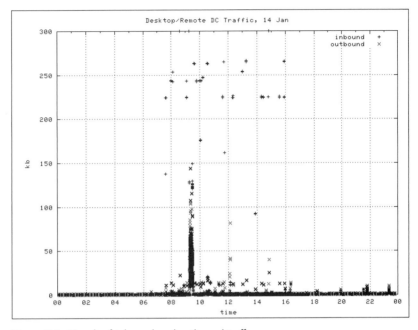

Figure 8-8: Graph of inbound and outbound traffic

According to the key, the data points of the inbound traffic are plus signs (+). The outbound traffic data points appear as x characters. gnuplot will also use different colors for the data points. (Figure 8-8 is a bit easier to understand in color, but this book is in black and white because I want it to be affordable.) Having two different data point characters helps, but not much. It's better to show both types of traffic simultaneously, but not intermingled.

To make this graph easier to understand at a glance, graph outbound traffic as negative numbers, like so:

```
gnuplot > plot "inbound.txt" using ($1+edt):($2/kb>300 ? 300 : $2/kb) \
        > title "inbound", \
        > "outbound.txt" using ($1+edt):($2/kb>300 ? ❶ -300 : ❷ -$2/kb)
title "outbound"
```

You've made only two minor changes here, placing minus signs in your outbound graph's plot statement at ❶ and ❷. Figure 8-9 shows the resulting graph.

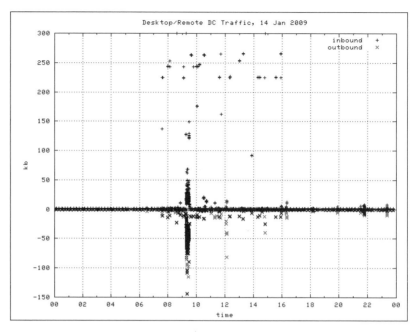

Figure 8-9: Utilization diagram with outbound traffic as negative numbers

As you can see in this graph, it's clear that you're receiving much more traffic than you send, and you receive it much more frequently. The inbound and outbound clipping levels are unchanged, but the outbound traffic never approaches the clipping level. You can also see that you have a big utilization spike just after 9 AM EST.

To get another look at this data, you could graph it with impulses like so:

```
gnuplot> plot "inbound.txt" using ($1+edt):($2/kb>300 ? 300 : $2/kb) \
    > title "inbound" with impulses, \
    > "outbound.txt" using ($1+edt):($2/kb>300 ? -300 : -$2/kb) \
    > title "outbound" with impulses
```

The result resembles Figure 8-10.

With proper graphs, anyone—even your manager—can understand network utilization. Figure 8-10 makes it clear that desktops are exchanging traffic with remote domain controllers, even though Microsoft insisted that clients should contact their local domain controller only. You can now resolve the problem with documented facts rather than guesses and intermittent packet sniffer snapshots.

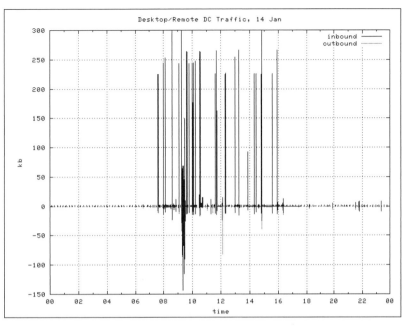

Figure 8-10: Impulse utilization diagram with outbound traffic as negative numbers

Automating Graph Production

Although you'll always need to have some ad hoc reporting ability, you'll find that you need certain graphs over and over again. You should make producing these graphs so easy that one of your flunkies can do it, or you can even schedule graph production with cron. The best way to manage this is through scripting and automation. gnuplot is very scripting-friendly, and the following script processes yesterday's flow files to generate a bidirectional traffic graph.

NOTE   *This script is not optimized. In a real environment, you'd send email via Perl, but I don't want to waste a page on that example when you probably already have a standard way to send mail on your systems. Too, this script uses insecure temp files, and you shouldn't use such files on a shared system. In short, do not use this script as is; rather, use it as a guide for writing a script that fits your own needs in the best Perl you can maintain. Who told you to listen to me, anyway?*

```perl
#!/usr/bin/perl

#where are our flow files?
$logdir="/var/log/flows/";
#flow file version
$version=5;

#get yesterday's date
@T=localtime(time-86400);
$year=$T[5]+1900;
$month=$T[4]+1;
```

```
unless ($month>9) {
    $month = '0'.$month;
}
$day=$T[3];

$filePrefix="ft-v0$version.$year-$month-$day";

#generate the reports and prepare them for graphing

system ("flow-cat $logdir$filePrefix* | flow-nfilter -F DCtoDesktops | flow-
report -S octets > /tmp/DCtoDesktop.txt");

system ("flow-cat $logdir$filePrefix* | flow-nfilter -F DesktopsToDC | flow-
report -S octets > /tmp/DesktopToDC.txt");

system ("sed '1,2d' /tmp/DesktopToDC.txt > /tmp/outbound.txt");
system ("sed '1,2d' /tmp/DCtoDesktop.txt > /tmp/inbound.txt");

#run gnuplot
open GNUPLOT, "| gnuplot";
print GNUPLOT <<gnuplot_settings;
set terminal jpeg
set output "/tmp/desktop-DC.jpeg"
set xdata time
set timefmt x "%s"
set format x "%H"
set xlabel "time"
set ylabel "kb"
set title "Desktop/DC Traffic, $day $month $year"
edt = -18000
kb=125
set grid
plot "/tmp/inbound.txt" using (\$1+edt):(\$2/kb>300 ? 300 : \$2/kb) \\
    title "inbound" with impulses, \\
    "/tmp/outbound.txt" using (\$1+edt):(\$2/kb>300 ? -300 : -\$2/kb) \\
    title "outbound" with impulses
gnuplot_settings
close GNUPLOT;

#send mail
system ("mutt -s \"Traffic for $day $month $year\" -a /tmp/desktop-DC.jpeg
mwlucas@localhost < /dev/null");
```

Admittedly, some of the commands here are a little long, but there's no interface to run flow reports directly from within Perl. You replace sed with textbook Perl routines, but you're already using system() calls all over the place.

Beginning with run gnuplot, you configure gnuplot entirely within this script. You could also load most of your gnuplot configuration from a file.

And as for sending mail (at the end of the script), you probably already have a preferred way to send mail from your servers. If you don't, I recommend Perl's MIME::Lite module. Otherwise, look at programs such as mutt or metamail.

Comparison Graphs

The easiest way to compare traffic from multiple time periods is to overlay one graph atop another; doing so helps you evaluate the impact of system changes on the network. You can use the same type of linear interpolation for this as well, with some needed changes to the graph techniques and the time values.

In the following report, you'll compare inbound and outbound Internet traffic from two different 24-hour periods, A and B. The data is in two files: *inboundA.txt* and *inboundB.txt*. I've already removed the column names from the top of these files.

Data Normalizing

To make the graphs overlay each other, you need to adjust the data times. Bandwidth values are largely unchanged, but the time values are problematic. The simplest way to do this is to subtract a value from each set of data so that each graph starts at time zero.

When you use sort -key in the output section of your linear-interpolated report, the earliest time in your file appears at the top. For example, look at the top of *inboundA.txt*.

```
# ['/usr/local/bin/flow-rptfmt']
unix-secs  octets
❶ 1229488610 1033.430171
1229488611 1033.430171
1229488612 1033.430171
...
```

InboundA.txt begins in epochal second 1229488610 (❶). You subtract 1,229,488,610 from every time value to turn it into an offset from zero. Similarly, *inboundB.txt* begins in epochal second 1230179749. You store these values in gnuplot, and while you're defining constants, you'll also define the number of octets in a kilobyte.

```
gnuplot> inboundA=1229488610
gnuplot> inboundB=1230179749
gnuplot> kb=125
```

NOTE *Those of you who check these dates will notice that they start about a minute apart. A difference of one minute in a small graph of a day's traffic is negligible. If you were graphing traffic within a single minute or creating a wide graph for a single hour you'd have to correct for this difference, but at this scale we don't care.*

Time Scale

You want to label the x-axis by time using "hours into the samples," but as things stand, the x-axis will be numbered in seconds. You can convert seconds into hours by configuring gnuplot's *tics*. A tic is a divider along an axis;

major tics are labeled, and minor tics are not. The previous graphs had a labeled tic every two hours and one minor tic halfway between each hour. Let's keep that value: Two hours is 7,200 seconds.

```
gnuplot> set xtics 7200
gnuplot> set mxtics 2
```

With these basic labels, you can now plot your data.

```
gnuplot> plot "inboundA.txt" using ($1-inboundA):($2/kb) with lines title "day
1 traffic", "inboundB.txt" using ($1-inboundB):($2/kb) with lines title "day 2
traffic"
```

The result should look something like Figure 8-11, except in color.

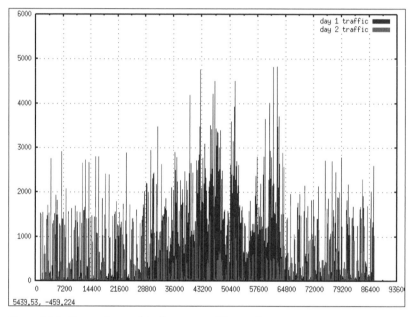

Figure 8-11: Comparisons of traffic on two different days

You can combine this sort of comparison graph with the graph that shows inbound and outbound traffic simultaneously and get an easy-to-understand comparison of traffic from two different time windows. Or you can make one day's traffic negative to make it easier to see. You can build graphs that show how much of your Internet traffic is web browsing from Monday through Friday, 9 AM to 5 PM, to show the impact of users on the network. Or you can compare your current network usage to the usage when your new Internet circuit was installed last year. gnuplot lets you visualize any data you have. If you want more sophisticated examples of using gnuplot with flow data, look for the CAIDA tools or the FloCon (*http://www.cert.org/flocon/*) proceedings.

9

EDGES AND ANALYSIS

 With the tools I've discussed throughout this book, you can analyze and present your data in just about any way you might need. In this chapter, you'll consider a couple of similar systems and learn how to connect them to your flow collector. Then you'll look at a couple of common use cases that illustrate what you can accomplish with flow analysis.

NetFlow v9

NetFlow version 9 is mostly used for IPv6 (although it can be extended to include other types of information as well) and is only rarely deployed. Although most NetFlow sensors support multiple versions, such as 5 or 7 in addition to 9, a few manufacturers make hardware that speaks only version 9. When version 9 becomes more widely used, flow-tools and its brethren will probably develop support for it. Until that time, however, how can you cope with NetFlow version 9 data?

Other free flow collectors accept version 9 flows. You can translate version 9 data into flow-tools format. I'll show how to use flowd[1] (*http://www .mindrot.org/projects/flowd/*), by the author of softflowd. To transform your data into a flow-capture record file, you first need to install flowd.

Installing flowd

If your operating system includes a flowd package, use it. If not, you should install flowd, but before you do, install the following software:

- BSD yacc (usually packaged as byacc on Linux systems)
- GNU make

Yes, that's GNU-style make plus BSD-style yacc.

The flowd software expects to run as the unprivileged user *_flowd*. Create this user before building the software.

Once yacc and make are installed, build flowd much like you would flow-tools or softflowd. The configure script includes a variety of options. Here, I build and install flowd under */usr/local/flowd*:

```
# configure --prefix=/usr/local/flowd
# gmake
# gmake install
```

That's it! You should get a configuration file and the program itself.

Configuring flowd

Where you control flow-capture with command-line arguments, flowd uses a configuration file. Most flowd configuration options are similar to options offered by flow-capture.

```
❶ logfile "/var/flow/router-v9/current"
❷ pidfile "/var/run/flowd.pid"
❸ listen on 0.0.0.0:6789
❹ flow source 192.0.2.1
❺ store ALL
❻ accept all
```

flowd stores flow records in the logfile at ❶. Like flow-capture's ft- files, a flowd log is a compressed binary file that you cannot view directly. Like most other software, flowd records its process ID in a PID file, as shown at ❷. Most systems store PID files in the directory */var/run*.

flowd must listen to the network, and at ❸ you specify an IP address and a UDP port, separated by a colon. If you were to use an IP of 0.0.0.0, flowd would listen for incoming flow data on all IP addresses on the system. To

---

1. I seriously considered using flowd for this book, but it doesn't yet have the variety of canned reports that flow-capture supports. I expect this to change over time, however, and if you need an IPv6 flow collector and are comfortable writing reports in Perl or Python, you should consider flowd.

restrict the IP addresses flowd accepts flow data from, list a router's IP address as a flow source, as shown at ❹.

Although flowd has comprehensive filtering features to let you record only certain types of flows, you tell flowd at ❺ to record everything and at ❻ to accept everything the sensor transmits.

Once you've finished editing your configuration file, start flowd, and tell your version 9 sensor to transmit data to this collector's IP address and port. When version 9 flow data arrives, flowd should record it in the logfile. Once you see the logfile grow larger, it's time to convert data to flow-tools format.

Converting flowd Data to Flow-tools

NetFlow version 9 includes the information expected in a NetFlow v5 record: source and destination addresses and ports, protocol numbers, packet counts, and so on. You need to automatically extract this information from the flowd log and import it into a flow-capture ft- file. Fortunately, Craig Weinhold's flowd2ft script does this for you. You can copy the script from the following listing or download it from *http://www.networkflowanalysis.com/*. Let's look at it.

```perl
#!/usr/bin/perl
# "flowd2ft" crontab script to move flowd capture files into flow-tools

# -- flow-tools variables
# where ft's flow-import is
❶ our $ftImport = "/usr/local/bin/flow-import";
# put a copy of the flow file here, for flowscan
❷ our $ftDir = "/var/flow/router-v5/ft";
# timezone for ft capture files
❸ our $ftTZ = "-0500";
# seconds per ft capture file and cron interval
❹ our $ftPeriod = 300;

# -- flowd variables
# where flowd-reader is
❺ our $flowdReader = "/usr/local/bin/flowd-reader";
# where flowd.conf is
❻ our $flowdConf = "/usr/local/etc/flowd.conf";
# SIGUSR1
our $flowdHup = "10";
our ($flowdPid, $flowdLog);

our ($sec,$min,$hour,$mday,$mon,$year,$wday,$yday,$isdst) =
localtime(time - $ftPeriod);
our $ftFile = sprintf("ft-v05.%04d-%02d-%02d.%02d%02d%02d$ftTZ", $year + 1900,
$mon + 1, $mday, $hour, $min, $sec);

❼   open(IN, $flowdConf) || die "Could not read $flowdConf";
while ( <IN> ) {
        if (/^\s*logfile ["]?([^"\s]+)/) { $flowdLog = $1; }
        if (/^\s*pidfile ["]?([^"\s]+)/) { $flowdPid = $1; }
}
```

```
    close(IN);

    exit if (! -f $flowdLog); # exit silently on empty file

    die "$flowdPid does not exist: $!" if (! -f $flowdPid);
    my $pid = `cat $flowdPid`;
❽   `mv $flowdLog $flowdLog.tmp`;
    die "$flowdPid ($pid) invalid: $!" if (! kill $flowdHup, $pid);
❾   `$flowdReader -c $flowdLog.tmp | $ftImport -f 2 -V 5 -z 1 > $ftDir/$ftFile`;
```

Before using this script, you'll need to set the configuration variables. At ❶ you hard-code the location of the flow-import program. At ❷ you point the script to the directory you want to use to store your created flow-capture files. At ❸ you give the script the time zone offset in minutes so that it can include that information in the filename just like flow-capture would. At ❹ you tell the script to create a new ft- file every 300 seconds, just as your usual flow-capture instances do.

The script also needs to know where the flowd-reader program (❺) is installed and where to find the flowd configuration (❻). At ❼ the script reads the flowd configuration file for the rest of its settings and then at ❽ moves the existing flowd file out of the way so that it can restart flowd and close the existing logfile. Finally, at ❾ it reads the freshly closed logfile and creates a new flow-capture file.

After configuring the script, run it once by hand. It should create a new ft- logfile in the destination directory and tell you how many flows it processed. If the script doesn't run correctly, check your settings and error and log messages. Once you're sure that your script is running properly, have your system run it every five minutes by making the appropriate entry in cron, as shown here:

```
*/5  *   *   *   *       /usr/local/bin/convert-flowd-ft.pl > /tmp/convert.log
```

You will now have flow records that are compatible with the rest of your flow reporting system. You can use these records to set up FlowScan, run flow-report, or do anything else you like.

sFlow

sFlow is a flow export technology invented by InMon that competes with Cisco's NetFlow. Many vendors, such as HP and Extreme, offer equipment that exports sFlow but not NetFlow. No need to despair, though: You can translate sFlow packets into NetFlow version 5 data and feed that to flow-tools.

NOTE   *If you have a lot of sFlow-based equipment, however, you should really look into an sFlow reporting system. I recommend converting sFlow to NetFlow when you have an existing flow-tools setup and a couple of sFlow devices that you'd like to integrate into that system, not when you have a data center full of sFlow hardware.*

Configuring sFlow Export with sflowenable

Some sFlow sensors can be configured through the GUI or command line, but a few sFlow sensors require configuration via SNMP. Although you could manually use SNMP GET and SET commands to set up sFlow, the fine folks at InMon offer a script to automate this process for you. Grab a copy of sflowenable from *http://www.inmon.com/technology/sflowenable/*.

sflowenable requires the net-snmp tools you probably already have installed on your network management workstation. It also requires GNU awk, also known as gawk. Some operating systems include gawk as the default awk; others have it as an add-on package. If sflowenable fails with cryptic awk errors, you have the wrong awk. Install gawk, and either edit the script to use gawk instead of awk or alias awk to gawk in your shell. Now say that three times fast.

Running sflowenable requires the sensor hostname and a read-write SNMP community, the collector IP, and the UDP port you want to receive sFlow data on.

```
sflowenable.sh sFlow-sensor community collector_IP collector_port
```

For example, to activate sFlow on the device bigSwitch, using the SNMP community LucasRulez, and to transmit the data to a sFlow collector on the host 192.0.2.15 on port 5515, I would run the following:

```
# sflowenable.sh bigSwitch LucasRulez 192.0.2.15 5515
```

You should see data coming to port 5515 on your collector almost immediately. But wait a minute—you have nothing that can listen to sFlow, let alone do anything with it! You'll handle that detail now.

Convert sFlow to NetFlow

The sflowtool program is a free sFlow collector, capture, and converter available from *http://www.inmon.com/technology/sflowTools.php*. Among its features, it can convert a sFlow data stream to NetFlow version 5 and send it to a Net-Flow collector. This is perfect for these purposes.

sflowtool is a simple program with no special prerequisites. Build it with the familiar ./configure, make, make install routine you've used repeatedly.

To have sflowtool convert and retransmit data, you need a port to listen for sFlow connections, a flow-capture host, and the flow-capture port.

```
sflowtool -p sflow_port -c flow-capture-host -d flow-capture-port > /dev/null &
```

In the earlier example, I assumed that you had a sFlow collector on port 5515. Let's assume you want to accept those sFlow packets, convert them to NetFlow, and retransmit them to a flow-capture instance running on the same host on port 5516. You would run sflowtool like this:

```
sflowtool -p 5515 -c localhost -d 5516 > /dev/null &
```

Now configure a `flow-capture` instance to record the flow data, and you have data from your sFlow-only device with no local scripts or conversion routines necessary.

Problem Solving with Flow Data

You've explored the usefulness of various flow analysis features throughout this book. Now you'll look at a few case studies of real problems and possible solutions. Some of these I've touched on earlier; others are completely new.

Finding Busted Software

Under normal circumstances, a small percentage of TCP connections break regularly on every network. Software stacks misbehave, clients try to connect to defunct printers, and users who ought to know better install freeware that behaves unspeakably. Perhaps the fastest way to use flow data to improve your network is to check for these broken connections, identify their sources and destinations, and discover what software on the affected machines is causing the problems. The following are two common groups of "broken" TCP connections:

SYN-only flows   A machine attempts to connect to a remote host that doesn't answer.

RST-only flows   A machine attempts to connect to a remote host that refuses the connection. You can write filters for each of these and report on them separately.

Broken Connection Filters

The following filters will capture these two types of broken TCP connection:

```
❶ filter-primitive syn-only
      type ip-tcp-flags
      permit 0x2
❷ filter-primitive rst-only
      type ip-tcp-flags
      permit 0x4

❸ filter-definition syn-only
      match ip-tcp-flags syn-only
❹ filter-definition rst-only
      match ip-tcp-flags rst-only
```

Here you define a primitive for SYN-only flows at ❶, a corresponding filter at ❸, an RST-only primitive at ❷, and its matching filter at ❹.

Checking for Resets

Now use the `rst-only` filter on a sample of typical traffic.

```
# flow-cat ❶ ft-v05.2010-01-22.10* | flow-nfilter -F rst-only | flow-report
-v ❷ TYPE=ip-address -v ❸ SORT=+flows
ip-address      flows octets packets duration
❹ 192.0.2.184   1186  14880  372     100
192.0.2.197     1186  14880  372     100
198.22.63.8     39    1720   43      4
72.21.91.20     23    920    23      0
192.0.6.197     23    1920   48      16
192.0.64.69     16    640    16      0
...
```

Choose records from a time where you expect "typical" traffic. For example, if your office is open only from 9 AM to 5 PM, the flow records from 2 AM will not represent normal use (although they're probably interesting to look at separately). On my network, I'm analyzing records at ❶ from 10 AM to 11 AM.

You're hunting for machines that are either sending or receiving abnormally large numbers of SYN-only or RST-only flows. Although you might initially view the data with `flow-print`, what you really want is a list of IP addresses and the number of matching flows, as offered by the `ip-address` report at ❷. I want to sort in decreasing order, as shown at ❸. In this hour, the first two hosts have 30 times more RST-only flows than the host in third place, as you can see at ❹. Something isn't behaving well there.

The next step is to check a few more time windows to see whether this behavior is consistent or whether these two hosts were just having trouble at a particular time. Assuming that the behavior is consistent, take a closer look at the RST-only traffic from the first host. In this example, I'm using the `ip-addr` report created in Chapter 4, so I don't need to differentiate between source and destination addresses yet:

```
# flow-cat ft-v05.2010-01-22.10* | flow-nfilter -F rst-only | flow-nfilter -F
ip-addr -v ADDR=192.0.2.184 | flow-print | less
srcIP          dstIP          prot srcPort dstPort octets   packets
192.0.2.184    192.0.2.197    6    443     33171   80       2
192.0.2.184    192.0.2.197    6    443     17866   80       2
192.0.2.184    192.0.2.197    6    443     64447   80       2
192.0.2.184    192.0.2.197    6    443     60076   80       2
192.0.2.184    192.0.2.197    6    443     13839   80       2
...
```

As you can see in the previous listing, each flow appears basically identical at first glance. The host 192.0.2.184 sends two TCP RSTs to 192.0.2.197, from port 443 to a high-numbered port. These are rejected HTTPS requests. If you were to view all traffic between these two hosts, you'd see that 192.0.2.197 makes HTTPS requests to 192.0.2.184, which then rejects them.

Running `flow-print` a second time with a format that includes timestamps, such as the following, shows that the client makes this request every few seconds:

```
flow-print -f 5
```

The host 192.0.2.197 is running a piece of software that is broken or misconfigured. Now go ask the system administrator what's going on.

Note that my test network is fairly small. In an enterprise data center, you might find dozens of different software packages behaving badly; I've personally seen misconfigured software try to contact other hosts hundreds of times a second. Although TCP RSTs don't usually consume enough bandwidth to cause problems, resolving these problems makes the software more efficient, reduces hardware requirements, and might reduce network traffic and service delays in unexpected ways.

Checking for Failed Connections

SYN-only flows show that a host requested a connection but nothing answered. Either the requested address is not on the network, the host at that address cannot answer the request, or the host is silently ignoring the request. Although you probably know whether your equipment is configured to silently ignore requests, identifying the first two types of hosts can be very useful. You'll identify IP addresses with high levels of SYN-only flows much like you checked for RST-only flows; only the filter changes.

```
# flow-cat ft-v05.2011-01-22.10* | flow-nfilter -F hamlin | flow-nfilter -F
syn-only | flow-report -v TYPE=ip-address -v SORT=+flows
ip-address       flows octets packets duration
❶ 192.0.2.13      8306  526240 16998   2390732
  118.126.4.66     256  10240  256     0
  112.110.75.169   224  40640  635     1828064
  192.0.2.158      193  24624  513     1430236
  192.0.2.233      158  24648  474     1421304
  ...
```

In this report, once again you have a clear outlier: the host 192.0.2.13 shown at ❶ has many more SYN-only flows than any other host. To see why, look at that host's traffic using the same technique you used for a particular RST-only host, as shown here:

```
# flow-cat ft-v05.2011-01-22.10* | flow-nfilter -F rst-only | flow-nfilter -F
ip-addr -v ADDR=192.0.2.13 | flow-print | less
  srcIP           dstIP           prot  srcPort dstPort octets  packets
❶ 192.0.2.13      192.0.2.16      6     26064   24      64      1
❷ 192.0.2.13      192.0.2.16      6     26064   26      64      1
❸ 192.0.2.13      192.0.2.16      6     26147   27      64      1
❹ 192.0.2.13      192.0.2.16      6     26148   28      64      1
```

192.0.2.13	192.0.2.16	6	26152	29	64	1
192.0.2.13	192.0.2.16	6	26149	30	64	1
192.0.2.13	192.0.2.16	6	26246	31	64	1
192.0.2.13	192.0.2.16	6	26248	32	64	1
192.0.2.13	192.0.2.16	6	26253	33	64	1

...

As you can see, the host 192.0.2.13 repeatedly tries to contact 192.0.2.16, first on port 24 at ❶ and then port 26 (❷), port 27 (❸), port 28 (❹), and so on. This particular data shows that 192.0.2.13 is trying every port between 1 and 1024 on 192.0.2.16. The connection attempts then move to 192.0.2.17.

This activity is indicative of a port scanner. Remember, not all port scanners scan ports sequentially—the key is to look for the same IP being hit at many ports in a relatively brief time. If 192.0.2.13 is your security workstation and you habitually scan your own network, this might be normal behavior. However, worms and intruders also use port scanners to identify vulnerable targets. If you don't know why this machine is scanning the network, find out!

One interesting thing in this output is that the port scan appears to skip port 25. Remember, you're checking for flows that reset immediately. If a host responds on a port, it won't appear on this list. In this case, 192.0.2.16 runs a mail server; viewing all the traffic between these hosts would show a flow to port 25 and an answering flow.

Investigating another IP with a high SYN-only count might produce results like these:

srcIP	dstIP	prot	srcPort	dstPort	octets	packets
221.194.136.17	192.0.2.158	6	35628	80	432	8
66.249.67.245	192.0.2.158	6	44008	80	240	4
221.194.136.17	192.0.2.158	6	35628	80	48	1
66.249.67.245	192.0.2.158	6	44008	80	60	1
65.55.207.118	192.0.2.158	6	52684	80	144	3
65.55.106.137	192.0.2.158	6	54180	80	144	3
65.55.106.185	192.0.2.158	6	21976	80	144	3

...

Each of these different source IP addresses is trying to connect to 192.0.2.158, all on TCP port 80. A quick check shows that this machine is a web server, and it does answer requests on port 80. Why do you see these SYN-only flows?

If your network equipment is reporting a flow, it certainly delivered the packet to the network node because delivering packets is a much higher-priority task than flow reporting! In this particular case, removing the syn-only filter from the flow-print command showed that the web server answered thousands of requests. flow-report told you that this host had 193 SYN-only flows during the hour you checked, but the web server just didn't answer these 193 requests. Maybe it ran out of memory or CPU. Perhaps the network card was saturated, or the web server software was reloaded.

Graphing the times the SYN-only packets appeared might give some answers, especially when compared with a graph of the number of connections opened at that time or list of times the server performs internal maintenance. As the network administrator, all you can say is that during this hour users got a "Page Cannot Be Displayed" or some similar error 193 times. Is this acceptable in your environment and situation? Probably not.

The nice thing with this type of result is that you know what part of the delivery system failed. The network delivered the packets, and the web server didn't answer. If the web server administrator reports that he's getting complaints about network timeouts, you can provide evidence that the timeouts aren't actually network problems and offer suggestions on how to fix the issues.

Identifying Worms

If you're on an enterprise network, worms cause something worse than system trouble. They cause meetings. With management. And because your antivirus software probably kicked up desktop alarms as the worm tried to propagate, those meetings will probably include senior managers who will ask inconvenient questions about how you spend your time.

Your best response is to find the worm source as quickly as possible. For example, in spring 2009, my employer's antivirus systems began spewing warnings about infection attempts from the Conficker virus. At a global company with tens of thousands of desktops, manually identifying virus sources could take countless man-hours and would require cooperation across umpteen time zones and multiple language barriers. Even though I had flow data for only three plants out of dozens around the world, flow analysis identified the sources in about 15 minutes and spared most of those meetings.

To find a worm, first identify the worm's propagation method. A few minutes on Google tells me that Conficker spreads through Microsoft's file-sharing port, on TCP/445. The worm probes every IP on its network to identify Windows hosts and infects any it finds. This is unusual behavior: Although many servers will receive connections from many different hosts, very few systems will try to reach every other host on a network.

You can use the ip-source-address-destination-count report to count the number of hosts a system tries to contact, as shown here:

```
# flow-cat ❶ ft-v05.2009-05-29.* | flow-nfilter -F ip-port -v ❷ PORT=445 |
flow-report -v ❸ TYPE=ip-source-address-destination-count -v OPTIONS=-header
-v ❹ FIELDS=-duration,-packets,-octets | ❺ sort -rnk 2 | less
  ip-source-address ip-destination-address-count flows
❻ 172.17.84.14      1851                          1711
❼ 172.17.84.13      1591                          1483
❽ 172.19.11.65      59                            225
  172.19.11.8       44                            60
  172.19.11.4       17                            38
  ...
```

As you can see, I begin at ❶ with the flow files for the time window when the worm attacked my local network. I then search at ❷ only for the flows going to or from port 445, and I run these flows through the ip-source-address-destination-count report at ❸. Unnecessary fields are removed at ❹ to make the output easier to read.

NOTE *Remember that this report and its counterpart, ip-destination-address-source-count, do not have built-in sorting functions. You must sort these externally, as shown at ❺. (One consequence of sorting externally is that the header for each column appears at the bottom of the list. I've restored the header to the top of this example to make it easier to understand. Do the same for your managers.)*

This report reveals two hosts that try to connect to a remarkably large number of other hosts: 172.17.84.14 connected or tried to connect to 1,851 different hosts on my data center network, as shown at ❻. Because the network has fewer than 500 active computers, this is immediately suspicious. The second host shown at ❼ has a similar profile, while the third at ❽ is my corporate file server, which has many fewer connections.

These two machines turned out to be on a test network in a different hemisphere. Without flow analysis, I could never have identified these machines. With analysis, an email documenting the results got me out of having to attend any of the follow-up meetings.

Traffic to Illegal Addresses

Is your firewall misconfigured? Yes. Yes, it is. You just don't know it.

Most firewalls use Network Address Translation (NAT) to connect hosts on private addresses to ones on the public Internet. If you have a complicated firewall policy and a firewall platform that encourages complicated or downright bizarre NAT rules,[2] it's easy to accidentally leak untranslated addresses onto your Internet-facing network. If you're running multiple firewalls using one policy, it becomes almost inevitable. Your ISP should filter internal addresses from your Internet circuits, so any traffic with private IP addresses on your external network is coming from you (or you and your ISP need to have a little talk).

It's easy to track down traffic from private addresses. First, define a filter that includes your internal addresses.

```
filter-primitive internal
    type ip-address-prefix
❶  permit 172.16.0.0/16
    permit 172.17.0.0/16
    permit 172.18.0.0/16

filter-definition internal
  match ip-source-address internal
  or
  match ip-destination-address internal
```

---

2. (Cough.) Checkpoint. (Cough.)

Here you identify at ❶ three blocks of IP addresses that are used internally and define a filter for them. Next, go to the directory where you store flow records for your Internet-facing network, filter for these addresses, and print the results.

```
# flow-cat * | flow-nfilter -F internal | flow-print | less
  srcIP            dstIP             prot  srcPort  dstPort  octets    packets
❶ 172.16.84.151    137.118.232.3     6     33892    25       40        1
  172.16.84.151    94.190.193.162    6     43729    25       309       1
  172.16.84.151    123.118.100.174   6     25051    25       339       1
  172.16.84.151    189.70.172.2      6     33724    2015     133       1
  172.16.84.151    212.242.180.151   6     33724    11906    133       1
❷ 172.16.84.130    198.22.66.10      17    4132     53       132       1
  172.16.84.130    198.22.62.19      17    38897    53       132       1
  ...
```

Each of these flows passed through a firewall rule with an improper NAT configuration. In other words, these rules are broken, and they will impact you in unexpected ways. For example, the line at ❶ shows a host trying to send email from a private address. The connection never completes, of course. If this is your backup mail exchanger, you'll have a nasty surprise when your primary breaks. Similarly, at ❷ you also have a host trying to make name service queries from a private address. Fixing these in advance will reduce future outages.

Traffic to Nonexistent Hosts

Theoretically, removing network servers should reduce network usage. Unfortunately, that's not always true.

At one point, certain desktops on my employer's corporate network would not become useful until more than five minutes after the user entered their username and password. This is slow even for commodity operating systems. Although not every workstation was affected, most of those that were impacted were at remote locations where I lacked diagnostic equipment. I had a user try one of these workstations at a specific time and then checked the flow records to see whether that workstation had tried to contact anything at my data center during that window.

As it turned out, most of the traffic from that workstation during that time was trying to reach my Novell login server, which had been turned off a few days before. The workstation still had the client installed, however. Apparently the Novell client software insisted on trying to contact the login server even though it had been told to shut down. Removing the Novell client from that client resolved the slow login issues.

With one problem identified, I next used FlowGrapher to diagram traffic from that remote plant to the disconnected server's IP address. For two hours every morning, this traffic consumed almost 25 percent of the plant's network connection. Although removing the disabled client had previously been considered unnecessary, this evidence changed people's minds.

Strictly speaking, this wasn't a network problem, but diagnosing it required involvement by a network administrator and resolving it reduced the number of network complaints. And remember, all a network engineer wants is for his users to shut up.

Afterword

I'm certain that most of you get along fabulously with each and every one of your co-workers, your work environment is a delight and a joy, and your IT group is a seamless, cohesive team without bitter bickering or belabored backbiting. Those of you unfortunate enough to work in a less supportive environment should read this.

Flow analysis will change your problem-solving capacities. You'll solve odd issues that have haunted your network for years. You'll conclusively show that problems that everyone has comfortably blamed on the network are actually server or software problems. You'll even be able to dig up a whole list of weird problems that other people are causing on the network. All of this will quickly change your relationship with your co-workers and management.

Systems administration and network engineers have a long tradition of being difficult to work with; we even have archetypes like the Bastard Operator from Hell. Now that you have evidence, it's tempting to make those who doubted you suffer for their intransigence. Now that you have evidence, though, you can afford to be generous. When something is your problem, admit it. When you show that something isn't your problem, however, say something like "Here's the evidence identifying the problem. Although this is clearly not a network issue, I'm happy to help you solve your problem." Admittedly, this is much less satisfying than using words like "you loser." Unlikely as it seems, a positive attitude can change co-worker and management attitudes about the network staff and can improve your life.

And if not, well, at least you'll know for certain that it's not your problem. And it's *never* too late to call someone a doofus.

INDEX

or logical operator, in filter
definition, 76–77
organization name, on web
page, 144
$organization variable, 129
origination of flows, 94
OSPF, filter to match, 61
outbound traffic, determining for
flow, 124
outliers, eliminating from graph,
166–167
OutputDir directive, for CUFlow, 125
output-interface match type, 75
output-interface report, 100

P

packages, installing flow-tools
from, 25
packet-capture software, 37
packet-filtering firewalls, 45
packet-sampled flows, 19
packet size distribution, in
flow-report default
report, 84
packet-size report, 96
packet sniffer, 10
packets
dropped
by interface counter, 38
number in softflowd
process, 37
number in flow, 42
packets per flow
filtering on, 73
in flow-report default report, 84
report, 97
packets per second (pps), 98
packets per second filters, 74
packets report, 97
password protection, for Flow-
Viewer website, 140
PATH environment variable, 25
path variable
for flow-report, 108
setting to pipe, 113
percent-total option, in
flow-report, 91

percentages, displaying in reports,
90–91
perfile() function, 137
Perl scripts, 6, 117
permit statement, 80
pie charts, in FlowViewer, 148
ping requests, 14, 54
pipe symbol (|), 108
plot command (gnuplot), 159,
162–163
plotting program, 6
port mirroring, switch for, 33
port monitoring, switch for, 33
port number primitives, 62
port scanner, 185
"port unreachable" ICMP type, 55
PORT variable, 79
ports
common number assignments,
44–45
common protocol
assignments, 44
printing names, 43–44
report on used, 94
reports combining IP addresses
with, 96
vs. services, 45
showing in hex, 46–47
source or destination filters,
70–71
pps report, 98
prefix-mask, for address format, 112
primitives, 58–59, 61–70
Autonomous System (AS), 69–70
for BGP, 67–70
comments for, 62
comparison operators, 65
vs. conditions, 60
counter, 66–67, 73
double, 67, 74
emailServers, 78
ICMP type and code, 63–64
for interface numbers, 69
IP address, 72
ip-address-mask, 64–65
ip-address-prefix, 64–65
for IP addresses, 64

IP protocol, 61–62
names for, 59
port number, 62
subnet, 64–65
TCP control bit, 63
time, 66
printed reports, in FlowViewer, 149
printing
graphs to files, 168
protocol and port names, 43–44
setting cutoff for, 148
to wide terminal, 45
private IP addresses, flows from, 100
private network segments, flows
from, 24
probe, 11. *See also* sensors
problem solving with flow data,
182–189
process ID, of softflowd process, 37
promiscuous mode, preventing, 29
PROT (protocol) variable, 79
Protocol statement, for CUFlow, 126
protocols
common number assignments,
44–45
filtering by, 61
in FlowViewer, 147
generating graphs for, 130
printing names, 43–44
report on, 95–96
PSH (push) bit, 50

R

RAM, 22
ranges of ports, primitives for, 62
Real Time header, 83
rebooting, and Cisco router interface numbering, 68, 100
recipient, report on flows by, 92
records field, in flow-report, 83
redirecting output to files, 113
remote facilities, flows from, 24
report options, in detail report, 82
report types, 82
ReportClasses configuration value,
in FlowScan, 123
reporting system, 11

reports. *See also* flow-report program
analyzing individual flows from,
88–89
applying filters, 109–110
customizing, 107–110
definitions, 107
displaying headers, hostnames
and percentages, 90–91
format and output, 108
in HTML, 91
parameters in FlowViewer, 146,
147–148
removing columns, 109
reversing sampling, 110–111
$reports_directory, 144
$reports_directory variable, 142
$reports_short variable, 142
reset-only flows, 107–110
resets, checking for, 183–184
response packet, 16
reversing, sampling, 110–111
Round Robin Database (RRD), 121
converting data to graphs, 129
files from FlowTracker, 152
router interface, filtering by, 75
Router statements, for CUFlow, 126
routers, as sensors, 11
routing, interfaces, and next hops
reports, 99–103
RPTOPT variable, in flow-report, 86, 91
RRD. *See* Round Robin Database
(RRD)
$rrddir variable, 129
RRDtool, 141
rrdtool_bin_directory, 144
RST (reset) bit, 51
rst-only filter, 109–110, 183
RST-only flow, 63, 182
RTG, 4

S

sample time, in FlowGrapher, 151
sampled packets, 19
sampling multiplier, in
FlowTracker, 153
sampling rate, 31–32
sampling, reversing, 110–111

startup script
    for `flow-capture`, 27
    for FlowScan, 123, 128
`stat-definition`
    combining with `stat-report`, 110
    for customized flow report,
        107–108
`stat-report`
    combining with `stat-definition`,
        110
    for customized flow report,
        107–108
    filters in, 111
    time information use by,
        113–114
stat.cfg file, 82, 107, 160–161
statistics reports, in FlowViewer,
        149–150
`strftime` library, 113
subnet primitives, 64–65
Subnet statement, for CUFlow, 124
SubNetIO module, in FlowScan, 123
summary-detail report, 82, 85
switches, as sensors, 11
SYN-ACK packet, 16
SYN-only flow, 182
    primitive matching flow with
        only, 63
SYN request, 16
SYN (synchronize) bit, 50
system resources, for collectors, 22

T

`tail` command, 145
`tar` command, 25
TCP (Transmission Control
        Protocol), 44
    broken connections, 182
    common port assignments, 44
    control bit filters, 71
    control bits, 50–52
    defining ports for separate
        tracking, 126
    failed connections, 184–186
    flags, 45
    primitive for traffic, 59

TCP control bit primitives, 63
TCP flags
    in FlowViewer, 147
    symbolic names, 135
TCP flows, 16–17
The TCP/IP Guide (Kozierok), 9
TCP three-way handshake, 17
`tcpdump`, 29
`tcpflags`, exporting, 136
termination of flows, 95
test.plt file, 160
three-way handshake, 17
throughput matrix, 101
time
    on graphs, 162
    need for synchronization, 49
    use to direct output, 113–114
"time exceeded" PCMP type, 54
time filters, 73
time primitives, 66
time scale for graph, 175–176
timeouts, flow export and, 18
title of graph, in `gnuplot`, 159
total bankwidth report, 160–168
totals option, in `flow-report`, 90–91
traceroute, 99
tracker, 152
    viewing, 153–154
$tracker_directory, 143
Tracking Set Label, in
        FlowTracker, 153
Tracking Type, in FlowTracker, 153
`$trackings_title` variable, 144
traffic size reports, 96–97
traffic speed reports, 97–99
training of network administrators, 2
transit provider, 105
Transmission Control Protocol. *See*
        TCP (Transmission Con-
        trol Protocol)
troubleshooting
    collectors, 29
    FlowViewer, 145–146
Type of Service flag in
        FlowViewer, 147
`TYPE` variable, in `flow-report`, 85

U

UDP (User Datagram Protocol), 44
  common port assignments, 44
  flow-capture listening to port, 27
UDP flows, 15–16
unidirectional bandwidth report, 168–170
Unix epoch time, 6
URG (urgent) bit, 51
user complaints, 1–2
$user_hyperlink, 144
users
  creating for FlowScan, 122
  of FlowViewer, 140
  name for running web server, 141
UTC (Coordinated Universal Time)
  converting to local time, 163
  time zone offset from, 28
uunet AS primitive, 74

V

VAR_ADDR primitive, 79–80
variable-driven filters, 79
  defining, 79–80
variables, 86
  command line for setting, 107
  creating, 80
VAR_PORT primitive, 79–80
VAR_PROT primitive, 79–80
viewing flows, 41–55
VRRP cluster, 30

W

WaitSeconds setting, for FlowScan, 123, 124
wanted() function (*Cflow.pm*), 134
web farms, 132
web interface
  from FlowScan, 121
  for FlowViewer, 144
web servers
  for FlowViewer, 141
  response from, 88
  TCP flows, 16
webTraffic filter, 76
Webview Netflow Reporter, 155
Weinhold, Craig, 179
whois, 106–107
wide-screen display, for flow-print output, 48–49
wide terminal, printing to, 45
Windows, Calculator program, 52
worms, 93
  identifying, 186

X

X server, 6
  for gnuplot, 158
xheader option, in flow-report, 90

Y

y-axis label, on graphs, 164–165

Z

zero-packet flows, 83

The Electronic Frontier Foundation (EFF) is the leading organization defending civil liberties in the digital world. We defend free speech on the Internet, fight illegal surveillance, promote the rights of innovators to develop new digital technologies, and work to ensure that the rights and freedoms we enjoy are enhanced — rather than eroded — as our use of technology grows.

PRIVACY EFF has sued telecom giant AT&T for giving the NSA unfettered access to the private communications of millions of their customers. eff.org/nsa

FREE SPEECH EFF's Coders' Rights Project is defending the rights of programmers and security researchers to publish their findings without fear of legal challenges. eff.org/freespeech

INNOVATION EFF's Patent Busting Project challenges overbroad patents that threaten technological innovation. eff.org/patent

FAIR USE EFF is fighting prohibitive standards that would take away your right to receive and use over-the-air television broadcasts any way you choose. eff.org/IP/fairuse

TRANSPARENCY EFF has developed the Switzerland Network Testing Tool to give individuals the tools to test for covert traffic filtering. eff.org/transparency

INTERNATIONAL EFF is working to ensure that international treaties do not restrict our free speech, privacy or digital consumer rights. eff.org/global

EFF.ORG

ELECTRONIC FRONTIER FOUNDATION

Protecting Rights and Promoting Freedom on the Electronic Frontier

EFF is a member-supported organization. Join Now! www.eff.org/support

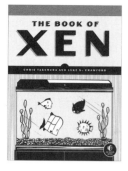

THE BOOK OF™ XEN
A Practical Guide for the System Administrator

by CHRIS TAKEMURA *and* LUKE S. CRAWFORD

Xen allows administrators to run many virtual operating systems on one physical server, including Linux, BSD, OpenSolaris, and Microsoft Windows. In the process, users save money on hardware, maintenance, and electricity. Not only is Xen open source, the Xen hypervisor (the virtual machine monitor) is the best-performing hypervisor available. *The Book of Xen* explains everything a system administrator needs to know to use this powerful technology, with coverage of installation, networking, virtualized storage, and managing guest and host operating systems. Written for administrators who have worked with *nix before but who may be new to virtualization, *The Book of Xen* covers both the basics and the trickier aspects of Xen administration, like profiling and benchmarks, migration, XenSource administration, and hardware assisted virtualization (HVM).

OCTOBER 2009, 312 PP., $49.95
ISBN 978-1-59327-186-2

THE ART OF ASSEMBLY LANGUAGE, 2ND EDITION

by RANDALL HYDE

Widely respected by hackers of all kinds, *The Art of Assembly Language* teaches programmers how to understand assembly language and how to use it to write powerful, efficient code. Using the proven High Level Assembler (HLA) as its primary teaching tool, *The Art of Assembly Language* leverages your knowledge of high-level programming languages to make it easier for you to quickly grasp basic assembly concepts. Among the most comprehensive references to assembly language ever published, *The Art of Assembly Language, 2nd Edition* has been thoroughly updated to reflect recent changes to the HLA language. All code from the book is portable to the Windows, Linux, Mac OS X, and FreeBSD operating systems.

MARCH 2010, 760 PP., $59.95
ISBN 978-1-59327-207-4

NAGIOS, 2ND EDITION
System and Network Monitoring

by WOLFGANG BARTH

Nagios, which runs on Linux and most *nix variants, can be configured to continuously monitor network services such as SMTP, POP3, HTTP, NNTP, SSH, and FTP. It can also supervise host resources (processor load, disk and memory usage, running processes, log files, and so on) and environmental factors, such as temperature and humidity. *Nagios, 2nd Edition* is your guide to getting the most out of this versatile and powerful monitoring tool.

OCTOBER 2008, 728 PP., $59.95
ISBN 978-1-59327-179-4